Lecture Notes in Computer Science 12155

More information about this series at http://www.springer.com/series/7407

André Brinkmann · Wolfgang Karl ·
Stefan Lankes · Sven Tomforde ·
Thilo Pionteck · Carsten Trinitis (Eds.)

Architecture of Computing Systems – ARCS 2020

33rd International Conference
Aachen, Germany, May 25–28, 2020
Proceedings

 Springer

Editors
André Brinkmann ⓘ
Johannes Gutenberg University of Mainz
Mainz, Germany

Wolfgang Karl
Karlsruhe Institute of Technology
Karlsruhe, Germany

Stefan Lankes
RWTH Aachen University
Aachen, Germany

Sven Tomforde ⓘ
Christian-Albrecht University of Kiel
Kiel, Germany

Thilo Pionteck ⓘ
Otto-von-Guericke University Magdeburg
Magdeburg, Germany

Carsten Trinitis ⓘ
Technical University of Munich
Garching b. München, Germany

ISSN 0302-9743   ISSN 1611-3349   (electronic)
Lecture Notes in Computer Science
ISBN 978-3-030-52793-8   ISBN 978-3-030-52794-5   (eBook)
https://doi.org/10.1007/978-3-030-52794-5

LNCS Sublibrary: SL1 – Theoretical Computer Science and General Issues

This Springer imprint is published by the registered company Springer Nature Switzerland AG
The registered company address is: Gewerbestrasse 11, 6330 Cham, Switzerland

Preface

The 33rd edition of the International Conference on Computer Architecture (ARCS 2020) was planned to be held at RWTH Aachen University, one of the oldest technical universities in Germany and a member of the German TU9-association of technical universities. The conference would have taken place during May 25–28, 2020, and therefore in the middle of the 150th anniversary celebrations of RWTH Aachen.

The coronavirus disease COVID-19, nevertheless, completely changed the way of living in Germany, Europe, and all over the world in 2020. The physical execution of nearly all scientific conferences had to be stopped, as borders were closed and all bigger events had to be canceled to confine the spread of the disease and therefore to save lives. This of course also hit ARCS 2020 and the Organizing Committee made the decision to cancel the networking event for our community in the exciting city of Aachen. Due to the extraordinary situation only these conference proceedings were published. In addition, the organization team offered the possibility to publish videos of the contributions in order to foster the dissemination of the results.

The ARCS conference series has over 30 years of tradition reporting leading-edge research in computer architecture and operating systems. ARCS addresses the complete spectrum from fully integrated, self-powered embedded systems up to high-performance computing systems and provides a platform covering newly emerging and cross-cutting topics, such as autonomous and ubiquitous systems, reconfigurable computing and acceleration, neural networks and artificial intelligence, as well as outlooks on future topics such as post-Moore architectures and organic computing.

The focus of the 2020 conference was set on concepts and tools for incorporating self-adaptation and self-organization mechanisms in high-performance computing systems. This includes upcoming approaches for runtime modifications at various abstraction levels, ranging from hardware changes to goal changes and their impact on architectures, technologies, and languages. The conference was organized by the special interest group on "Architecture of Computing Systems" of the GI (Gesellschaft für Informatik e. V.) and ITG (Informationstechnische Gesellschaft im VDE).

ARCS 2020 attracted 33 submissions from authors in 15 countries worldwide, including China, Colombia, South Korea, Venezuela, and the USA. Each submission was reviewed by a diverse and dedicated Program Committee. 3 submissions received 3 qualified reviews and the remaining 30 submissions got 4 or even 5 reviews, leading to a total of 116 reviews.

The Program Committee selected 12 submissions to be published in the proceedings, which corresponds to a 37% paper acceptance rate. The accepted papers cover a variety of topics from the ARCS core domains, including scheduling, near-data processing, HW architectures, or the application of transactional memory.

ARCS has a long tradition of hosting associated workshops. The following three workshops were organized in conjunction with the main conference this year and we decided to include the accepted papers within the conference proceedings:

- 14th GI/ITG Workshop on Parallel Systems and Algorithms (PASA 2020)
- 6th FORMUS^{3}IC Workshop
- Third Workshop on Computer Architectures in Space (CompSpace 2020)

We thank the many individuals who contributed to ARCS 2020, in particular the members of the Program Committee and all the additional external reviewers for their time and effort in carefully reviewing and judging the submissions. We further thank all authors for submitting their work to ARCS and presenting accepted papers as video contributions. The workshops were organized and coordinated by Carsten Trinitis, the proceedings were compiled by Thilo Pionteck, publicity was managed by Lena Oden, and the website was maintained by Markus Hoffmann. Thanks to all these individuals and all the many other people who helped in the organization of ARCS 2020.

May 2020

André Brinkmann
Wolfgang Karl
Stefan Lankes
Sven Tomforde

Organization

General Chairs

Stefan Lankes   RWTH Aachen University, Germany
Wolfgang Karl   Karlsruhe Institute of Technology, Germany

Program Chairs

Sven Tomforde   University of Kiel, Germany
André Brinkmann   Johannes Gutenberg University Mainz, Germany

Workshop and Tutorial Chair

Carsten Trinitis   Technical University of Munich, Germany

Publicity Chair

Lena Oden   FernUniversität in Hagen, Germany

Publication Chair

Thilo Pionteck   Otto von Guericke University Magdeburg, Germany

Web Chair

Markus Hoffmann   Karlsruhe Institute of Technology, Germany

Program Committee

Mladen Berekovic   Universität zu Lübeck, Germany
Jürgen Brehm   Leibnitz Universität Hannover, Germany
André Brinkmann   Johannes Gutenberg University Mainz, Germany
Uwe Brinkschulte   Goethe-Universität Frankfurt am Main, Germany
João M.P. Cardoso   Universidade do Porto, Portugal
Thomas Carle   Institut de Recherche en Informatique de Toulouse,
                                      France
Ahmed El-Mahdy   Egypt-Japan University of Science and Technology,
                                      Egypt
Lukas Esterle   Aarhus University, Denmark
Dietmar Fey   Friedrich-Alexander-Universität Erlangen-Nürnberg,
                                      Germany
Giorgis Georgakoudis   Lawrence Livermore National Laboratory, USA

Additional Reviewers

Christoph Borchert	Osnabrück University, Germany
Peter Brand	Friedrich-Alexander-Universität Erlangen-Nürnberg, Germany
Hugues Cassé	Institut de Recherche en Informatique de Toulouse, France
Boris Dreyer	Technische Universität Darmstadt, Germany
Jorge Echavarria	Friedrich-Alexander-Universität Erlangen-Nürnberg, Germany
Farnam Khalili Maybodi	University of Siena, Italy
Kevin Kremer	Johannes Gutenberg University Mainz, Germany
Leon Li	University of California, San Diego, USA
Diogo Marques	Universidade de Lisboa, Portugal
Rolf Meyer	Universität zu Lübeck, Germany
Nuno Neves	INESC-ID Lisboa, Portugal
Elbruz Ozen	University of California, San Diego, USA
Marco Procaccini	University of Siena, Italy
Oskar Pusz	Leibnitz Universität Hannover, Germany
Paul Renaud-Goud	Institut de Recherche en Informatique de Toulouse, France
Amin Sahebi	University of Siena, Italy
Frederic Schimmelpfennig	Johannes Gutenberg University Mainz, Germany
Ladislav Steffko	University of California, San Diego, USA
Ramon Wirsch	Technische Universität Darmstadt, Germany
Mahdi Zahedi	Delft University of Technology, The Netherlands

6th FORMUS^{3}IC Workshop

Program Committee

Dietmar Fey	Friedrich-Alexander-Universität Erlangen-Nürnberg, Germany
Jens Harnisch	Infineon AG, Germany
Martin Hobelsberger	Hochschule München, Germany
Jose Daniel Gracia Sanchez	Universidad Carlos III de Madrid, Spain
Ralph Mader	Continental AG, Germany
Vaclav Matousek	University of West Bohemia, Czech Republic
Avi Mendelson	Technion University, Israel
Jürgen Mottok	Ostbayerische Technische Hochschule Regensburg, Germany
Tobias Schüle	SIEMENS AG, Germany
Andreas Sailer	Vector, Germany
Christian Siemers	Clausthal University of Technology, Germany
Michael Wong	Codeplay, UK

Third Workshop on Computer Architectures in Space (CompSpace)

Program Committee

Carsten Trinitis	Technical University of Munich, Germany
Sebastian Rückerl	Technical University of Munich, Germany
Nicolas Appel	Technical University of Munich, Germany

14th Workshop on Parallel Systems and Algorithms (PASA)

Program Committee

Martin Dietzfelbinger	Technische Universität Ilmenau, Germany
Steffen Christgau	Zuse Institute Berlin, Germany
Andreas Döring	IBM Zürich, Switzerland
Norbert Eicker	Jülich Supercomputing Centre, Germany
Thomas Fahringer	Universität Innsbruck, Austria
Dietmar Fey	Friedrich-Alexander-Universität Erlangen-Nürnberg, Germany
Rolf Hoffmann	Technische Universität Darmstadt, Germany
Klaus Jansen	Christian-Albrechts-Universität zu Kiel, Germany
Ben Juurlink	Technische Universität Berlin, Germany
Wolfgang Karl	Karlsruhe Institute of Technology, Germany
Jörg Keller	Fernuniversität in Hagen, Germany
Stefan Lankes	RWTH Aachen University, Germany
Christian Lengauer	University of Passau, Germany
Erik Maehle	Universität zu Lübeck, Germany
Ulrich Margull	Technische Hochschule Ingolstadt, Germany
Ernst W. Mayr	Technical University of Munich, Germany
Ulrich Meyer	Goethe-Universität Frankfurt am Main, Germany
Friedhelm Meyer auf der Heide	Universität Paderborn, Germany
Juergen Mottok	Ostbayerische Technische Hochschule Regensburg, Germany
Wolfgang Nagel	Technische Universität Dresden, Germany
Michael Philippsen	Friedrich-Alexander-Universität Erlangen-Nürnberg, Germany
Harald Räcke	Technical University of Munich, Germany
Karl Dieter Reinartz	Hochstädt, Germany
Christian Scheideler	Universität Paderborn, Germany
Bettina Schnor	Universität Potsdam, Germany
Martin Schulz	Technical University of Munich, Germany
Uwe Schwiegelshohn	Technische Universität Dortmund, Germany
Peter Sobe	Hochschule fr Technik und Wirtschaft Dresden, Germany
Carsten Trinitis	Technical University of Munich, Germany
Rolf Wanka	Friedrich-Alexander-Universität Erlangen-Nürnberg, Germany

Contents

FORMUS^{3}IC Workshop

Workshop on Computer Architectures in Space (CompSpace)

Workshop on Parallel Systems and Algorithms (PASA)

Main Concerence

Approximate Data Dependence Profiling Based on Abstract Interval and Congruent Domains

Mostafa Abbas[1]([✉])(iD), Rasha Omar[1]([✉])'(iD), Ahmed El-Mahdy[1,3]([✉])(iD),
and Erven Rohou[2]([✉])(iD)

[1] Egypt-Japan University of Science and Technology (E-JUST), Alexandria, Egypt
{mostafa.abbas,rasha.omar,ahmed.elmahdy}@ejust.edu.eg
[2] Univ Rennes, Inria, CNRS, IRISA, Rennes, France
erven.rohou@inria.fr
[3] Alexandria University, Alexandria, Egypt

Abstract. Although parallel processing is mainstream, existing programs are often serial, and usually re-engineering cost is high. Data dependence profiling allows for automatically assessing parallelisation potential; Yet, data dependence profiling is notoriously slow and requires large memory, as it generally requires keeping track of each memory access. This paper considers employing a simple abstract single-trace analysis method using simple interval and congruent modulo domains to track dependencies at lower time and memory costs. The method gathers and abstracts the set of all memory reference addresses for each static memory access instruction. This method removes the need for keeping a large shadow memory and only requires a single pair-wise analysis pass to detect dependencies among memory instructions through simple intersection operations. Moreover, the combination of interval and congruent domains improves precision when compared with only using an interval domain representation, mainly when the data is not accessed in a dense access pattern. We further improve precision through partitioning memory space into blocks, where references in each block abstracted independently. An initial performance study is conducted on SPEC CPU-2006 benchmark programs and polyhedral benchmark suite. Results show that the method reduces execution time overhead by $1.4\times$ for polyhedral and $10.7\times$ for SPEC2006 on average; and significantly reduces memory by $109780\times$ and $6981\times$ for polyhedral and SPEC2006 respectively; the method has an average precision of 99.05% and 61.37% for polyhedral and SPEC respectively. Using memory partitioning resulted in improving mean precision to be 82.25% and decreasing memory reduction to be $47\times$ for SPEC2006 suite.

Keywords: Data dependence profiling · Dynamic binary analysis · Congruent domains · Interval domains

A. El-Mahdy—On-leave from Alexandria University.

A. Brinkmann et al. (Eds.): ARCS 2020, LNCS 12155, pp. 3–16, 2020.
https://doi.org/10.1007/978-3-030-52794-5_1

1   Introduction

Data dependence profiling is an essential step towards deciding on parallelising loops, especially for heterogeneous parallel platforms, where the cost of re-engineering originally serial programs is high. However, obtaining the profiles is generally a costly operation as it requires instrumenting all memory access instructions; hence it suffers from significant memory consumption and runtime overhead (i.e., separate records for every accessed memory address). Therefore, profilers rely on approximation methods, trading-off accuracy with analysis overhead. One typical method is sampling the execution trace, where only a portion of the trace is analysed [5,23]. However, sampling is prone to missing some dependence arcs and losing the most recent relationships. Other profilers tackle the runtime overhead by parallelising runtime analysis [10,17,24].

This paper considers performing a form of abstract analysis for all memory references over the whole program. The analysis borrows from the well-known abstract interpretation static analysis method, which is used to generate an abstract collective program state for all possible execution traces [1,6,18]. Here, we specialise the method to analyse only one execution trace (profiling trace). Moreover, we do not perform abstract computations or interpretations over the abstract state; instead, we rely on the underlying execution system to generate the current state and use a corresponding abstract operation (Union) to gather and approximate the state. In other words, the main aim is to generate an abstract single-trace semantics, from the current execution trace.

The advantage of this approach is that we dramatically reduce the memory size required for the analysis, as there is no need to have a shadow memory, which is typical in profilers. Moreover, we only perform pair-wise operations on the static memory access instructions after gathering their trace state, to identify data-dependence, thus also significantly reducing profiling time. The trade-off here is precision or false dependencies, while the sensitivity or true dependencies are never missed.

In this paper, for each dynamic memory access operation, we use a corresponding abstract operation that joins the current memory access address with the current abstracted set of seen addresses for the corresponding memory access instruction, thus generating an abstract single-trace semantic for all static memory instructions. The abstraction uses a composite abstract domain, consisting of interval and congruent domains. The former provides an approximation of the covered range, and the latter provides information about the access pattern. We partition the memory address space into blocks and associate a value from the composite domain for each block, to further improve precision.

This paper has the following contributions:

- Utilise abstract interval and congruent domains to approximate the accessed memory location for each static memory access instruction.
- Conduct an initial performance investigation using polyhedral benchmark and SPEC CPU-2006 benchmark suites using the Pin system [14].

- Utilise the gathered semantics to detect pair-wise memory data dependencies (RAW, WAR, and WAW) from binary files at runtime for all static memory access instructions.

This paper is organised as follows: Sect. 2 discusses related work. Section 3 provides an overview of abstract interpretation and defines the interval and congruent domains and their corresponding operations. Section 4 discusses our profiling algorithm. Section 5 presents our initial results. Finally, Sect. 6 concludes our paper and discusses future work.

2   Related Work

2.1   Static Analysis

Abstract interpretation is a static analysis method that generates a collective program semantics at each program point. The method relies on generating abstract equations that generate the collective program semantics at each program point. Abstract interpretation is not generally used in the context of data dependence analysis for imperative programs (functional programs have in-depth treatment, e.g., [3]); nevertheless, there are attempts in this direction [8,16].

Ricci [20] is an early attempt to consider dependence analysis by combining interval and bisection domains; the latter is used to maintain relations among pairs of variables. The technique is applied at the source level on some kernels. Moreover, the use of the bisection domain helped to reduce the interval width, whereas in our approach we consider the density of the elements in the interval, as well conducting the analysis on the binary level; however, we do not generate collective semantics for all possible traces; we only consider the profiling trace, which is typical for profilers.

The use of the congruence domain in abstract interpretation is described in detail in Bydge's master thesis [4]. This paper adopts the same definitions and operations for that domain. However, the thesis does not consider program parallelisation.

Tzolovski [22] has discussed possible data dependence abstractions, which included direction and distance vectors as defined by Maydan et al. [15]. In this paper, we explore an initial practical implementation of simple dependence detection and leave more elaborate possible abstractions for future work.

SecondWrite [11] is a static binary rewriter tool. It analyses the dependence in regular loops in binary programs and workout to rewrite a parallelised binary version. SecondWrite translates the *x86* binary input to the intermediate format of the LLVM Compiler and then uses the *x86* back-end LLVM to write the output binary. They make use of the LLVM IR rich infrastructure, such as control-flow analysis, data-flow analysis, and optimisation passes to generate a parallel alternative version according to which loop can be partitioned.

2.2   Dynamic Analysis

Li et al. [13] introduce a profiler for the sequential and parallel program based on LLVM. They tackle the runtime overhead by parallelising the profiler. The profiler records memory accesses using signatures to achieve efficiency in space, (as an approximate representation, concept from transactional memory [21]) rather than instrument every memory access. The serial profiler has a 190× slowdown on average for NAS benchmarks and a 191× slowdown on average for Starbench programs and consumed memory up to 7.856 GB. By using lock-free parallel design, the runtime overhead reduces to 78× for NAS and 93× for Starbench. By using a signature with 100 million slots, the memory consumption reduces to 649 MB (NAS) and 1390 MB (Starbench), with accuracy less than 0.4% false-positive rate and less than 0.1% false-negative rate.

Chen et al. [5] implement a data dependence profiling tool on top of the Intel's Open Research Compiler (ORC) to provide information about the dynamic behaviour of data dependence in programs, mainly for nested loops.

They study two approximation methods: shadow memory and sampling techniques, as a trade-off to mitigate both space and runtime overhead. The tool speculatively ignores dependence edges (between the source and the sink) that have low probability. The threshold value of this low probability can be determined by the overhead of a data mis-speculation process according to the target machine. The slowdown ranges from 16% to 167% on SPEC CPU2000 benchmarks compared to the original execution time by using a sampling rate of 0.0001 to 0.1, respectively, and with a precision ranging from 30% to 10% in missing dependence edges.

Vanka et al. [23] implement a set-based profiling approach coupled with software signatures. The key insight is that set-level tracking provides a better trade-off between accuracy and performance. At compile time, they identify the essential dependence relationships according to a specific optimisation (i.e. speculative code motion) for profiling at runtime. The profiling analysis working on sets, figuring out set's relationships dependence, rather than working with pair-wise dependence relationships. The set-based profiler is implemented as an IR level pass in LLVM and applied to SPEC2000 benchmarks for presenting results. They achieved a slowdown 2.97× with the accuracy range from 0.15 and 0.17, measured by normalised average Euclidean distance.

Norouzi et al. [19] implement an extension of DiscoPoP data dependence profiler that uses a hybrid (static and dynamic) approach in reporting the existence of data dependence in the polyhedral loops. The static dependence analysis part excludes the detected dependent memory access instructions in the annotated area by PLUTO (an auto-parallelising compiler for polyhedral loops) and hence excludes them in the dynamic analysis. Finally, static and dynamic dependencies are merged in an appropriate way to be used later in suitable parallelisation discovery tools. It is clear that if no polyhedral loops are detected in a program, the hybrid approach turns into purely dynamic. By conducting experiments on Polybench and NAS Parallel Benchmarks suits, they achieved a median profiling-time reduction by 62% compared to DiscoPoP profiler framework.

Li et al. [12] introduce a profiling method based on repeatedly skipping memory operations in loops. They used DiscoPoP to implement the profiler. The experiments on NAS Parallel Benchmarks and Starbench parallel benchmark suite show a reduction on runtime overhead by 42.5% on average. The reduction runtime mainly comes from the data dependence building phase, where updating the shadow memory remains as the traditional way. The effect of this approach results from the existence of sequencing memory access patterns in loops (e.g. arrays), if not exists, the profiling suffers from extra runtime overhead due to the extra conditions compared to traditional one.

3   Proposed Method Formulation

3.1   Gathering Single-Trace Semantics Dynamically

Our method differs from typical abstract interpretation in that we obtain the abstract collective semantics for a single-trace of the program, instead of all traces. Also, we rely on abstracting the collective semantics for only memory read and write operations, not all program points. Moreover, instead of generating abstract equations, and statically solve or interpret them, we rely on obtaining actual read and write addresses values at runtime from the underlying execution environment, and collect the obtained concrete values into collected abstract semantics (i.e. all possible referenced address seen for each memory instruction). In other words, we define a corresponding operation that collects the semantics. Thus, for a memory access operation i reading or writing from/to address a, we define the abstract collective semantics, Σ at this operation as:

$$\Sigma_i = \Sigma_i \cup \alpha(\{a\}) \tag{1}$$

Where $\Sigma \in \mathbb{D}_A$; and $\mathbb{D}_A$ is an abstract domain with partial lattice with ordering relation $\cup$, moreover, $\alpha()$ is an abstraction function that abstracts the current concrete partial collective semantic set into an abstract one. We also adopt a composite abstract domain that consists of interval and congruence domains. The congruent domain is helpful to represent stride memory access patterns, and the interval domain considers the lower and upper limits of memory access address. It is worth mentioning that abstract interpretation guarantees sound analysis, where the obtained collective semantics is always a superset of the concrete collective semantics.

3.2   The Interval Domain

The interval domain [7] is an abstract domain that can determine safe lower and upper limits of program variables. The abstract interval domain, $\mathbb{D}_I$, is defined as:

$$\mathbb{D}_I = \{[a, b]\}, \forall a \leq b \in \mathbb{Z} \tag{2}$$

The $\cup$ and $\cap$ operators are defined as:

$$[a, b] \cup [a', b'] = [\min(a, a'), \max(b, b')] \tag{3}$$

$$[a, b] \cap [a', b'] = \begin{cases} [\max(a, a'), \min(b, b')] \text{ if } \max(a, a') \leq \min(b, b') \\ \phi \text{ otherwise} \end{cases} \tag{4}$$

3.3 The Congruence Domain

The congruence domain [9] consists of abstract values denoted, $aZ + b$, Where $b \in \mathbb{Z}$ and $a \in \mathbb{N}$. We will call a the modulo and b the remainder. A congruence relation (c, b) is defined as $c \equiv b \mod a$. The set of all C such that $c \in C$ and $c \equiv b \mod a$, is $C = \{aZ + b : \forall Z \in \mathbb{Z}\}$.

Thus, we define the abstract congruent, $\mathbb{D}_{CG}$, domain as:

$$\mathbb{D}_{CG} = \{aZ + b\}, \forall a, b \in \mathbb{N} \tag{5}$$

The $\cup$ and $\cap$ operators are defined as:

$$(aZ + b) \cup (a'Z + b') = \gcd\{a, a', |b - b'|\}Z + \min\{b, b'\} \tag{6}$$

$$(aZ + b) \cap (a'Z + b') = \begin{cases} \text{lcm}\{a, a'\}Z + b'' \text{ if } b \equiv b' \mod \gcd\{a, a'\} \\ \phi \text{ otherwise} \end{cases} \tag{7}$$

Where $b'' \equiv b \mod a$ and also $b'' \equiv b' \mod a'$.

4 Profiling Framework

4.1 Pin Framework

Pin [14] is a framework for dynamic binary instrumentation framework. Similar to other frameworks, users can observe the running code, detect intensive functions and loops, monitor parameters, and modify the code while it runs. Pin framework provides an API to let users build custom tools called Pintools, which in turn dynamically instruments the compiled binary files in the user space application. By inserting an appropriate runtime analysis routine for a kind of instructions, we can understand the behaviour of a given binary program.

Our profiler inserts instrumentation code dynamically into the binary code for each memory read/write operation; which is mainly callbacks to the corresponding runtime analysis routines. The profiler can operate on three different modes. The first one performs conventional profiling, where the second one performs a comprehensive (i.e. pairwise method) profiling. Both the first and second modes can be considered as a different perspective of ground truth for the underlying data dependence, as it provides an exhaustive, accurate data dependence results. However, it suffers from immense memory and runtime overhead. The third operation mode performs the proposed profiling technique. Our implementation focuses only on memory references, where data dependence between registers can be easily detected by convenient static analysis.

4.2   Conventional Profiling Technique

For each executing memory instruction, the runtime analysis records the effective memory address and corresponding instruction address as a key, value, and mode (read/write) tuple in a hash table. The hash table, thus, keeps track of the last instruction accessed that memory address.

The analysis routine can then construct a corresponding dependence arc at runtime when a memory write operation happens, marking out a dependence relation (i.e. RAW, WAR, WAW) between the current and the last instruction that accessed the same memory location, i.e. a dependence relation between the current memory instruction and the closest prior instruction(s) which depends on. This method is close to the baseline algorithms of previous work (e.g. [12]).

4.3   Comprehensive Profiling Technique

Conventional data dependence profiling aims to capture dependencies among executing instructions; i.e. memory references, not static instructions. Another approach, as defined by Bernstein Conditions [2], is to compare the set of all accessed memory locations for each instruction; a depending pair would have a non-empty intersection.

This analysis requires capturing the set of all data references for each static memory instruction, which results in great storage, and complexity of $O(n^2)$ intersections, where n is the stored memory address. This analysis is close to the baseline algorithms of previous work [5,10]. Our proposed method (described below) essentially abstracts this method, significantly reducing the storage requirements.

4.4   Abstract Profiling Technique

The third profiling operating mode is the proposed abstract approximate profiling. As in the previously mentioned profiling techniques, the profiler inserts a callback to the runtime analysis routine for each memory access instruction.

The input to the proposed algorithm is effectively a memory access trace. The trace can be generated dynamically by an underlying execution environment or read from an off-line trace file, that has been collected before. The trace is defined as the sequence of the tuples (inst, mode, address), where 'inst' refers to the memory instruction address, 'mode' refers to whether the instruction is read or write, and finally 'address' is the effective memory address accessed by the instruction.

At runtime, the analysis routine manipulates memory addresses by converting them into corresponding abstract interval and congruent domain values, and accumulating them to the recorded (abstract) addresses, according to Eqs. 3 (referred to as $\alpha_{Interval}$) and 6 (referred to as $\alpha_{Congruent}$) as mentioned above. Here, each static memory instruction has its hash table entry for collecting abstract profiling data. The substantial difference from conventional profiling is that the profiler stores only the abstract set of seen memory addresses, for each memory instruction (i.e. limited number of entries related to the number of static memory instructions). Finally, we compute the intersection between those intervals/congruence values of memory instructions (read or write) according to the aforementioned Eqs. 4 and 7, indicating the potential of the existence of dependence. The intersection conditions require both interval and congruent domain to intersect.

It is worth noting that abstract profiling (as well as comprehensive profiling) cannot distinguish between WAR/RAW dependence, where ordering relations are not kept. In future work, we will consider abstracting this order by keeping distance information among instructions.

4.5 Experimental Study

Figure 1 demonstrates the effectiveness of interval and congruent domain in exploring data dependence between memory references. Figure 1-(a) shows an example where statements S1 and S2 are independent, as each memory access has its separate index values (e.g. one is even, and the other is odd). The upper (not shaded) part of Table 1 shows the corresponding assembly instructions, their addresses, and interval/congruence analysis results. Apparently, there is no intersection using the congruence domain, thus no dependence, even though the intervals intersect. On the other hand, Fig. 1-(b) shows another example where S3 and S4 are independent also, as each part of the array are accessed in two different loops. The shaded part of Table 1 shows its corresponding results. It is clear that there is no intersection in the interval domain, thus no dependence, even though the congruent domain intersects. By considering both congruent and interval intersections for reporting a dependence, this can provide for the better potential to improve precision. Thus both abstract domains provide a safe approximation to the concrete domain (i.e. absence of dependence in one abstract domain is sufficient to decide the absence of dependence on the concrete domain).

Table 1. The output results show the effect of the different domains on analysis.

Inst. Address	Inst. Loc.	Assembly code	Interval domain	Congruence domain
f3ed7cb	S1	movsd qword ptr [rax+rdx*8], xmm0	[7e3e0, 7e420]	10 Z + 7e3e0
f3ed7e1	S2	movsd xmm1, qword ptr [rax+rdx*8]	[7e3d8, 7e418]	10 Z + 7e3d8
0c048f2	S3	movsd qword ptr [rax+rdx*8], xmm0	[7b698, 7b6b0]	8 Z + 7b698
0c04942	S4	movsd xmm2, qword ptr [rax+rdx*8]	[7b6b8, 7b6d8]	8 Z + 7b6b8

Abstract profiling may introduce false dependence arcs. Figure 2-(a) show a simple example that clarifies the causes of the false-positive relationships that may happen. This example does not have any real data dependence relationships because of the writes at $S1$ only access memory exclusively in the range between $ExprMIN$ and $ExprMAX$ of the array a, while, the reads at $S2$ happen elsewhere. Figure 2-(b) shows the reported dependence graph contains two false-positive arcs. One arc between $S1$ and $S2$ because the interval of $S1 = [ExprMIN, ExprMax]$ intersects with the interval of $S2 = [IMIN, IMAX]$ and the related congruent values also intersect. The other arc between $S2$ and itself representing WAW dependence.

We can enhance the precision by partitioning the memory address space into blocks (with a block size of 2^k bits) and abstracting each block address space. For the previous example, the false positive eliminated if $S1$ and $S2$ access different blocks of memory, and hence there is no intersection between the two instruction's memory blocks. In this study, we did experiments for various memory block size, as demonstrated in the next section.

```
for( i = IMIN;  i < IMAX;  i++)        for  (i = IMIN;  i < IMAX/2;  i++){
   if  ( i%2 == 0 )                        a[ i ] = ...;    //  S3
      a[ i ] = ...;    // S1              }
   else                                 for  (i = IMAX/2;  i < IMAX;  i++){
      ... = a[ i ];   // S2                ... = a[ i ];  //  S4
                                        }
            (a)                                        (b)
```

Fig. 1. Two examples are showing the effect of the different domains on analysis.

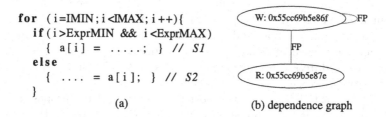

```
for  (i=IMIN; i<IMAX; i++){
   if( i>ExprMIN && i<ExprMAX)
      { a[ i ] = .....; } // S1
   else
      { .... = a[ i ]; } // S2
}
```
            (a)   (b) dependence graph

Fig. 2. A simple example is showing a case of false-positive dependence arcs.

5 Results

We have evaluated the proposed profiling method over fifteen kernels from the polyhedral benchmark suite (PolyBench/C 3.2) and eleven programs from SPEC CPU 2006 benchmark suite to asses both the accuracy of the profiled dependencies and performance. We have conducted experiments on a machine with Intel Core I7, 16 GB memory and running Ubuntu release 18.04 (64-bit) operating system. For this study, we considered detecting two data dependence classes: RAW/WAR and WAW.

The profiling results form polyhedral benchmark suite seems pretty optimistic for our method. Results show that the method reduces execution time overhead by 1.4× on average and having a significant memory reduction 109780× on average of memory space with 100% of sensitivity and 99.05% on average of precision compared to comprehensive profiling baseline. The following part elaborates in more details SPEC profiling results, which is more challenging.

Table 2. Abstract analysis of SPEC2006 benchmarks.

Benchmark name	Dyn. Mem. Inst (millions)	Static. Mem. Inst	Memory Red. Conventional (X)	Memory Red. Comprehensive (X)	Sensitivity (%) TP/(TP+FN)	Precision 1 (%) TP/(TP+FP)	Precision 2 (%) TP/(TP+FP)
401.bzip2	2,701 (29.9%)	3,068	2044.0	22032.3	100	54.1	70.4
403.gcc	653 (17.3%)	59,465	30.7	366.2	100	16.0	45.3
429.mcf	1,227 (41.2%)	743	17472.3	46907.8	100	95.9	100.0
445.gobmk	571 (22.0%)	5,744	43.0	205.9	100	17.8	80.2
456.hmmer	5,310 (38.3%)	1,132	110.8	409.3	100	39.3	83.6
458.sjeng	3,280 (20.8%)	3,269	2391.8	2489.7	100	41.1	61.4
462.libquantum	40 (17.8%)	313	58.8	201.5	100	62.0	79.6
464.h264ref	27,145 (31.7%)	10,854	856.8	1903.6	100	17.8	33.2
471.omnetpp	284 (24.6%)	2,931	168.6	390.9	100	31.1	38.4
473.astar	6,071 (28.0%)	1,698	708.5	1863.7	100	54.0	66.4
483.xalancbmk	71 (25.5%)	32,884	7.8	21.8	100	13.5	16.5

Table 2 discusses the abstract analysis profiler results. The first two columns list the benchmark programs and their dynamic read and write instruction counts (and their per cent relative to all dynamic instructions), which in turn affects the amount of runtime analysis overhead for each program. The third column lists the static memory instructions, which affects the memory overhead for the proposed abstract profiling. The fourth and fifth columns show an extreme reduction in memory usage overhead, averaging 2172× and 6981× compared to conventional and comprehensive, respectively. It is clear that our proposed profiler significantly saves memory when compared with both baseline profiling. It needs only four memory records to keep abstract data for each static memory access instruction (i.e. min and max address values for the interval domain, and a and b values for the congruent domain) compared to keeping all the executed data memory access address. This advantage enables scalability in profiling memory-intensive program, especially in low memory devices.

Finally, the last three columns report the accuracy of the proposed profiler in terms of sensitivity and precision. The sensitivity (recall) of the proposed abstract analysis achieved 100% accuracy in detecting all occurred data dependencies (as expected). The positive predictive value (precision) is calculated in the seventh and eighth columns, precision 1 and precision 2, compared to conventional and Comprehensive profiling baseline, respectively[1]. Results indicate that our system intends to overestimate the dependence relations; this is expected due to the underlying abstraction concept. However, the sensitivity metric is generally essential, as not missing a dependence is more important than reporting wrong dependence because it would affect the correctness of the parallelisation decision. Both sensitivity and precision are formulated by calculating TP (true

---

[1] We use two metrics as conventional profiling edges connect two dynamic instruction instances, whereas comprehensive profiling connects two static instructions; thus, ground truth is represented differently in each case.

positive; how many actual dependence pairs are detected by the proposed profiler), FN (false negative; how many missed dependence pairs), and FP (false positive, how many dependence pairs reported but are wrong). It is worth mentioning that the precision is low (61.4% on average), due to successive calls to the same functions, which leads to having some clusters of data corresponding to each call.

Figure 3 shows the slowdown for each benchmark program. We can notice the differences in runtime overhead in each benchmark program between conventional, comprehensive, and abstract profiling. Notably, the runtime overhead of abstract profiling is better than the comprehensive (10.7×) and the conventional (1.4×) profiling techniques on average, where it saves memory but needs runtime processing for every dynamic memory instruction. In future work, we will work on tackling the runtime overhead. Figure 4 shows the precision analysis and memory reduction for different memory block size. It is clear that block size is a decreasing function of precision and an increasing function of memory reduction. Block size of 2^{12} bits seems to be a good design point as memory reduction is still significant (47× average memory reduction) with 82.25% precision.

SD^3 [10] as related work, implemented on Pin and used a SPEC2006 to present the results compared to the pairwise method as a baseline (i.e. comprehensive). The SD^3 baseline has more runtime overhead than our baseline implementation. For example, the slowdown baseline of 462.*libquantum* and 456.*hmmer* is 90× and 210× respectively; moreover, most of the reminder SPEC programs fail due to lack of memory resources (consumes more than10 GB memory). On the other side, our implementation of the baseline has a slowdown 7.42× and 71.54×, respectively for the same two programs, and a slowdown of all tested programs 402.4× on average. Serial SD^3 has 289× slowdown on average for the top 20 hottest loops. The parallelised version of SD^3 shows a 70× slowdown on average (8 tasks on 8 cores). The proposed profiler shows 37.4× on average for profiling the whole program, and a memory reduction 6981× on average.

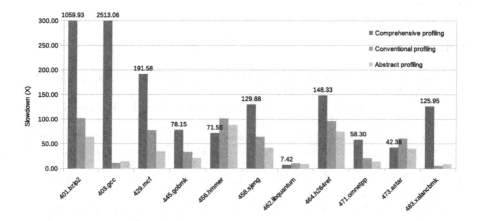

Fig. 3. Abstract profiling overhead on SPEC2006 benchmark.

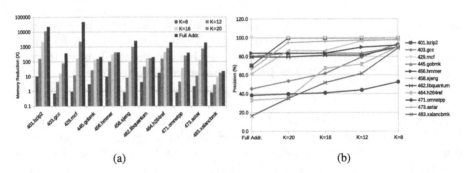

(a)   (b)

Fig. 4. Memory reduction and precision analysis for different memory block size.

Moreover, our technique applies to other approaches that intend to mitigate profiling overhead like sampling and parallelisation, which we aim to investigate in the future.

6   Conclusions and Future Work

This paper has considered employing a simple abstract representation based method for detecting data dependence at the binary level. This approach has combined both an interval and congruent abstract domains to detect data dependence relations, as well as abstracting partitioned memory sub address spaces. We have implemented this approach on the Pin dynamic binary instrumentation framework and conducted an initial performance study on both SPEC and polyhedral benchmark suite. Results show perfect recall rate of 100% with a significant memory reduction in comparison with the profiling baseline. Future work includes considering more elaborate abstract properties such as dependence vectors as integrating this profiling method with an automatic parallelisation framework.

References

1. Abstract Interpretation in a Nutshell. http://www.di.ens.fr/%7Ecousot/AI/ IntroAbsInt.html. Accessed 24 February 2018
2. Bernstein, A.J.: Analysis of programs for parallel processing. IEEE Trans. Electron. Comput. **5**, 757–763 (1966)
3. Bueno, F., De La Banda, M.G., Hermenegildo, M.: Effectivness of abstract interpretation in automatic parallelization: a case study in logic programming. ACM Trans. Program. Lang. Syst. (TOPLAS) **21**(2), 189–239 (1999)
4. Bygde, S.: Abstract interpretation and abstract domains. Master's thesis, Västerås, Sweden, May 2006
5. Chen, T., Lin, J., Dai, X., Hsu, W.-C., Yew, P.-C.: Data dependence profiling for speculative optimizations. In: Duesterwald, E. (ed.) CC 2004. LNCS, vol. 2985, pp. 57–72. Springer, Heidelberg (2004). https://doi.org/10.1007/978-3-540-24723-4_5

6. Cousot, P.: A gentle introduction to abstract interpretation. In: The 9th International Symposium on Theoretical Aspects of Software Engineering, Nanjing, China, September 2015, pp. 1–46. http://www.di.ens.fr/~cousot/publications. www/slides-public/PCousot-TASE-2015-AI-tutorial-4-1.pdf

7. Cousot, P., Cousot, R.: Abstract interpretation: a unified lattice model for static analysis of programs by construction or approximation of fixpoints. In: Proceedings of the 4th ACM SIGACT-SIGPLAN Symposium on Principles of Programming Languages, pp. 238–252 (1977)

8. Cousot, P., Cousot, R.: Abstract interpretation: past, present and future. In: Proceedings of the Joint Meeting of the Twenty-Third EACSL Annual Conference on Computer Science Logic (CSL) and the Twenty-Ninth Annual ACM/IEEE Symposium on Logic in Computer Science (LICS), pp. 1–10 (2014)

9. Granger, P.: Static analysis of arithmetical congruences. Int. J. Comput. Math. **30**(3–4), 165–190 (1989)

10. Kim, M., Kim, H., Luk, C.K.: SD3: a scalable approach to dynamic data-dependence profiling. In: 2010 43rd Annual IEEE/ACM International Symposium on Microarchitecture, pp. 535–546. IEEE (2010)

11. Kotha, A., Anand, K., Smithson, M., Yellareddy, G., Barua, R.: Automatic parallelization in a binary rewriter. In: 43rd Annual IEEE/ACM International Symposium on Microarchitecture, pp. 547–557. IEEE (2010)

12. Li, Z., Beaumont, M., Jannesari, A., Wolf, F.: Fast data-dependence profiling by skipping repeatedly executed memory operations. In: Wang, G., Zomaya, A., Perez, G.M., Li, K. (eds.) ICA3PP 2015. LNCS, vol. 9531, pp. 583–596. Springer, Cham (2015). https://doi.org/10.1007/978-3-319-27140-8_40

13. Li, Z., Jannesari, A., Wolf, F.: An efficient data-dependence profiler for sequential and parallel programs. In: IEEE International Parallel and Distributed Processing Symposium, pp. 484–493. IEEE (2015)

14. Luk, C.K., et al.: Pin: building customized program analysis tools with dynamic instrumentation. In: Conference on Programming Language Design and Implementation (2005)

15. Maydan, D., Amarsinghe, S., Lam, M.: Data dependence and data-flow analysis of arrays. In: Banerjee, U., Gelernter, D., Nicolau, A., Padua, D. (eds.) LCPC 1992. LNCS, vol. 757, pp. 434–448. Springer, Heidelberg (1993). https://doi.org/10.1007/3-540-57502-2_63

16. Midkiff, S.P.: Automatic Parallelization: An Overview of Fundamental Compiler Techniques. Morgan & Claypool Publishers, San Rafael (2012)

17. Moseley, T., Shye, A., Reddi, V.J., Grunwald, D., Peri, R.: Shadow profiling: hiding instrumentation costs with parallelism. In: International Symposium on Code Generation and Optimization (CGO 2007), pp. 198–208. IEEE (2007)

18. Nielson, F., Nielson, H.R., Hankin, C.: Principles of Program Analysis. Springer, Heidelberg (2015). https://doi.org/10.1007/978-3-662-03811-6

19. Norouzi, M., Ilias, Q., Jannesari, A., Wolf, F.: Accelerating data-dependence profiling with static hints. In: Yahyapour, R. (ed.) Euro-Par 2019. LNCS, vol. 11725, pp. 17–28. Springer, Cham (2019). https://doi.org/10.1007/978-3-030-29400-7_2

20. Ricci, L.: Automatic loop parallelization: an abstract interpretation approach. In: Proceedings. International Conference on Parallel Computing in Electrical Engineering, pp. 112–118. IEEE (2002)

21. Sanchez, D., Yen, L., Hill, M.D., Sankaralingam, K.: Implementing signatures for transactional memory. In: 40th Annual IEEE/ACM International Symposium on Microarchitecture (MICRO 2007), pp. 123–133. IEEE (2007)

22. Tzolovski, S.: Data dependences as abstract interpretations. In: Van Hentenryck, P. (ed.) SAS 1997. LNCS, vol. 1302, pp. 366–366. Springer, Heidelberg (1997). https://doi.org/10.1007/BFb0032756
23. Vanka, R., Tuck, J.: Efficient and accurate data dependence profiling using software signatures. In: Proceedings of the Tenth International Symposium on Code Generation and Optimization, pp. 186–195 (2012)
24. Yu, H., Li, Z.: Multi-slicing: a compiler-supported parallel approach to data dependence profiling. In: Proceedings of the 2012 International Symposium on Software Testing and Analysis, pp. 23–33 (2012)

Evaluating Dynamic Task Scheduling with Priorities and Adaptive Aging in a Task-Based Runtime System

Thomas Becker[1(✉)] and Tobias Schüle[2]

[1] Karlsruhe Institute of Technology, Kaiserstr. 12, 76131 Karlsruhe, Germany
thomas.becker@kit.edu
[2] Siemens AG, Corporate Technology, 81739 Munich, Germany
tobias.schuele@siemens.com

Abstract. The high degree of parallelism of today's computing systems often requires executing applications and their tasks in parallel due to a limited scaling capability of individual applications. In such scenarios, considering the differing importance of applications while scheduling tasks is done by assigning priorities to the tasks. However, priorities may lead to starvation in highly utilized systems. A solution is offered by aging mechanisms that raise the priority of long waiting tasks. As modern systems are often dynamic in nature, we developed a two-level aging mechanism and analyzed its effect in the context of 6 dynamic scheduling algorithms for heterogeneous systems. In the context of task scheduling, aging refers to a method that increases the priority of a task over its lifetime. We used a task-based runtime system to evaluate the mechanism on a real system in two scenarios. The results show a speed up of the average total makespan in 9 out of 12 conducted experiments when aging is used with the cost of additional waiting time for the applications/jobs with higher priority. However, the job/application with the highest priority is still finished first in all cases. Considering the scheduling algorithms, Minimum Completion Time, Sufferage, and Relative Cost benefit in both experiments by the aging mechanism. Additionally, no algorithm significantly dominates all other algorithms when total makespans are compared.

Keywords: Dynamic task scheduling · Task priorities · Heterogeneous architectures

1 Motivation

Modern computing systems used in fields like embedded and high performance computing feature a high degree of parallelism and are often equipped with additional accelerators, e.g. GPUs. This parallelism can be used to execute different functionality or applications in parallel as not all applications are able to exploit the available computational power due to a lack of scaling capability. However, executing multiple applications and their corresponding tasks in parallel can be

© Springer Nature Switzerland AG 2020
A. Brinkmann et al. (Eds.): ARCS 2020, LNCS 12155, pp. 17–31, 2020.
https://doi.org/10.1007/978-3-030-52794-5_2

problematic if a certain quality of service is required or expected for a subset of the applications. A common way to express differing importance of applications or functionality in non-safety-critical systems is to assign priorities accordingly. In highly utilized systems though, static task priorities can lead to the starvation of certain tasks. Starvation can be avoided by applying aging mechanisms. Aging refers to the technique of raising the priority of tasks that have waited a certain amount of time in the system for execution. This is not to be confused with hardware aging, where the fault rate of a hardware component increases over its lifetime.

Today's computing systems are often dynamic in nature, which means that the set of tasks to be executed does not remain static, and tasks' start times may be unknown as they may be triggered by signals or user interactions. Therefore, we focus on dynamic scheduling algorithms and add an adaptive aging mechanism that considers the current system state and load.

Generally, heterogeneous architectures present many challenges to application developers. A state-of-the-art solution is offered by task-based runtime systems that abstract from the underlying system and provide helpful functionality for developers. To utilize these features, we integrate our work into an existing task-based runtime system, the Embedded Multicore Building Blocks (EMB^2), an open-source runtime system and library developed by Siemens. In summary, we make the following contributions:

- We integrate 6 dynamic scheduling algorithms into a task-based runtime system and add the ability to consider task priorities.
- We develop a two-level adaptive aging mechanism to extend the scheduling module.
- We evaluate the algorithms without and with aging on a real system and investigate their behavior in terms of different metrics.
- We analyze the effect of aging in these experiments.

The remainder of this paper is structured as follows: In Sect. 2 we briefly discuss the problem statement and the necessary fundamentals of our work. EMB^2 is shortly introduced in Sect. 3. Section 4 presents the extensions made to EMB^2 and the scheduling algorithms we implemented. The experimental setup and the obtained results are presented in Sect. 5. Finally, we discuss related work (Sect. 6) and conclude with directions for future work (Sect. 7).

2   Fundamentals and Problem Statement

The basic scheduling problem comprises a set of n tasks $T := \{t_1, \ldots, t_n\}$ that has to be assigned to a set of m processing units $P := \{p_1, \ldots, p_m\}$. Next to mapping a task t_i to a processing unit p_j, scheduling also includes the assignment of an ordering and time slices. In the case of heterogeneous systems, the processing units p_j may have different characteristics, which can lead to varying executions times for a single task on different units [22]. Scheduling problems are generally considered to be NP-hard [10].

As there is no algorithm that can solve all scheduling problems efficiently, there exist many heuristics. Generally, these can be classified into static and dynamic algorithms [20]. The main difference is that static algorithms make all decisions before a single task is executed, whereas dynamic algorithms schedule tasks at runtime. Hence, static algorithms have to know all relevant task information beforehand, while dynamic ones do not need full information and are able to adapt their behavior.

This work targets tasks that may potentially create infinite task instances for execution and whose start times may be unknown. Therefore, we focus on dynamic scheduling algorithms. Additionally, we allow adding priorities to tasks. In general, task priorities can be set before runtime for every instance of this task and remain static over its lifecycle, or they are dynamically set for every task instance at runtime and may change over time [5]. The earliest deadline first (EDF) algorithm [9] is a well-known example with dynamic task priorities. Each task instance is assigned the priority $p = \frac{1}{d}$ when it arrives in the system, where d is the deadline of this instance. Contrary to EDF, rate-monotonic scheduling [16] assigns static priorities. Each task is assigned the priority $p = \frac{1}{r_i}$, where r_i is the period of task t_i. In this work, an application developer is allowed to assign a static priority to a task, which is then used for all instances of this task. However, we also utilize an *aging* mechanism that is allowed to increase the priority of a single task instance in order to improve fairness if the waiting time of an instance is considered too long. In addition, it has to be noted that we do not support task preemption.

3   Embedded Multicore Building Blocks

EMB^2 [21] is a C/C++ library and runtime system for parallel programming of embedded systems.[1] One of the challenges EMB^2 aims to solve is to reduce the complexity of heterogeneous and parallel architectures for application developers. EMB^2 builds on MTAPI, a task model that allows several implementation variants for a user-defined task. An application developer defines a specific functionality (kernel), e.g., a matrix multiplication, and is then allowed to provide one or multiple implementations for this task. Thereby, the application development can be separated from implementing specific kernels and the underlying hardware. These kernels targeting specific accelerators can then be optimized by hardware experts.

MTAPI additionally allows a developer to start tasks and to synchronize on their completion, where the actual execution is controlled by the runtime system. Thereby, the developer has to guarantee that only tasks that are ready to execute and have their dependencies fulfilled are started. MTAPI's tasks are more light-weight than a thread and distributed among worker threads for execution. Execution takes place concurrently to other tasks that have been started and it is allowed to start new tasks within a task.

---

[1] https://embb.io/.

In previous work, we already extended EMB^2 to support sophisticated scheduling on heterogeneous architectures [2]. For this purpose, we added a general processing unit abstraction that allows grouping identical units into groups. All processing units are represented by an OS-level worker thread that is used to execute the tasks mapped to this processing unit. Furthermore, we added a monitoring component to EMB^2 that monitors task execution. In the current version, the component measures task execution times including potentially necessary data transfers. The measurements are stored within a history database with the task's problem size as key. The stored data is then used to predict execution times of upcoming tasks to improve scheduling decisions. Finally, we added an abstract scheduler module and six dynamic scheduling heuristics for heterogeneous architectures to EMB^2.

As of yet, necessary data transfers for the execution on accelerators are not considered separately. This means that a task executed on an accelerator always transfers its data on and off the accelerator regardless of its predecessor and successor tasks. The high-level architecture of EMB^2 can be seen in Fig. 1.

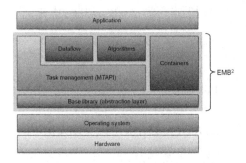

Fig. 1. High-level architecture of EMB^2 [21]

4   Dynamic Scheduling Algorithms

This section presents the extensions added to EMB^2 to support task priorities, the algorithms that have been integrated into EMB^2, and the adaptive aging mechanism used to increase fairness.

We selected the algorithms on the basis of their runtime overhead, since scheduling decisions have to be made as fast as possible in dynamic systems, their implementation complexity, and their ability to work with limited knowledge about the set of tasks to be executed. The selected heuristics can be classified into immediate and batch mode. Immediate mode considers tasks in a fixed order, only moving on to the next task after making a scheduling decision. In contrast, batch mode considers tasks out-of-order and so delays task scheduling decisions as long as possible, thereby increasing the pool of potential tasks to choose from.

4.1   EMB² Extensions

Both the abstract scheduler module and each processing unit abstraction created for [2] comprise queues to store tasks. The scheduler queue stores all tasks ready to execute, while the processing unit queues store all tasks assigned to this specific unit. For EMB² to be able to support different task priorities, each queue was replaced by a set of queues with one queue for every priority level. Assigned tasks and tasks ready to execute are then stored in queues according to their current priority.

4.2   Immediate Mode Heuristics

Minimum Completion Time (MCT). [1] combines the execution time of a task t_i with the estimated completion time ct of the already assigned tasks of a processing unit p_j. In total, MCT predicts the completion time ct of a task t_i and assigns t_i to the processing unit p_j that minimizes ct of t_i.

4.3   Batch Mode Heuristics

Min-Min. [12] extends the idea of MCT by considering the complete set of currently ready-to-execute tasks. The heuristic then assigns the task t_i that has the earliest completion time to the processing unit p_j that minimizes the completion time of t_i $ct(t_i)$. In general, the core idea is to schedule shorter tasks first to encumber the system for as short a time as possible. This can lead to starvation of larger tasks if steadily new shorter tasks arrive in the system.

Max-Min. [15] is a variant of Min-Min and based on the observation that Min-Min often leads to large tasks getting postponed to the end of an execution cycle, needlessly increasing the total makespan because the remaining tasks are too coarse-granular to partition equally. So, Max-Min schedules the tasks with the latest minimum completion time first, leaving small tasks to pad out any load imbalance in the end. However, this can lead to starvation of small tasks if steadily new longer tasks arrive.

RASA. [18] is a combination of both Min-Min and Max-Min. It uses them alternatively for each iteration, starting with Min-Min if the number of resources is odd, and Max-Min otherwise.

Sufferage. [15] ranks all tasks ready-to-execute according to their urgency based on how much time the task stands to lose if it does not get mapped to its preferred resource. The ranking is given by the difference between the task's minimum completion time and the minimum completion time the task would achieve if the fastest processing unit would not be available.

Relative Cost (RC). [17] uses the new metric rc, which divides ct of a task t_i by its average ct over all processing units, to rank tasks. RC both uses a static and a dynamic variant of the relative cost metric to compute the final metric. The static variant is defined as $\gamma_s(t_i, p_j) = \frac{et(t_i, p_j)}{et_{avg}(t_i)}$, where $et(t_i, p_j)$ is the execution time of task t_i on processing unit p_j, and $et_{avg}(t_i)$ is the average execution time of t_i over all processing units. $\gamma_d(t_i, p_j)$, the dynamic variant is defined as $\gamma_d(t_i, p_j) = \frac{ct(t_i, p_j)}{ct_{avg}(t_i)}$, where $ct(t_i, p_j)$ is the completion time of t_i on p_j, and $ct_{avg}(t_i)$ is the average ct of t_i over all processing units. The second variant is dynamic as ct is updated after each time a task is mapped to a processing unit. The variants are then combined into $rc = \gamma_s(t_i, p_j)^\alpha \cdot \gamma_d(t_i, p_j)$, where $\alpha \in [0, 1]$ determines the effect of the static costs. In this work, we use $\alpha = 0.5$. RC then maps the task with minimum rc to p_j that minimizes $ct(t_i)$.

4.4 Aging Mechanism

We added a two-level aging mechanism to the scheduling module of EMB^2 to avoid starvation of tasks. The first level was integrated directly into the scheduler module. Tasks ready to execute are stored into priority-specific ready-queues. Therefore, if there are n distinct priority levels, n separate ready-queues are created. Each time the scheduler is activated, each non-empty queue with a priority lower than the set maximum priority is checked for potential aging candidates if at least two times the amount of active processing units of tasks are currently ready to execute. So, the aging mechanism is only activated if at least $2 \cdot p$ tasks are currently enqueued with p being the number of active processing units. A task in a ready-queue is selected for priority promotion if the task is older than the average task waiting time multiplied with a threshold factor α_{prom}. After a task is promoted to a new priority queue by increasing its priority, the task is pushed to the back of the queue and its waiting time reset.

The second level of the aging mechanism targets the processing units' waiting queues. Each processing unit possesses priority-specific queues, where assigned tasks are stored. Again, if there are n distinct priority levels, each processing unit possesses n separate waiting queues. A task is assigned to the priority level, which it last had in the scheduler. As long as a processing unit is active, i.e. at least one waiting queue is non-empty, each non-empty queue with a priority lower than the set maximum priority is checked for potential aging candidates. Again, a task in a waiting queue is selected for priority promotion if the task is older than the average queue waiting time multiplied with a threshold factor α_{prom}. Actually, different threshold factors α_{prom} can be used. However in this work, we use $\alpha_{prom} = 1.7$ for both levels. This value was determined empirically as a compromise to reduce overall priority promotion while still enabling the promotion for long-waiting tasks. Again, the waiting time of a task is reset after a promotion and it is pushed to the back of the new queue.

5   Experiments

As benchmarks we considered two different scenarios with all benchmark tasks providing both a CPU and a GPU OpenCL implementation. The first scenario consists of three independent heterogeneous tasks with differing priorities and has already been used in our previous work [2]. This benchmark resembles dynamic systems as the task instances are started sporadically, thereby adding a random component to the starting point of a task instance.

For the second scenario, we execute two benchmarks of the Rodinia benchmark suite [4], hotspot3D and particlefilter, in parallel with different priorities. Both benchmarks distribute their work over several parallel tasks.

All experiments were conducted ten times with and without aging. For each experiment, we measured the makespan of each application or job, and the total makespan of all tasks. We then computed the average, the minimum, and the maximum. The makespan is defined as the time from start to finish of an application or task. Additionally, we measured the flow time of each task and again computed the average, the minimum, and the maximum. The flow time of t_i is defined as $t_{i,flow} = t_{i,finish} - t_{i,release}$, where $t_{i,release}$ is the release time or system arrival time of t_i and $t_{i,finish}$ is the finish time of t_i. So, $t_{i,flow}$ is basically the time t_i spends in the system. It has to be noted that the flow time is usually dominated by a task's waiting time. This potentially leads to large differences between minimum, average, and maximum values.

5.1   Experimental Setup

The experiments were performed on a server with two Intel Xeon E5-2650 v4 CPUs with 12 cores at 2.2 GHz each and dynamic voltage and frequency scaling enabled, an NVIDIA Tesla K80, and 128 GB of 2.4 GHz DDR4 SDRAM DIMM (PC4-19200). The software environment includes Ubuntu 18.04.3, the Linux 4.15.0-74.84-generic kernel, glibc 2.27, and the nvidia-410.48 driver. EMB^2 was compiled with the GCC 7.4.0 compiler. We limited EMB^2 to 16 CPU cores for the experiments in order to increase the system load and simulate a highly utilized system.

The scheduling algorithms presented in Sect. 4 operate in the so-called pull mode. In pull mode, the scheduler gets triggered iff at least one processing unit is idle. We chose this mode because it allows the scheduler to collect a set of tasks, which is needed to benefit from the batch mode heuristics.

5.2   Independent Heterogeneous Jobs

We chose three video-processing tasks that have both an OpenCL and a CPU implementation for the first scenario:

- J_1 (**Mean**): A 3×3 box blur.
- J_2 (**Cartoonify**): Performs a Sobel operator with a threshold selecting black pixels for edge regions and discretized RGB values for the interior. The Sobel operator consists of two convolutions with different 3×3 kernels followed by the computation of an Euclidean norm.
- J_3 (**Black-and-White (BW)**): A simple filter which replaces (R,G,B) values with their greyscale version ($\frac{R+G+B}{3}, \frac{R+G+B}{3}, \frac{R+G+B}{3}$).

All operations were applied to the *kodim23.png* test image. The three operations execute for 72.8 ms, 165.97 ms, and 11.4 ms on the CPU and 3.4 ms, 3.1 ms, and 3.1 ms on the GPU. We assigned Mean the priority 1, Cartoonify the priority 2, and Black-and-White the priority 0 with 2 being the highest and maximum priority in the system. A sporadic profile was used to create task instances of these three jobs. New task instances were released with a minimum interarrival time of $\frac{1}{k}$ s, where k is the parameter to control the load, plus a random delay drawn from an exponential distribution with parameter $\lambda = k$. By varying k, we can generate a range of different loads. The evaluation workload consists of

Table 1. Makespan results of the independent heterogeneous jobs experiment

		MCT	Min-Min	Max-Min	Suff	RASA	RC
Cartoonify	min w/o aging	1.43 s	1.46 s	1.45 s	1.46 s	1.42 s	1.44 s
	min w/ aging	1.68 s	1.64 s	1.79 s	1.51 s	1.79 s	1.59 s
	avg w/o aging	1.49 s	1.56 s	1.54 s	1.53 s	1.59 s	1.52 s
	avg w/aging	1.88 s	1.87 s	2.22 s	1.68 s	2.25 s	1.82 s
	max w/o aging	1.64 s	1.70 s	1.65 s	1.74 s	1.78 s	1.65 s
	max w/ aging	2.38 s	2.24 s	3.67 s	2.23 s	3.71 s	2.69 s
Mean	min w/o aging	2.17 s	2.31 s	2.35 s	2.36 s	2.29 s	2.35 s
	min w/ aging	2.20 s	2.69 s	2.46 s	2.48 s	2.43 s	2.70 s
	avg w/o aging	2.29 s	2.45 s	2.49 s	2.48 s	2.51 s	2.46 s
	avg w/ aging	2.37 s	2.86 s	2.71 s	2.60 s	2.62 s	2.85 s
	max w/o aging	2.55 s	2.82 s	2.70 s	2.86 s	2.93 s	2.70 s
	max w/ aging	2.57 s	3.08 s	3.23 s	2.68 s	3.14 s	3.06 s
BW	min w/o aging	2.38 s	2.75 s	2.79 s	2.83 s	2.68 s	2.85 s
	min w/ aging	2.28 s	2.42 s	2.72 s	2.52 s	2.35 s	2.56 s
	avg w/o aging	2.51 s	2.92 s	2.98 s	2.95 s	2.96 s	2.97 s
	avg w/ aging	2.46 s	2.57 s	2.98 s	2.74 s	2.58 s	2.80 s
	max w/o aging	2.77 s	3.27 s	3.23 s	3.32 s	3.38 s	3.27 s
	max w/ aging	2.70 s	2.74 s	3.23 s	2.84 s	2.75 s	2.99 s
Total	min w/o aging	2.38 s	2.75 s	2.79 s	2.83 s	2.68 s	2.85 s
	min w/ aging	2.31 s	2.69 s	2.72 s	2.62 s	2.52 s	2.70 s
	avg w/o aging	2.51 s	2.92 s	2.98 s	2.95 s	2.96 s	2.97 s
	avg w/ aging	2.47 s	2.86 s	3.03 s	2.74 s	2.82 s	2.90 s
	max w/o aging	2.77 s	3.27 s	3.23 s	3.32 s	3.38 s	3.27 s
	max w/ aging	2.70 s	3.08 s	3.67 s	2.82 s	3.71 s	3.06 s

3000 tasks corresponding in equal proportions to instances of all three jobs. We conducted the experiment for $k = 2000$ to simulate a heavily utilized system. The results of the makespan measurements can be seen in Table 1.

They show that for 5 out of 6 algorithms the average total makespan is improved by adding the aging mechanism, with Max-Min being the only algorithm where the makespan increases by 1.6%. On average over all algorithms, the average makespan is improved by about 3.75%. Sufferage profits the most with an improvement of about 7.5%. Considering the single applications, aging increases the average makespan for Cartoonify by about 26.9% and for Mean by about 8.9% compared to a decrease of 6.7% for Black-and-White. Especially for Max-Min and RASA, which uses Max-Min, the average makespan of Cartoonify suffers from an increase of over 40%. Other noteworthy results are an increase of over 13.7% for the maximum measured total makespan for Max-Min and of over 9.5% for RASA, which correlates with an increase of 123.1% and 108% respectively for Cartoonify. Comparing the algorithms, MCT achieves the best average total makespan with and without aging while Max-Min achieves the worst result in both cases. Sufferage gets the second best results in both cases.

Further, we obtained results for the flow time $t_{i,flow}$ of each task instance t_i and then computed the minimum, average and maximum flow time for all three jobs. Table 2 lists the results.

The results show a significant increase, by 95.2% on average, in the average flow time for Cartoonify in 5 out of 6 experiments, with RC being the exception. For Cartoonify, this correlates with an increase in the maximum flow time for each algorithm. In contrast, the average flow time for both Mean and Black-and-White decreases for each algorithm by 13.1% on average and 25.67% on average,

Table 2. Flow time results of the independent heterogeneous jobs experiment

		MCT	Min-Min	Max-Min	Suff	RASA	RC
Cartoonify	min w/o aging	1.54 ms	1.61 ms	1.46 ms	1.49 ms	1.46 ms	1.48 ms
	min w/ aging	1.77 ms	2.00 ms	1.47 ms	1.56 ms	1.51 ms	1.61 ms
	avg w/o aging	214.01 ms	239.59 ms	222.93 ms	229.04 ms	233.67 ms	220.88 ms
	avg w/ aging	477.43 ms	355.65 ms	427.44 ms	230.28 ms	730.11 ms	202.69 ms
	max w/o aging	1047.54 ms	948.90 ms	1500.34 ms	1137.52 ms	1000.74 ms	1124.99 ms
	max w/ aging	1306.71 ms	1553.85 ms	3624.45 ms	1454.86 ms	3313.17 ms	1838.82 ms
Mean	min w/o aging	1.81 ms	1.72 ms	1.62 ms	1.72 ms	1.64 ms	1.64 ms
	min w/ aging	2.99 ms	6.05 ms	1.65 ms	1.81 ms	1.66 ms	1.79 ms
	avg w/o aging	1073.45 ms	1208.23 ms	1206.62 ms	1261.46 ms	1145.06 ms	1226.23 ms
	avg w/ aging	904.87 ms	1092.57 ms	1030.84 ms	1073.86 ms	886.34 ms	1213.63 ms
	max w/o aging	1498.08 ms	2570.64 ms	2708.11 ms	2513.19 ms	2180.18 ms	2605.41 ms
	max w/ aging	1459.64 ms	26617.62 ms	3196.53 ms	1904.88 ms	2830.09 ms	2883.13 ms
BW	min w/o aging	1.41 ms	1.69 ms	1.33 ms	1.41 ms	1.44 ms	1.57 ms
	min w/ aging	1.76 ms	1.76 ms	1.49 ms	1.37 ms	1.48 ms	1.73 ms
	avg w/o aging	1744.71 ms	2085.71 ms	2085.25 ms	2142.52 ms	2016.48 ms	2123.33 ms
	avg w/ aging	1400.28 ms	1333.99 ms	1946.73 ms	1587.36 ms	1263.95 ms	1517.70 ms
	max w/o aging	2365.10 ms	2823.32 ms	3116.59 ms	2914.91 ms	2817.72 ms	3026.06 ms
	max w/ aging	2089.93 ms	2161.86 ms	3210.39 ms	2321.71 ms	2402.84 ms	2666.41 ms

respectively. This shows the effect of the aging mechanism as the waiting time for task instances of both jobs is reduced by increasing their priority. For Black-and-White, this also correlates with a decrease in the maximum flow time measured.

5.3   Parallel Applications

The second scenario consists of two Rodinia benchmark applications, Hotspot3D and Particlefilter, executed in parallel. **Hotspot3D** iteratively computes the heat distribution of a 3D chip represented by a grid. In every iteration, a new temperature value depending on the last value, the surrounding values, and a power value is computed for each element. We chose this computation as kernel function for a parallelization with EMB^2 and parallelized it over the z-axis. The CPU implementation then further splits its task into smaller CPU specific subtasks. This is done manually and statically by the programmer to use the underlying parallelism of the multicore CPU and still have a single original CPU task that handles the same workload as the GPU task. For the evaluation, we used a $512 \times 512 \times 8$ grid with the start values for temperature and power included in the benchmark, and 1000 iterations. The average runtime on the CPU is 5.03 ms and 7.36 ms on the GPU.

Particlefilter is a statistical estimator of the locations of target objects given noisy measurements. Profiling showed that *findIndex()* is the best candidate for a parallelization. *findIndex()* computes the first index in the cumulative distribution function array with a value greater than or equal to a given value. As *findIndex()* is called for every particle, we parallelized the computation by dividing the particles into work groups. The CPU implementation again further divides those groups into subtasks. We used the standard parameters 128 for both matrix dimensions, 100 for the number of frames, and 50000 for the number of particles for the evaluation. The average task runtime on the CPU is 17.8 ms and 6.5 ms on the GPU. Table 3 shows the makespan results without and with aging respectively for this experiment.

Overall, the average total makespan is improved by a speed up of about 3.16% when aging is used and the average total makespan improves for 4 out of 6 algorithms, with Min-Min and RASA being the exceptions. In this scenario Max-Min improves most by using aging with a speed up of about 4.5%. The individual average makespans decrease by 0.6% for Particlefilter and by 1.6% for Hotspot3D. It is also noteworthy that the minimum obtained makespan of Hotspot3D decreases by over 13% for both Max-Min and Sufferage. When the algorithms are compared, Min-Min achieves the best average total makespan without aging and Max-Min the best result with aging, with Min-Min getting the second best result.

Again, we additionally monitored the flow time $t_{i,flow}$ for all task instances t_i and computed the minimum, average, and maximum over all instances for both applications. The results are shown in Table 4.

Table 3. Makespan results of the Rodinia benchmarks experiment

		MCT	Min-Min	Max-Min	Suff	RASA	RC
Particlefilter	min w/o aging	26.46 s	26.52 s	25.97 s	26.57 s	26.62 s	25.61 s
	min w/ aging	27.25 s	25.96 s	26.37 s	26.82 s	26.23 s	26.42 s
	avg w/o aging	27.61 s	27.73 s	27.82 s	27.72 s	27.56 s	27.85 s
	avg w/ aging	27.76 s	27.17 s	27.49 s	27.61 s	27.62 s	27.67 s
	max w/o aging	28.79 s	27.92 s	28.83 s	28.54 s	28.79 s	29.56 s
	max w/ aging	28.62 s	28.37 s	28.55 s	28.97 s	29.15 s	29.47 s
Hotspot3D	min w/o aging	26.84 s	27.82 s	29.91 s	30.52 s	26.63 s	30.22 s
	min w/ aging	26.27 s	25.37 s	26.02 s	25.93 s	25.33 s	27.82 s
	avg w/o aging	30.93 s	30.59 s	31.44 s	31.38 s	30.71 s	31.78 s
	avg w/ aging	30.70 s	30.59 s	30.03 s	30.96 s	30.64 s	30.93 s
	max w/o aging	32.60 s	32.18 s	32.02 s	32.28 s	32.09 s	33.46 s
	max w/ aging	31.81 s	31.91 s	31.71 s	32.47 s	31.83 s	33.16 s
Total	min w/o aging	26.84 s	27.82 s	29.91 s	30.52 s	26.63 s	30.22 s
	min w/ aging	27.42 s	26.68 s	26.62 s	26.82 s	26.48 s	27.82 s
	avg w/o aging	30.93 s	30.59 s	31.44 s	31.38 s	30.71 s	31.78 s
	avg w/ aging	30.81 s	30.72 s	30.09 s	31.05 s	30.76 s	30.93 s
	max w/o aging	32.60 s	32.18 s	32.02 s	32.28 s	32.09 s	33.46 s
	max w/ aging	31.81 s	31.91 s	31.71 s	32.47 s	31.83 s	33.16 s

The results show a decrease in the minimum and maximum flow time of Hotspot3D for 5 and 4 algorithms, respectively. This correlates with shorter waiting times caused by a priority raise. The averages roughly remain unchanged. This can be explained by the much larger number of tasks for Hotspot3D, which are executed after Particlefilter is finished and thereby dominate the average for Hotspot3D.

Table 4. Flow time results of the Rodinia benchmarks experiment

		MCT	Min-Min	Max-Min	Suff	RASA	RC
Particlefilter	min w/o aging	4.58 ms	4.56 ms	4.52 ms	4.92 ms	4.59 ms	4.34 ms
	min w/ aging	4.29 ms	4.37 ms	4.68 ms	4.65 ms	4.18 ms	4.45 ms
	avg w/o aging	42.16 ms	42.10 ms	43.93 ms	43.61 ms	42.19 ms	42.21 ms
	avg w/ aging	43.35 ms	41.98 ms	43.46 ms	41.69 ms	42.66 ms	43.47 ms
	max w/o aging	564.30 ms	568.94 ms	606.79 ms	663.52 ms	528.12 ms	723.96 ms
	max w/ aging	636.67 ms	506.50 ms	490.95 ms	639.28 ms	651.32 ms	543.53 ms
Hotspot3D	min w/o aging	2.34 ms	1.96 ms	2.15 ms	1.92 ms	1.94 ms	1.67 ms
	min w/ aging	1.63 ms	1.65 ms	1.62 ms	1.63 ms	2.33 ms	1.62 ms
	avg w/o aging	13.33 ms	13.06 ms	13.27 ms	13.16 ms	13.25 ms	13.49 ms
	avg w/ aging	13.31 ms	13.28 ms	13.16 ms	13.31 ms	13.17 ms	13.37 ms
	max w/o aging	932.72 ms	801.60 ms	838.39 ms	686.93 ms	648.79 ms	819.58 ms
	max w/ aging	709.43 ms	674.13 ms	656.37 ms	938.87 ms	664.43 ms	735.07 ms

6   Related Work

Known existing task-based runtime systems such as HALadapt [14], the TANGO framework [8], and HPX [11] do not employ task priorities to distinguish application importance. StarPU [3], though, supports assigning a priority per processing unit type to a task. Compared to our work, StarPU does not adapt priorities at runtime.

Task or job scheduling algorithms with priorities are usually employed in the context of real-time systems, especially hard real-time systems with strict deadlines. These algorithms can be classified by the way they assign priorities [5]. Algorithms like EDF [9] or least laxity first (LLF) [6] assign each task instance a different priority. Thereby, EDF assigns each instance an individual static priority based on its deadline (see Sect. 2), whereas the priorities assigned by LLF are dynamically adapted as the laxity, the remaining time until a task has to be started to fulfill its deadline, decreases over time [5]. Contrary to this, algorithms like RMS [16] set a static priority that applies to each instance. The work of this paper differs from these algorithms as our tasks do not possess deadlines. In our work, an application developer is allowed to set a priority for a task that then applies to each instance. However, we additionally utilize an aging mechanism to increase fairness, i.e. priorities may be dynamically adapted.

Similarly to EDF, list scheduling algorithms [22–24] prioritize and then order individual task instances by computing metrics like the upward rank used by the heterogeneous earliest finish time (HEFT) heuristic.

Kim et al. [15] consider task priorities and deadlines in the context of dynamic systems, where the arrival of tasks is unknown. The paper uses three priority levels, high, medium, low, that can be assigned to task instances. The priorities are combined with the tasks' deadlines to compute the worth of executing a task. Thereby, a scheduling order is created. In contrast to our approach, priorities are not dynamically adapted to avoid starvation.

Aging mechanisms have been employed in several other works. Kannan et al. [13] implemented three priority queues and task instances get promoted to a higher priority level after a fixed time interval. Similarly, the priority of a task also gets promoted at fixed time intervals in [19]. In [7], a counter is decreased after high priority tasks are executed. If a threshold is reached, a low priority task is executed next.

7   Conclusion and Future Work

In this work, we developed an adaptive aging mechanism and integrated it in combination with six different dynamic scheduling algorithms into the task-based runtime system EMB^2. We evaluated the scheduling algorithms in two scenarios with task priorities, a benchmark consisting of three independent heterogeneous jobs with a sporadic profile, and two Rodinia benchmarks executed in parallel. Thereby, the experiments were conducted without and with the developed aging mechanism to examine its effects.

The results show a slight improvement in total average makespan (average speed up of 3.75% and 3.16%) for 5 out of 6 algorithms in the first and for 4 out of 6 algorithms in the second scenario. As expected, this correlates with an increase in the average makespan for the applications with higher priorities caused by additional waiting time (the total time spent in queues in the scheduler and processing unit). This is also reflected in the flow time measurements. The average increase of 95.2% for the average flow time of the Cartoonify benchmark is exemplary for this statement. However, the average flowtime and the average makespan of the application/job with the highest priority remain lowest over all applications/jobs in all experiments. In return, the aging mechanism reduces the waiting time which is reflected by improvements of the average makespan and the average flow time of the job/application with the lowest priority (25% decrease in average flowtime for black-and-white). A comparison between the scheduling algorithms shows that no algorithm dominates the other ones considering the average total makespan. MCT, Sufferage, and RC, though, are able to profit in all experiments by using aging.

In summary, our adaptive aging mechanism slightly improves the overall makespan in most experiments while reducing the time a low priority task has to wait for its execution, thereby increasing fairness, and still securing the fastest execution and shortest time spent in the system for the job with the highest priority. In the future, supplemental evaluations are necessary to further solidify these conclusions. Furthermore, additional optimization goals next to fairness and makespan, like energy consumption, have to be considered.

References

1. Armstrong, R., Hensgen, D., Kidd, T.: The relative performance of various mapping algorithms is independent of sizable variances in run-time predictions. In: Seventh Proceedings of the Heterogeneous Computing Workshop (HCW 1998), pp. 79–87, March 1998. https://doi.org/10.1109/HCW.1998.666547
2. Becker, T., Karl, W., Schüle, T.: Evaluating dynamic task scheduling in a task-based runtime system for heterogeneous architectures. In: Schoeberl, M., Hochberger, C., Uhrig, S., Brehm, J., Pionteck, T. (eds.) ARCS 2019. Lecture Notes in Computer Science, vol. 11479, pp. 142–155. Springer, Cham (2019). https://doi.org/10.1007/978-3-030-18656-2_11
3. Bramas, B.: Impact study of data locality on task-based applications through the Heteroprio scheduler. PeerJ Comput. Sci. **5**, e190 (2019). https://doi.org/10.7717/peerj-cs.190. https://hal.inria.fr/hal-02120736
4. Che, S., et al..: Rodinia: a benchmark suite for heterogeneous computing. In: Proceedings of the 2009 IEEE International Symposium on Workload Characterization (IISWC), IISWC 2009, pp. 44–54. IEEE Computer Society, Washington, DC (2009). https://doi.org/10.1109/IISWC.2009.5306797
5. Davis, R.I., Burns, A.: A survey of hard real-time scheduling for multiprocessor systems. ACM Comput. Surv. **43**(4), 1–44 (2011). https://doi.org/10.1145/1978802.1978814
6. Dertouzos, M.L., Mok, A.K.: Multiprocessor online scheduling of hard-real-time tasks. IEEE Trans. Softw. Eng. **15**(12), 1497–1506 (1989)

7. Dhivya., P., Sangamithra., V., KamalRaj, R., Karthik, S.: Improving the resource utilization in grid environment using aging technique. In: Third International Conference on Computing, Communication and Networking Technologies (ICCCNT 2012). pp. 1–5, July 2012. https://doi.org/10.1109/ICCCNT.2012.6395912

8. Djemame, K., et al.: TANGO: transparent heterogeneous hardware architecture deployment for energy gain in operation. CoRR abs/1603.01407 (2016). http://arxiv.org/abs/1603.01407

9. Garey, M.R., Johnson, D.S.: Computers and Intractability: A Guide to the Theory of NP-Completeness. W. H. Freeman & Co., New York (1990)

10. Graham, R., Lawler, E., Lenstra, J., Kan, A.: Optimization and approximation in deterministic sequencing and scheduling: a survey. In: Hammer, P., Johnson, E., Korte, B. (eds.) Discrete Optimization II, Annals of Discrete Mathematics, vol. 5, pp. 287–326. Elsevier (1979)

11. Heller, T., Diehl, P., Byerly, Z., Biddiscombe, J., Kaiser, H.: HPX - An open source C++ Standard Library for Parallelism and Concurrency. In: Proceedings of OpenSuCo 2017 (OpenSuCo 2017), Denver, Colorado, USA, November 2017, p. 5 (2017)

12. Ibarra, O.H., Kim, C.E.: Heuristic algorithms for scheduling independent tasks on nonidentical processors. J. ACM **24**(2), 280–289 (1977). https://doi.org/10.1145/322003.322011. http://doi.acm.org/10.1145/322003.322011

13. Kannan, G., Thamarai Selvi, S.: Nonpreemptive priority (NPRP) based job scheduling model for virtualized grid environment. In: 3rd International Conference on Advanced Computer Theory and Engineering (ICACTE), vol. 4, pp. V4-377–V4-381, August 2010. https://doi.org/10.1109/ICACTE.2010.5579461

14. Kicherer, M., Nowak, F., Buchty, R., Karl, W.: Seamlessly portable applications: managing the diversity of modern heterogeneous systems. ACM Trans. Archit. Code Optim. **8**(4), 42:1–42:20 (2012). https://doi.org/10.1145/2086696.2086721. http://doi.acm.org/10.1145/2086696.2086721

15. Kim, J.K., et al.: Dynamically mapping tasks with priorities and multiple deadlines in a heterogeneous environment. J. Parallel Distrib Comput. **67**(2), 154–169 (2007). https://doi.org/10.1016/j.jpdc.2006.06.005. http://www.sciencedirect.com/science/article/pii/S0743731506001444

16. Liu, C.L., Layland, J.W.: Scheduling algorithms for multiprogramming in a hard-real-time environment. J. ACM **20**(1), 46–61 (1973). https://doi.org/10.1145/321738.321743

17. Wu, M.-Y., Shu., W: A high-performance mapping algorithm for heterogeneous computing systems. In: Proceedings 15th International Parallel and Distributed Processing Symposium. IPDPS 2001, pp. 6 pp, April 2001

18. Parsa, S., Entezari-Maleki, R.: RASA: a new task scheduling algorithm in grid environment. World Appl. Sci. J. **7**, 152–160 (2009)

19. Pathan, R.M.: Unifying fixed- and dynamic-priority scheduling based on priority promotion and an improved ready queue management technique. In: 21st IEEE Real-Time and Embedded Technology and Applications Symposium, pp. 209–220 (2015)

20. Rajak, N., Dixit, A., Rajak, R.: Classification of list task scheduling algorithms: a short review paper. J. Ind. Intell. Inf. **2** (2014). https://doi.org/10.12720/jiii.2.4.320-323

21. Schuele, T.: Embedded Multicore Building Blocks: Parallel Programming Made Easy. Embedded World (2015)

22. Topcuoglu, H., Hariri, S., Wu, M.-Y.: Task scheduling algorithms for heterogeneous processors. In: Proceedings of the Eighth Heterogeneous Computing Workshop (HCW 1999), pp. 3–14, April 1999. https://doi.org/10.1109/HCW.1999.765092
23. Xu, Y., Li, K., Hu, J., Li, K.: A genetic algorithm for task scheduling on heterogeneous computing systems using multiple priority queues. Inf. Sci. **270**, 255–287 (2014). https://doi.org/10.1016/j.ins.2014.02.122. http://www.sciencedirect.com/science/article/pii/S002002551400228X
24. Zhao, H., Sakellariou, R.: An experimental investigation into the rank function of the heterogeneous earliest finish time scheduling algorithm. In: Kosch, H., Böszörményi, L., Hellwagner, H. (eds.) Euro-Par 2003. LNCS, vol. 2790, pp. 189–194. Springer, Heidelberg (2003). https://doi.org/10.1007/978-3-540-45209-6_28

An Architecture for Solving the Eigenvalue Problem on Embedded FPGAs

Alwyn Burger[1]([envelope]) [ID], Patrick Urban[1] [ID], Jayson Boubin[2] [ID],
and Gregor Schiele[1] [ID]

[1] University of Duisburg-Essen, 47057 Duisburg, Germany
{falwyn.burger,gregor.schiele}@uni-due.de,
patrick.urban@stud.uni-due.de
[2] The Ohio State University, Columbus, OH, USA
boubin.2@osu.edu
http://www.uni-due.de/es, http://www.osu.edu

Abstract. Resource-limited embedded devices like Unmanned Aerial Vehicles (UAVs) often rely on offloading or simplified algorithms. Feature extraction such as Principle Component Analysis (PCA) can reduce transmission data without compromising accuracy, or even be used for applications like facial detection. This involves solving eigenvectors and values which is impractical on conventional embedded MCUs.

We present a novel hardware architecture for embedded FPGAs that performs eigendecomposition using previously unused techniques like squared Givens rotations. That leads to a 3x performance improvement for 16×16 covariance matrices over similar approaches that use much larger FPGAs. Offering higher than 30 fps at only 68.61 μJ per frame, our architecture creates exciting new possibilities for intelligent mobile devices.

Keywords: Hardware architecture · FPGA · Feature extraction

1 Introduction

Eigendecomposition and feature extraction have been the focus of continued research for many years [19,25,26]. Algorithms like principle component analysis (PCA) allow us to simplify a dataset to only its important features by identifying its distinguishing eigenvectors. By projecting data into a reduced eigenspace (the space described by the eigenvectors), we can simplify problems like facial detection and recognition to a comparison of a few eigenvalues, i.e. the relative weight of each eigenvector. More applications of these techniques are being developed, e.g. in the field of convolutional neural networks (CNNs) where PCA can find dominant features and compress network structures [12].

However, PCA's batched nature and computational complexity makes it infeasible for resource-limited devices. In power-limited applications such as Unmanned Aerial Vehicles (UAVs) that rely on camera feeds, feature extraction

© Springer Nature Switzerland AG 2020
A. Brinkmann et al. (Eds.): ARCS 2020, LNCS 12155, pp. 32–43, 2020.
https://doi.org/10.1007/978-3-030-52794-5_3

could offer data size reduction through local preprocessing. Adding the online learning capabilities of incremental PCA (IPCA) further allows the devices to incorporate incoming images into the training set – thereby continuously improving its performance.

To enable this, an accelerator architecture is required that efficiently performs eigendecomposition on an embedded FPGA. This offers improved energy efficiency for small devices over GPUs, and additionally provides flexibility over ASICs as it can be reconfigured to deploy another accelerator at runtime. Delegating this complex computational task to a local FPGA promises considerably improved processing power over doing everything on a MCU.

However, most techniques for doing eigendecomposition such as the QR algorithm [11] strongly depend on trigonometric functions or square roots to compute a Givens rotation matrix [14] which are resource inefficient on such devices. Although alternatives like Squared Givens Rotations (SGR) [9] would be considerably more efficient, they introduce scaling issues and have to the authors' knowledge not been successfully used in the QR algorithm.

In this paper we present a revolutionary hardware architecture design for performing eigenvalue decomposition (EVD) on an embedded FPGA. By using a number of state-of-the-art optimization techniques in a novel way, our system is capable of increasing processing speed by 3–4x over current literature without compromising accuracy.

Our main contributions are

1. a highly resource-optimized computing architecture for solving eigenvalue problems,
2. that is scalable from tiny embedded FPGAs to standard desktop models through a fully homogeneous network of processing elements,
3. and offers pipelined single clock processing elements for maximum processing speed.

We present our solution by looking at related work in Sect. 2, followed by an overview of our solution in Sect. 3. The details of the technical contributions follows in Sect. 4, after which we evaluate our solution in Sect. 5. Finally, we study the application case of UAVs in Sect. 6 and conclude with some final thoughts in Sect. 7.

2   Related Work

Incremental PCA [1,6] is a relatively recent development. It offers us the crucial benefit of online training and avoids the expansion of the covariance matrix as the training dataset is expanded. Conventional eigensolver algorithms have been found to be ill-suited to GPU architectures [18] even though they can achieve nearly 5x speedup over CPUs. QR decomposition (which computes a single iteration of the QR algorithm) specifically has been implemented using different GPU-based accelerator architectures [17,18].

Similar to our approach, Guerrero-Ramírez et. al. [15] presented the first eigensolver based on systolic arrays that implements the QR algorithm using

FPGAs. These arrays describe a network of processing elements, where each partially computes a function and passes to their neighbors. In this case, they iteratively calculate trigonometric functions. Their implementation improved processing time by a factor of 1.17x–1.37x compared to CPU architectures.

A slower solution that includes a full PCA solver was shown by Korat [19]. It uses significantly more FPGA resources than the previously mentioned work, and showed that some of the components such as mean calculation and data normalization are very inefficient on FPGAs.

Ultimately, these authors were limited by having to iteratively approximate trigonometric functions using the COordinate Rotation DIgital Computer (CORDIC) algorithm [21] – causing severe slowdown for more processed bits [23]. Additionally, their resource consumption is impractically high for an embedded FPGA. Other projects that use systolic arrays for QR decompositions on FPGAs [8,27] have similar limitations. To the best of the authors' knowledge our work represents the first FPGA implementation of the QR algorithm using systolic arrays based on an algorithm that does not rely on trigonometric functions.

3   Solution Design

At the core of our EVD (see Fig. 1) is the triangular systolic array (a) to perform QR decomposition. It is composed of two types of nodes: boundary (b) on the diagonal of the triangular matrix and internal (c) off the diagonal. This iteratively computes the eigenvalues and eigenvectors of a provided covariance matrix, entering in a skewed order (d). The QR-array results can be fed back into the system using the buffer (e) until the result converges, at which point the deskewed output (f) is presented. The scaled output of each step of the QR array is down-scaled (g).

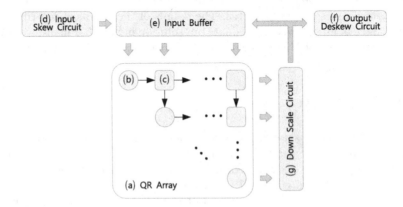

Fig. 1. Parallel triangular systolic array processor to determine the eigenvalues and eigenvectors by calculating the QR decomposition based on SGR in an iterative manner.

The starting point for our solution is the QR decomposition. We first consider a real symmetric matrix A_0 of dimensions $n \times n$, which is the covariance matrix for the PCA to be applied. The rank of this matrix corresponds with the number of eigenvectors being computed, effectively controlling the number of features being extracted. The approximate determination of the eigenvalues and eigenvectors is done with the QR algorithm. It is an iterative application of the QR decomposition, which factorizes a matrix by means of plane rotations, e.g. Givens rotations.

Each QR iteration is given as:

$$[Q_i, R_i] = qrd(A_i) \tag{1}$$
$$A_{i+1} = R_i Q_i \tag{2}$$

and is performed n times over the matrix A until its diagonal elements converge to the eigenvalues. The collection of eigenvectors Q themselves could be determined by calculating the product of all these orthogonal matrices Q_i:

$$Q = \prod_{i=0}^{n} Q_i \tag{3}$$

Using SGR allows us to first use A_i to compute R_i, and even to solve Eq. 1 by processing the identity matrix I to compute Q_i. The orthogonal similarity transformation A_{i+1} follows by processing R_i. Furthermore, the eigenvectors Q in Eq. 3 can be determined efficiently by processing each computed Q_i. As all of these are processed in the same way, we can reuse the processing elements for improved efficiency.

Each iteration in the QR algorithm thus consists of the input sequence $S = \{A, Q, R\}$. The problem remains that all R_i and Q_i are scaled by the SGR, meaning it cannot be directly used for further iterations.

4 Technical Implementation Contributions

Our primary contribution addresses the internal structure of the processing elements in the QR array. We improve upon the latency of current state-of-the-art algorithms by using the square-root-free algorithm proposed by Döhler [9] to avoid the associated latency. It allows our processing elements to have a latency of only one clock cycle.

Although SGR has been used for *QR decomposition*, it has not been applied to the *QR algorithm* due to scaling problems. Since results should be fed through multiple iterations, this would cause overflow errors. To the authors' best knowledge SGR has therefore not been used for EVD using the QR algorithm.

4.1 SGR Result Scaling

The SGR algorithm scales each calculated QR decomposition [9], which means that it cannot be used for the QR algorithm directly. Especially when using fixed-point representation, this will quickly cause overflow.

We found the result to be as shown in Eq. 4, which shows that the eigenvalues λ_i found on the diagonal of $R*$ are squared. Additionally, other values are linearly scaled with the value of λ_i^2. Similarly, each column in $Q*$ is scaled.

$$
\overset{\text{A}}{\begin{bmatrix} a_{11} & \cdots & a_{1n} \\ a_{21} & \cdots & a_{2n} \\ \vdots & \ddots & \vdots \\ a_{n1} & \cdots & a_{nn} \end{bmatrix}} \xrightarrow[\text{QR}]{\text{SGR}} \overset{\text{R*}}{\begin{bmatrix} \lambda_1^2 & \lambda_1 r_{12} & \cdots & \lambda_1 r_{1n} \\ 0 & \lambda_2^2 & \cdots & \lambda_2 r_{2n} \\ \vdots & \vdots & \ddots & \vdots \\ 0 & 0 & \cdots & \lambda_n^2 \end{bmatrix}} \overset{\text{Q*}}{\begin{bmatrix} \lambda_1 q_{11} & \cdots & \lambda_n q_{1n} \\ \lambda_1 q_{21} & \cdots & \lambda_n q_{2n} \\ \vdots & \ddots & \vdots \\ \lambda_1 q_{n1} & \cdots & \lambda_n q_{nn} \end{bmatrix}} \tag{4}
$$

A well-known approach for determining reciprocal square roots [10] is given by iteratively solving the Newton Method

$$
y_{i+1} = \frac{1}{2}(3y_i - y_i^3 x_{in}) \qquad y_0 = 0.5 \tag{5}
$$

until it converges to $y = \frac{1}{\sqrt{x_{in}}}$. However, this can be slow under a bad *initial guess* y_0 very different from the actual result. An interesting approach to this was coined for the video game *Doom*[1], where the initial guess is varied depending on the input value.

Extending on this concept, we have developed a novel way to use lookup-tables (LUTs) for using this with fixed-point numbers. By choosing from a pre-computed set of appropriate y_0 based on the input x_{in}, we can reduce the number of iterations required for convergence. Given a sufficiently large LUT with 128 24-bit entries to create a very accurate initial guess, we can directly solve Eq. 5 in a single iteration.

4.2 Shared Division

Solving EVD using SGR requires two divisions [7,9,20], which for a matrix width of n would result in $\frac{1}{2}(n^2 - n)$ dividers. Since they are non-trivial to implement in hardware (particularly the reciprocal of the divisor), this would be very resource-intensive.

Therefore, we studied the schedule of active nodes in the array as shown in Fig. 2. As division is only required in diagonal mode, this shows that only one division occurs per row. This allows us to share the dividers more efficiently, and to reduce the required number to n. For a 16×16 covariance matrix, this leads to a reduction of 104 divider circuits.

4.3 HDL Optimizations

Similarly, large binary multipliers occupy substantial logic resources in FPGAs. One can build a sequential circuit using multiplexers on the inputs that cycles a single multiplier for multiple usages. The basic idea is to first get the result of A * B in a register, then to multiply that by C.

---

[1] https://github.com/id-Software/DOOM.

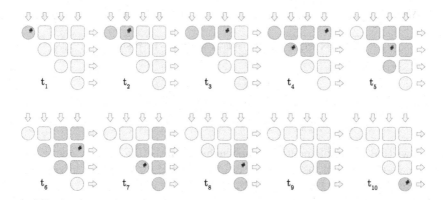

Fig. 2. Propagation through the array at time t_i highlighting the active nodes

Additionally, the DSPs are optimized using a technique called *retiming*, which involves moving registers across combinatorial logic to improve the design performance without affecting the input or output behavior of the circuit [22]. Despite the optimized interconnection in dedicated logic, adder chains used to implement binary multipliers in DPS slices cause delays.

Based on anecdotal evidence, this technique improved our maximum frequency possible from 247.64 MHz to 373.13 MHz. This increase of 50.67% greatly boosts performance, as the worst case slack is greatly improved.

5   Evaluation

Before our approach can be applied to a practical system, we must first evaluate how well it performs. It is aimed at embedded FPGAs that have been shown to be very capable in applications such as small neural networks [5,24]. Not only must we ensure that our design is efficient enough to fit this resource-constrained class of FPGAs, but also that the resulting performance is adequate to offer real-world usability.

5.1   Resource Utilization

Firstly, we consider the resource consumption on the FPGA. As detailed in Sect. 4, the greatest impact on this is through the size of the processed matrix. Larger matrix sizes enable the computation of more eigenvectors at increased complexity, thereby extracting more identifiable features. Therefore, we varied this size in Table 1 and captured the number of resources consumed by each solution.

Note that these results are an absolute number and is valid for the entire 7 series devices from Xilinx, as they are all based on the same architecture. This provides a convenient way to choose the correct FPGA to use for a specific application, based on the limiting hardware resource. For example, the Spartan 7 range varies in available DSP slices from 10 on the S6 to 160 on the S100. It

Table 1. Synthesis results for Xilinx-7 series FPGAs in absolute numbers

Matrix width	Logic cells	Flip-flops	DSP slices
4×4	3,940	1,497	15
8×8	11,616	5,548	45
16×16	36,165	21,612	153

also shows that the implemented homogeneous architecture is easily adaptable to larger-scale deployment, as a larger FPGA could simply support a larger matrix and thereby enable larger inputs and more complex applications.

To put these numbers in context, we compare them to the most recently published CORDIC-based eigensolvers [15, 19] in Fig. 3. We consider specifically the logic cells and DSP slices, as these are commonly the limiting factors.

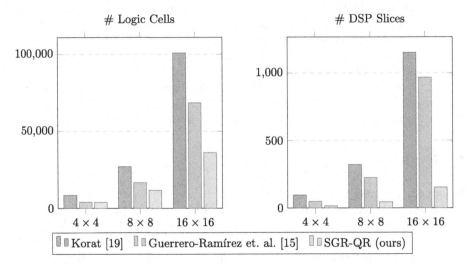

Fig. 3. Comparison of the resource utilization of different matrix sizes with related work

Omitting the additional logic required by a CORDIC-based approach significantly improves our resource consumption, as almost half of the logic cells are saved. More importantly, the number of DSP blocks are reduced by almost 85%. This allows us to use FPGAs with significantly fewer resources, or to support a larger covariance matrix.

5.2   Throughput

Before the system's throughput rate can be calculated, the maximum operating frequency f_{max} must be determined using a static time analysis. Table 2 lists the maximum possible clock rates for all targets as the matrix size is varied. As the other solution is not open source, only the clock frequencies achievable in [15] are provided for comparison. Unsurprisingly, the maximum clock rate at which the implemented design can be operated decreases with increasing logic density.

Table 2. Maximum operating frequencies in [MHz] depending on the matrix width

Target	f_{max} matrix width		
	4×4	8×8	16×16
XC7S100	239.01	228.31	219.11
XC7A100	265.75	237.87	237.98
XC7K70	339.90	272.18	252.46
EP4SGX230 [15]	235.32	220.15	201.35

To determine the throughput rate, the combined latency of the processing elements must be considered. Each has a latency of $p = 6$ clock cycles. The number of iterations to be performed is set to $k = 30$ for a direct comparison with related work.

Firstly, the latency of initially filling the FIFO buffers is $L_{FIFO} = 3n - 1$ cycles, where n is again the matrix width. Each of the QR iterations requires $L_{QR} = 24n - 6$ while the inverse square root consumes a constant $L_{Sqrt} = 12$ clock cycles.

This leads to a model of the overall latency L and throughput T of

$$L(n, k) = L_{FIFO} + k \cdot (L_{QR} + L_{Sqrt}) \tag{6}$$

$$T(n, k) = \frac{f_{max}}{L(n, k)} = \frac{f_{max}}{24nk + 3n + 6k - 1} \text{ solutions/s} \tag{7}$$

where each solution refers to a complete calculation of all eigenvalues and -vectors [15]. The maximum operating frequency f_{max} results from the static timing analysis results shown in Table 2.

Figure 4 compares the throughput of our approach to a CORDIC-based approach [15] and a desktop CPU. The SGR-QR was implemented on a Xilinx Spartan-7 XC7S100, and a fixed point representation of 24 bits was chosen to match the input signals in each DSP48 block. Note that the frequency of the memory is assumed to be at least as fast as the main clock f_{max}.

The SGR-QR is faster than the CORDIC-based approach implemented on the considerably larger Virtex-7 (3.81x for 4×4 to 4.26x for 16×16 matrices). The benefits of our highly parallel architecture over higher clocked CPUs become particularly evident for larger matrices. This is due to our approach's linear runtime, while CPU implementations are commonly $O(N^3)$ and single-threaded.

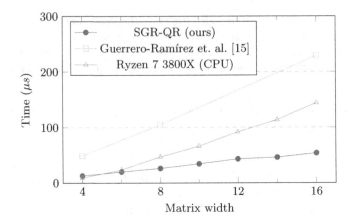

Fig. 4. Time in μs required to compute a single eigenpair of different matrix sizes

5.3 Estimated Power Usage

Using the maximum clock frequency from Table 2, the implementation results for a number of embedded FPGAs from the Xilinx-7 Family are shown in Table 3.

Table 3. Implementation results for matrix size 16×16

Target	LUT	FF	DSP	Power [W]
Spartan-7 XC7S100	49%	17%	96%	1.402
Artix-7 XC7A100	49%	17%	64%	1.379
Artix-7 XC7A200	23%	8%	21%	1.238
Kintex-7 XC7K70	76%	26%	64%	1.425
Kintex-7 XC7K160	31%	11%	26%	1.214

Apart from the proportional resource consumption for a number of devices, the estimated power usage is also provided by the Vivado software of Xilinx. This is the active consumption of the device, highlighting the importance of processing speed to offset the cost of keeping the FPGA powered.

6   Application Case Study

Our system is designed with high energy and resource efficiency in mind in order to support the small, battery-powered devices used in many pervasive or organic computing applications. One example is a fully autonomous aerial system (FAAS) that combines unmanned aerial vehicles (UAV), edge computers, and data centers to create intelligent systems. They should autonomously explore their environment and accomplish high level goals without human intervention [3], which requires expensive techniques such as facial detection.

UAVs typically only carry small batteries with flight times between 15 and 25 min and therefore rely on offloading tasks to edge and cloud systems [4]. Transferring images between edge and UAV is costly, taking on the order of seconds in prior work [4]. Prior work on micro aerial vehicles with in-situ vision systems performed detections locally on UAV. Increased frame rates and decreased power-consumption were achieved by downsampling (5–12 fps) and compressing incredibly small images (17 fps) to be used as input to neural networks [2,13]. In aerial applications this can lead to loss of critical information contained in small regions. Instead, our system can be used as a local facial detection algorithm or as preprocessing to reduce offloaded data to only the important features.

Therefore, we evaluated our architecture design using the well-known FDDB dataset [16]. A sliding window of 250×250 pixels is moved over an input image of resolution 640×480. The covariance matrix varies with the number of training images from 4 to 16 faces. For this dataset, 95% of the variance could be described with 62.5% of vectors – offering substantial data reductions. Processing speed of an EVD on the Spartan 7 S100 for different size covariance matrices are presented in Fig. 5. Using a naive classifier, increasing the matrix size from 4×4 to 16×16 increased the accuracy from 44.6% to 55.5% (in line with similar approaches [16]).

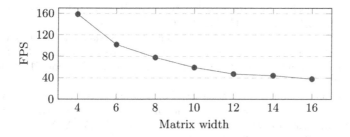

Fig. 5. Frames per second for facial detection application

The speed is reduced for larger matrices, but even at 16×16 the performance remains above 30fps. This shows the trade-off between speed and complexity, which can be combined with Table 3 to tailor the hardware choice. Each device's power usage allows us to estimate the energy usage per frame to between 3.14 μJ for $n = 4$ and 68.61 μJ for $n = 16$. Although related work does not provide this information, we are confident that our system is more energy efficient, as transmitting even an image preview (720×900) can take a UAV 1.4 s [4].

7   Conclusion and Future Work

We presented our approach for EVD on an embedded FPGA. Through optimizations like systolic arrays and dynamically scaling SGR results, we achieved an improvement of 3x performance over other approaches. Additionally, the architecture is resource optimized enough to be used even on small embedded FPGAs like a Xilinx Spartan 7.

In future work, we hope to implement this onto a set of drones augmented with FPGAs for real-world experiments. We also plan to investigate using this feature extraction method as a preprocessor for CNNs. By using the reconfigurability of the FPGA, we can switch between EVD to perform a learning feature extraction on incoming data followed by a neural network. This provides processing complexity heretofore impractical on embedded devices used in organic computing applications.

Acknowledgements. The authors acknowledge the financial support by the Federal Ministry of Education and Research of Germany in the KI-Sprung LUTNet project (project number 16ES1125).

References

1. Artac, M., Jogan, M., Leonardis, A.: Incremental PCA for on-line visual learning and recognition. In: Object Recognition Supported by User Interaction for Service Robots, vol. 3, pp. 781–784. IEEE (2002). https://doi.org/10.1109/icpr.2002.1048133
2. Boroujerdian, B., Genc, H., Krishnan, S., Cui, W., Faust, A., Reddi, V.: MAVBench: micro aerial vehicle benchmarking. In: 51st Annual IEEE/ACM International Symposium on Microarchitecture (MICRO), pp. 894–907. IEEE (2018). https://doi.org/10.1109/MICRO.2018.00077
3. Boubin, J., Chumley, J., Stewart, C., Khanal, S.: Autonomic computing challenges in fully autonomous precision agriculture. In: IEEE International Conference on Autonomic Computing (ICAC), pp. 11–17 (2019). https://doi.org/10.1109/ICAC.2019.00012
4. Boubin, J.G., Babu, N.T., Stewart, C., Chumley, J., Zhang, S.: Managing edge resources for fully autonomous aerial systems. In: Proceedings of the 4th ACM/IEEE Symposium on Edge Computing, pp. 74–87. ACM (2019). https://doi.org/10.1145/3318216.3363306
5. Burger, A., Qian, C., Schiele, G., Helms, D.: An embedded CNN implementation for on-device ECG analysis. In: IEEE International Conference on Pervasive Computing and Communications Workshops (PerCom Workshops) (2020)
6. Cardot, H., Degras, D.: Online principal component analysis in high dimension: which algorithm to choose? arXiv preprint arXiv:1511.03688 (2015)
7. Cerato, B., Masera, G., Viterbo, E.: Enabling VLSI processing blocks for MIMO-OFDM communications. VLSI Design **2**, 11 (2008). https://doi.org/10.1155/2008/351962
8. Chen, D., Sima, M.: Fixed-point CORDIC-based QR decomposition by Givens rotations on FPGA. In: International Conference on Reconfigurable Computing and FPGAs, pp. 327–332. IEEE (2011). https://doi.org/10.1109/ReConFig.2011.38
9. Döhler, R.: Squared givens rotation. IMA J. Numer. Anal. **11**(1), 1–5 (1991). https://doi.org/10.1093/imanum/11.1.1
10. Ercegovac, M.D., Lang, T., Muller, J.M., Tisserand, A.: Reciprocation, square root, inverse square root, and some elementary functions using small multipliers. IEEE Trans. Comput. **49**(7), 628–637 (2000). https://doi.org/10.1109/12.863031

11. Francis, J.G.: The QR transformation a unitary analogue to the LR transformation–Part 1. Comput. J. **4**(3), 265–271 (1961). https://doi.org/10.1093/comjnl/4.3.265
12. Garg, I., Panda, P., Roy, K.: A low effort approach to structured CNN design using PCA. IEEE Access **8**, 1347–1360 (2019). https://doi.org/10.1109/ACCESS.2019.2961960
13. Genc, H., Zu, Y., Chin, T.W., Halpern, M., Reddi, V.J.: Flying IoT: toward low-power vision in the sky. IEEE Micro **37**(6), 40–51 (2017). https://doi.org/10.1109/MM.2017.4241339
14. Golub, G.H., Van Loan, C.: Matrix Computations, 4th edn. The Johns Hopkins University Press, Baltimore (2013)
15. Guerrero-Ramírez, J.E., Velasco-Medina, J., Arce, J.C.: Hardware design of an eigensolver based on the QR method. Analog Integr. Circ. Sig. Process **82**(1), 125–134 (2014). https://doi.org/10.1109/LASCAS.2013.6519065
16. Jain, V., Learned-Miller, E.: FDDB: a benchmark for face detection in unconstrained settings. Technical report. UM-CS-2010-009, University of Massachusetts, Amherst (2010)
17. Johansen, T.A.H.: On the improvement and acceleration of eigenvalue decomposition in spectral methods using GPUs. Master's thesis, UiT Norges arktiske universitet (2016)
18. Kerr, A., Campbell, D., Richards, M.: QR decomposition on GPUs. In: Proceedings of 2nd Workshop on General Purpose Processing on Graphics Processing Units, pp. 71–78. ACM (2009). https://doi.org/10.1145/1513895.1513904
19. Korat, U.A., Alimohammad, A.: A reconfigurable hardware architecture for principal component analysis. Circuits Syst. Signal Process. **38**(5), 2097–2113 (2018). https://doi.org/10.1007/s00034-018-0953-y
20. Ma, L., Dickson, K., McAllister, J., McCanny, J.: MSGR-based low latency complex matrix inversion architecture. In: 9th International Conference on Signal Processing, pp. 410–413. IEEE (2008). https://doi.org/10.1109/ICOSP.2008.4697158
21. Meher, P.K., Valls, J., Juang, T.B., Sridharan, K., Maharatna, K.: 50 years of cordic: algorithms, architectures, and applications. IEEE Trans. Circuits Syst. I Regul. Pap. **56**(9), 1893–1907 (2009). https://doi.org/10.1109/TCSI.2009.2025803
22. Pan, P., Lin, C.C.: A new retiming-based technology mapping algorithm for LUT-based FPGAs. In: Proceedings of the 1998 ACM/SIGDA Sixth International Symposium on Field Programmable Gate Arrays, pp. 35–42. ACM (1998). https://doi.org/10.1145/275107.275118
23. Ren, M.: Cordic-based Givens QR decomposition for MIMO detectors. Ph.D. thesis, Georgia Institute of Technology (2013)
24. Schiele, G., Burger, A., Cichiwskyj, C.: The elastic node: an experimentation platform for hardware accelerator research in the internet of things. In: Proceedings of the IEEE International Conference on Autonomic Computing, ICAC, pp. 84–94 (2019). https://doi.org/10.1109/ICAC.2019.00020
25. Sorzano, C.O.S., Vargas, J., Montano, A.P.: A survey of dimensionality reduction techniques. arXiv preprint arXiv:1403.2877 (2014)
26. Turk, M.A., Pentland, A.P.: Face recognition using eigenfaces. In: Proceedings of the IEEE Computer Society Conference on Computer Vision and Pattern Recognition, pp. 586–591 (1991). https://doi.org/10.5120/20740-3119
27. Yu, H.: FPGA-based implementation of QR decomposition. Master's thesis, Arizona State University (2014)

ECC Memory for Fault Tolerant RISC-V Processors

Alexander Dörflinger[1(✉)], Yejun Guan[1], Sören Michalik[2], Sönke Michalik[2], Jamin Naghmouchi[2], and Harald Michalik[1]

[1] Institute of Computer and Network Engineering (IDA), Technische Universität Braunschweig, Braunschweig, Germany
{doerflinger,guan,michalik}@ida.ing-tu-bs.de
[2] Institute for Robotics and Process Control (IRP), Technische Universität Braunschweig, Braunschweig, Germany
{soeren.michalik,so.michalik,naghmouchi}@tu-braunschweig.de

Abstract. Numerous processor cores based on the popular RISC-V Instruction Set Architecture have been developed in the past few years and are freely available. The same applies for RISC-V ecosystems that allow to implement System-on-Chips with RISC-V processors on ASICs or FPGAs. However, so far only very little concepts and implementations for fault tolerant RISC-V processors are existing. This inhibits the use of RISC-V for safety-critical applications (as in the automotive domain) or within radiation environments (as in the aerospace domain). This work enhances the existing implementations Rocket and BOOM with a generic Error Correction Code (ECC) protected memory as a first step towards fault tolerance. The impact of the ECC additions on performance and resource utilization are discussed.

Keywords: BOOM · Cache · Error correction code · Fault injection · RISC-V · Rocket · Scrubbing · Single Event Effects

1 Introduction

The free and open RISC-V Instruction Set Architecture (ISA) has attracted an active community building processor cores and ecosystems, which makes it competitive to established processor designs. There is a strong growth forecast for the number of RISC-V cores in industrial-, consumer-, and other areas [13]. However, there are only a few approaches of fault-tolerant RISC-V designs for safety-critical and radiation-tolerant applications, which would open its use for the automotive and areospace domain. An exploitation of this market potential requires compliance with corresponding safety standards.

Mitigation of transient faults is one important mechanism for fault-tolerant electronics. ISO26262 [10] names error detection to increase the diagnostic coverage, which is required for electronics of higher safety levels. Furthermore, aerospace systems operating in environments with increased radiation levels are

© Springer Nature Switzerland AG 2020
A. Brinkmann et al. (Eds.): ARCS 2020, LNCS 12155, pp. 44–55, 2020.
https://doi.org/10.1007/978-3-030-52794-5_4

subject to non-destructive Single Event Effects (SEEs). An effective mitigation technique for hereby caused soft errors in memories are again error correction (and detection) codes [8]. Therefore, this paper will present how existing RISC-V implementations can be enhanced with Error Correction Codes (ECCs).

Contribution: This work devises and implements a highly configurable ECC protection for arbitrary memory structures and applies it to two different RISC-V processor systems. Some ECC implementations are already existing for RISC-V designs. However, they cover only parts of the memory structures of a processor core and/or are limited to small low-power solutions with processing power restrictions. The generic and configurable ECC approach of this work targets also large RISC-V cores for high performance computing and fully covers all memory structures. This prepares RISC-V for its use in safety-critical applications and radiation-intense environments. Together with further fault tolerance mechanisms (e.g., lockstep operation or other redundancy schemes), high performance RISC-V systems could be made available for the automotive and aerospace domain.

The rest of this paper is organized as follows: Sect. 2 presents existing fault tolerance concepts for RISC-V processors and Sect. 3 gives an introduction to the Chipyard[1] framework used within this work. A detailed description of the new ECC concept follows in Sect. 4. Results of its implementation are presented in Sect. 5.

2   Related Work

The SHAKTI-F design [9] mitigates SEEs by combining ECC with recomputation techniques. It features a relatively small 5-stage in-order microprocessor. However, its development has been discontinued and it is not maintained within the current SHAKTI-C class core anymore. Fault tolerance of caches, typically representing the largest and hence most susceptible memory structures within a processor system, is not addressed. The Klessydra microprocessor [4] based on PULPino[2] is a configurable 2 to 4-stage RISC-V implementation. Several time- and space redundancy techniques have been applied for fault tolerance. Again, error protection for larger memory structures has not been addressed yet.

Apart from SHAKTI-F and Klessydra (being free and open), some proprietary implementations are available targeting space applications. Microsemi (Microchip Technology Inc.) offers the Mi-V[3] ecosystem, which allows to instantiate RISC-V cores on their radiation tolerant FPGAs. Cobham Gaisler released the 64 bit NOEL-V[4] soft-core recently. However, just as the LEON3/4 processor, it is not fault tolerant by design; fault tolerant versions are built from radiation hardened standard cell libraries and are hence bound to specific technologies.

---

[1] https://chipyard.readthedocs.io/en/latest, UC Berkeley.

[2] https://pulp-platform.org.

[3] https://www.microsemi.com/product-directory/fpga-soc/5210-mi-v-embedded-ecosystem.

[4] https://www.gaisler.com/index.php/products/processors/noel-v.

Just as the LEON3/4 based System-on-Chips (SoCs) GR712 [5] and GR740 [6], NOEL-V uses *write-through* and *no-write allocate* cache policies. This guarantees that an erroneous cache line can be corrected by fetching its copy from a higher memory hierarchy level at any time. It makes an error correction code dispensable, because an error detection (e.g., parity bit) suffices. However, the hereby utilized write policies typically yield lower performance than *write-back* and *write allocate*.

The Rocket and BOOM RISC-V cores by UC Berkeley implement *write-back* and *write allocate* cache policies and are partly equipped with optional ECC. A Single Error Correction Double Error Detection (SEC-DED) code protects the caches of the SiFive U-series IPs (U54, U74) and SoC (FU540), which utilize the 5-stage in-order Rocket processor core. The BROOM tapeout [2] adds resilience methods to the 7-stage out-of-order BOOMv2 processor. Several techniques tolerate hard bit errors in L1 and L2 caches, which allows an aggressive reduction of the core voltage. However, the approach requires to know the position of erroneous bits beforehand (e.g. by running a built-in self-test). Hence, it cannot correct soft errors at arbitrary bit positions and does not increase fault tolerance.

3   Rocket and BOOM Processor Cores Within Chipyard

The Chipyard framework developed by UC Berkeley bundles RISC-V cores, peripherals, software compilers, simulators, and further tools for SoC development. It targets both FPGA implementations and ASIC design. Hardware components are programmed in the Chisel hardware description language (HDL). Chisel is based on object-oriented Scala and adds hardware construction primitives. Frequently utilized hardware elements are collected in a Chisel standard library (e.g., multiplexers, arbiters, counters, FIFO queues, etc.). As a modern programming language, it offers high abstraction, re-usability, and parameterization options. Compared to well-established HDLs such as Verilog and VHDL, the increased abstraction level results in a higher line of code efficiency and speeds up development times. However, it also adds complexity to simulation and netlist generation: Chisel code has to be compiled into an intermediate circuit representation (FIRRTL) before it is transformed into synthesizable Verilog.

Chipyard integrates two RISC-V implementations, which are both highly configurable. The 5-stage in-order Rocket core [1] offers both 32 and 64 bit register file widths, several branch prediction options, arbitrary cache sizes, and optional ISA extensions (MAFD). The core provides three privilege levels, addresses virtual memory, and is capable to boot Linux. Rocket is already equipped with the ECC options *Parity*, *SEC*, and *SEC-DED* for both L1I$ and L1D$ (tag and data each) which can be activated with limitations. Rocket provides blocking and non-blocking versions for the L1D$. The non-blocking version allows hit-under-miss requests, which enables the in-order processor to execute further instructions until the load data is used. However, this powerful non-blocking L1D$ variant does not support ECC in its tag field at all, and its implementation in the data field results in compile errors (several versions up to the current v1.3 have been tested without success).

Chipyard allows an easy replacement of the Rocket core with the 7-stage superscalar out-of-order BOOM core [3]. The instruction fetch unit is equipped with complex predictors (e.g., GShare and TAGE). A tapeout in TSMC 28 nm achieved 1.0 GHz and a Coremark of 3.77 per MHz [2], which makes BOOM one of the best performing RISC-V implementations. The BOOM utilizes the non-blocking L1D$ version of the Rocket, hence it is afflicted with the same ECC problems as described above. The L1I$ does not support any ECC implementation. Further resilience methods have been applied to the BOOM implementation [2]. However, they only target static hard errors and cannot mitigate arbitrary soft errors.

The cache resilience works on Rocket and BOOM are promising but not complete. ECC has been successfully applied only to the Rocket core, with restrictions. Memory structures apart from caches such as Branch Prediction Unit (BPU) tables and the Page Table Walker (PTW) are not protected. So far, the BOOM core lacks ECC protection for memories completely. Those gaps are closed in this work using a generic ECC memory described in the following section. The generic design makes it easy to apply it to all memory structures and is not limited to L1 caches. This work concentrates on the ECC integration in Rocket and BOOM; however, the parameterizable ECC memory interface allows to migrate the approach to other processor implementations as well.

4   Generic Error Correcting Memory Component

4.1   ECC Memory Requirements

Within the Rocket core only caches and one BPU table are implemented as memory arrays; all other buffers are mapped to registers due to their small size. This results in a small number of memory arrays ranging from 4 to 11, depending on the Rocket core configuration (Table 1). The more complex BOOM core additionally implements several buffers of the BPU and the PTW as memory arrays, due to their increased size. This results in 18 to 38 memory arrays within the BOOM core, depending on its configuration. The BOOM *Small* and *Medium* configurations differ mainly by their issue width; however, memory sizes and organization are very similar. The same applies for differences between *Large* and *Mega* configurations.

Enhancing all those memory arrays with ECC protection separately requires multiple and far-reaching code changes. For the Rocket core with FIRRTL transformation and simulation times ranging from 10 to 21 min[5], this would be still feasible. However, the BOOM core generation and simulation takes up to 185 min, making a custom ECC adaption of each memory array very laborious.

---

[5] Depending on its configuration; measured for `run-bmark-tests` on Intel i5-6500 3.20 GHz, 48 GB RAM.

Table 1. Number of memory arrays for selected Rocket and BOOM configurations

Core configuration	L1I$	L1D$	BPU	PTW	Sum
Rocket (Tiny)	2	2	0	0	4
Rocket (Big)	5	5	1	0	11
BOOM (Small)	5	5	7	1	18
BOOM (Medium)	5	5	7	1	18
BOOM (Large)	17	9	11	1	38
BOOM (Mega)	17	9	11	1	38

Hence, a generic ECC memory component has been developed separately, which can simply replace existing arrays and keeps the integration effort minimal.

The access scheme (e.g., single/dual-ported) and array organization (e.g., row of words) differs for each array, which has been considered during the development of the generic ECC protected memory called ECCmem. Hereby the newly created ECCmem component goes beyond existing IP such as Synopsis Design-Ware STAR ECC IP, the ARM Artisan embedded memory IP, and Xilinx ECC IP [14]. It is technology independent, i.e. not bound to any FPGA family or ASIC process, and additionally mitigates error accumulation, which is not addressed in any of the existing solutions.

4.2   ECCmem Component

Figure 1 depicts the overall ECCmem architecture. Dashed blocks are instantiated depending on configuration settings. The IOs `read/write request` and `response` make use of Chisel's Decoupled interface, wrapping the data vectors with a ready-valid pair. This interface abstraction allows a simple replacement of existing memories with the ECCmem module.

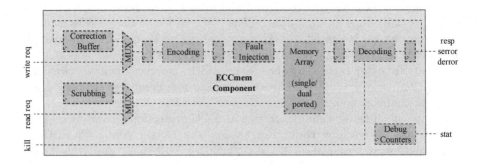

Fig. 1. Configurable ECCmem component

Depending on the capabilities of the selected ECC option, single and double errors are signaled through dedicated outputs (`serror`, `derror`) and tracked in error counter registers. Statistics on soft errors can be retrieved from further debug counters containing the number of read/write accesses, fault injection-, and error correction events. When relying on this error statistic information, reads from uninitialized data have to be precluded as they may result in inadvertent error events. One solution is to initialize the complete memory at boot time (applied e.g. to the BOOM data cache tag array). Another option is to set the kill signal, canceling read accesses to uninitialized data in subsequent clock cycles. This is a feasible solution for e.g. cache data arrays, because the initialization information can be retrieved from the coherency flags one clock cycle after issuing the read access.

Listing 1.1 gives an overview of the parameterization options of the ECCmem module, which satisfy the diverse requirements of memory arrays within the Rocket and BOOM implementations. The object oriented Chisel programming language makes it easy to handle the parameterization. Some ECCmem ports are conditional (depending on the configuration), which is not supported by other HDLs.

Listing 1.1. ECCmem Parameterization

```
class ECCmemParams(
    ecc_code: Code = SECDEDCode,
    reg_enc_input: Boolean = false,
    reg_enc_output: Boolen = false,
    reg_dec_input: Boolean = false,
    reg_dec_output: Boolean = false,
    depth: UInt = 1024,
    row_format: Vec[UInt],
    block_size: Int = 8,
    interleaving: Boolean = true,
    single_ported: Boolean = true,
    correction_buffer: UInt = 1,
    scrubbing: Boolean = true,
    scrubbing_interval: UInt = 4,
    fault_injection: Boolean = true,
    name: String
)
```

Encoding and Decoding. The ecc_code parameter allows to select different detection/correction codes. The current implementation supports the algorithms none, parity, and hamming codes (SEC, SEC-DED). Hsiao codes could be added in future for reduced area and delay overheads. Several reg_* options allow to insert registers at encoder/decoder inputs and outputs, which can be used to relax timing. In particular, the decoding path can result in long signal latencies, which may require corresponding register insertions.

Array Organization. The parameters depth, row_format, and block_size define the array organization (Fig. 2). The read/write data may be partitioned into several words within a row. Individual words may be accessed using a read-/write mask. A word can be further divided into blocks, which allows arbitrary ECC widths. This facilitates a fine-grained balancing of area overhead and encoding/decoding latency: the smaller the block size, the smaller its encoding/decoding latencies, but the higher its area overhead. Each block contains the original data and ECC bits being grouped together. The interleaving option shuffles bits of different blocks. It mitigates SEEs causing multi-bit errors in neighboring cells, because the erroneous bits will be spread across different blocks. With the single_ported option, the memory type can be selected. By default, a dual ported memory will be generated (e.g. required for BOOM data cache). Arrays with exclusive read/write access (e.g. BOOM instruction cache) benefit from the optimized resource utilization of single ported memory.

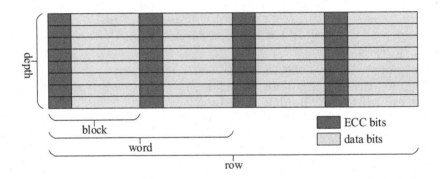

Fig. 2. ECCmem array organization

Correction Buffer. With the current ECC implementations (parity, SEC, SEC-DED), two or more accumulated errors cannot be corrected, and depending on the selected ECC algorithm, not even detected. When using codes with single error correction capabilities, the corrected data can be written back to memory. Any correction_buffer size greater 0 enables this error correction option. It mitigates error accumulation, because a single error typically gets corrected before a second SEE strikes the same block. In order to minimize the impact on the overall system, write back accesses are assigned with a lower priority than read and write requests. The corrected word is stored within a correction buffer until there is no concurrent write access (and in case of single-ported memory no concurrent read access). Corrected data must not overwrite updated data. Therefore, an entry within the correction buffer gets cleared once it senses a regular write access to the same memory address as the destination of corrected data. Once the correction buffer writes its content back to memory, the soft error has been removed. This error correction process typically completes before detection of a second error in another arbitrary word being read. However, systems with high read/write loads (i.e. long retention times in the correction buffer) and high expected error rates, may use a `correction_buffer` depth of >1.

Scrubbing. In the past, only very small numbers of SEE-caused soft errors were expected in on-chip memories such as caches of earth-bound applications, hence error accumulation has not been an issue [12]. However, the soft error rate increases exponentially with voltage decrease, and error accumulation has to be considered when relying on new technologies [7]. Furthermore, space applications can be exposed to multiple SEEs within minutes [11], depending on the FPGA or ASIC technology and the mission region. When operating under such conditions, the interval of system read accesses to memory arrays is not sufficient for preventing error accumulation. This applies for caches in particular: Cache line access patterns are hardly predictable, which increases the probability of error accumulation for less frequently accessed data regions.

To overcome this problem, the optional `scrubbing` option regularly reads the complete memory array, and guarantees a minimum interval of single bit error corrections. Again, the scrubbing mechanism is assigned with a lower priority than read requests (and write requests in case of single-ported memory) to eliminate any negative performance impact on the overall system. As depicted in Fig. 1, the scrubbing block generates continuous read accesses to memory. Once the decoding block detects a correctable error in one of the reads triggered by the scrubbing block, the corrected data will be passed to the correction buffer which handles the write back to memory. In order to prevent an overflow, a full correction buffer forces the scrubbing process to pause. Scrubbing adds high load on the read port of the memory, which can increase the power consumption. This effect can be limited by setting the `scrubbing_interval`, which defines together with the operating frequency and memory `depth` the scrubbing period (Eq. 1). When setting the `scrubbing_interval` to 0, the ECCmem component attempts to scrub the memory as fast as possible. In this case Eq. 1 gives only a lower bound of the scrubbing period, because any other regular read (and write) request stalls a scrubbing access.

$$\text{scrubbing period} = \frac{1}{f} \cdot \texttt{depth} \cdot (\texttt{scrubbing\_interval} + 1) \qquad (1)$$

Scrubbing accesses are distributed evenly in time for a balanced load distribution. To achieve this, a scrubbing counter decrements by 1 each clock cycle and triggers a scrubbing access to the next memory row once it hits 0 (① in Fig. 3). A scrubbing access increments the counter again by the defined `scrubbing_interval`. Higher priority accesses (read/write requests) delay the scrubbing access ②. Multiple high priority accesses could cause the scrubbing counter to underflow, which is prevented by stalling the scrubbing access ③.

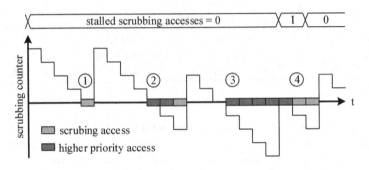

Fig. 3. Distributing scrubbing accesses in time

Stalled accesses are executed as soon as no other high priority access blocks the memory port ④.

Fault Injection. The `fault_injection` option allows sporadic injection of 1-bit and 2-bit errors with a user-defined probability into already encoded data (containing both data- and ECC bits). when writing to memory. This feature is used to test the functionality of the ECC, correction buffer, scrubbing, and debug counters. It further allows to simulate the processor behavior under SEEs, which can replace expensive radiation tests to some extent.

5   Evaluation

All memory arrays of Rocket and BOOM have been replaced with the ECCmem component described in Sect. 4. The integration did not require any far reaching changes, because the `read/write request` and `response` interfaces allowed a simple mapping to existing memories. The `kill` signal (compare Sect. 4.2) is generated correctly for all memories by determining the status of the memory content (initialized/uninitialized). The ECCmem is designed to have no effect on system performance (except when inserting additional register stages with a `reg_*` option). Both the write back of corrected data and the scrubbing mechanism are low prioritized, preventing to thwart read/write accesses. This has been verified running benchmark tests in a Verilator simulation for various Rocket and BOOM configurations (Table 2). Results for the Dhrystone benchmark are identical before and after integration of the ECCmem component.

Due to the similarity of the *Small*/*Medium* and *Large*/*Mega* variants regarding memory size and organization (Table 1), resource utilization results will be discussed for the *Small* and *Mega* configurations only, but apply for the *Medium* and *Large* variants respectively. Figure 4 (left) summarizes the resource utilization of BOOM implementations on the Xilinx Virtex UltraScale+ VCU118 evaluation board and the respective overhead for ECC protection. Figure 4 (right) plots the results for an ASIC synthesis in the GlobalFoundries 22 nm FDX technology (12 T), whereas area is reported for combinatorial cells, flip-flops, and

Table 2. Dhrystone results for different Rocket and BOOM configurations

Core configuration	Dhrystones/s
Rocket (Big)	1912
BOOM (Small)	1920
BOOM (Medium)	2526
BOOM (Large)	3521
BOOM (Mega)	3700

memory macros separately. The ECCmem components have been configured with default parameters, except for array specific attributes such as width, depth, and single/dual ported variants. Hence, a SEC-DED code is applied; scrubbing, error correction, and fault injection are activated.

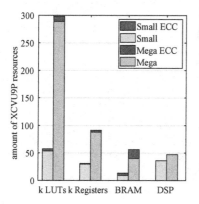 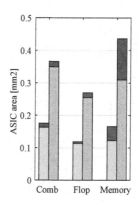

Fig. 4. Resource utilization of Small- and Mega BOOM configurations with and without ECC protection. Left: Xilinx Virtex UltraScale+ XCVU9P FPGA resources. Right: Area for GF 22 nm FDX technology after synthesis.

The FPGA resource overhead for ECC protected BOOM variants compared to original BOOM implementations is calculated in Table 3. It shows moderate overhead for logic (5.31%) and registers (3.44%) on average, but a large increase of RAM resources (41.68%). The ECC memory protection has no effect on DSP utilization. The area increase of the ASIC synthesis yields similar results.

For further evaluation of the increased RAM utilization, Fig. 5 depicts the RAM size for caches and other memory arrays within BOOM implementations with and without ECC protection. The overhead of RAM resources depends on the selected ECC `block_size`. Here the block size has been limited to 26 bits for all memories, which adds a maximum of 6 parity bits to each block. The block size can be only as large as the memory word size. Hence, very small word sizes result in high area overheads, as it is the case for e.g. the Branch Target Buffer

Table 3. Resource/area overhead of ECC protection for BOOM cores

Core config	FPGA resource overhead				ASIC area overhead		
	LUT	Regs	BRAM	DSP	Comb	Flop	Mem
Small BOOM	7.50%	3.47%	42.11%	0%	7.40%	4.52%	38.89%
Mega BOOM	3.11%	3.41%	41.25%	0%	4.82%	5.77%	40.85%
Average	5.31%	3.44%	41.68%	0%	6.11%	5.15%	39.87%

Bimodal Predictor table (BTB bim) with 1 bit words. In this case, applying TMR to this array is a more area efficient protection against SEEs.

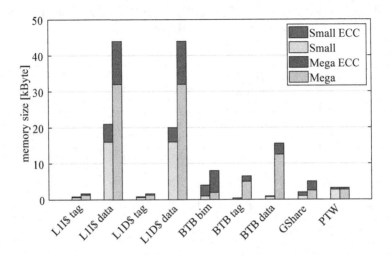

Fig. 5. ECC BRAM overhead for individual memories

6   Conclusion

In this paper we presented a generic solution to enhance existing RISC-V processor core implementations with ECC protected memory. When selecting codes with error correction capabilities, error accumulation can be mitigated by writing corrected data back to memory. Applying a scrubbing mechanism further reduces probabilities of error accumulation. As a reference implementation, all memory structures within the Rocket and BOOM cores have been replaced by the newly developed ECC protected memory. Logic and register overheads for the ECC protection are small, while RAM resource usage increases as expected for the applied hamming codes. Future work will complete the fault tolerance mechanisms for RISC-V processors by applying further redundancy techniques, which enables the use of RISC-V for safety-critical applications and the aerospace domain. Hereby, the remaining processor logic could be protected using TMR or lockstep techniques.

Acknowledgment. This work has been funded by BMWI under grant number 50 RK 1820 and is part of the DLR Raumfahrtmanagement Komponenteninitiative.

References

1. Asanović, K., et al.: The rocket chip generator. Technical report. UCB/EECS-2016-17, EECS Department, University of California, Berkeley, April 2016
2. Celio, C., Chiu, P., Asanović, K., Nikolić, B., Patterson, D.: Broom: an open-source out-of-order processor with resilient low-voltage operation in 28-nm cmos. IEEE Micro **39**(2), 52–60 (2019). https://doi.org/10.1109/MM.2019.2897782
3. Celio, C., Chiu, P.F., Nikolic, B., Patterson, D.A., Asanović, K.: Boom v2: an open-source out-of-order RISC-V core. Technical report. UCB/EECS-2017-157, EECS Department, University of California, Berkeley, September 2017
4. Cheikh, A., Cerutti, G., Mastrandrea, A., Menichelli, F., Olivieri, M.: The microarchitecture of a multi-threaded RISC-V compliant processing core family for IoT end-nodes. In: De Gloria, A. (ed.) ApplePies 2017. LNEE, vol. 512, pp. 89–97. Springer, Cham (2019). https://doi.org/10.1007/978-3-319-93082-4_12
5. Cobham Gaisler AB: GR712-UM, 2.12 edn. (2018)
6. Cobham Gaisler AB: GR740-UM-DA, 2.3 edn. (2019)
7. Dixit, A., Wood, A.: The impact of new technology on soft error rates. In: International Reliability Physics Symposium. pp. 5B.4.1–5B.4.7, April 2011. https://doi.org/10.1109/IRPS.2011.5784522
8. European Cooperation for Space Standardization - ECSS: ECSS-Q-HB-60-02A Space Product Assurance - Techniques for Radiation Effects Mitigation in ASICs and FPGAs Handbook, 1 edn., September 2016
9. Gupta, S., Gala, N., Madhusudan, G.S., Kamakoti, V.: SHAKTI-F: a fault tolerant microprocessor architecture. In: IEEE 24th Asian Test Symposium (ATS), pp. 163–168, November 2015. https://doi.org/10.1109/ATS.2015.35
10. International Organization for Standardization - ISO: ISO 26262 - Road Vehicles - Functional Safety, 2016 edn., April 2016
11. Michel, H., Guzmán-Miranda, H., Dörflinger, A., Michalik, H., Echanove, M.A.: SEU fault classification by fault injection for an FPGA in the space instrument SOPHI. In: NASA/ESA Conference on Adaptive Hardware and Systems (AHS), pp. 9–15, July 2017. https://doi.org/10.1109/AHS.2017.8046353
12. Mukherjee, S.S., Emer, J., Fossum, T., Reinhardt, S.K.: Cache scrubbing in microprocessors: myth or necessity? In: Proceedings of the 10th IEEE Pacific Rim International Symposium on Dependable Computing, pp. 37–42, March 2004. https://doi.org/10.1109/PRDC.2004.1276550
13. SEMICO Research Corporation: RISC-V Market Analysis The New Kid on the Block, cc315-19 edn., November 2019
14. Xilinx Inc.: ECC LogiCORE IP Product Guide, PG092, v2.0 edn. (2017)

3D Optimisation of Software Application Mappings on Heterogeneous MPSoCs

Gereon Führ[1]([✉]), Ahmed Hallawa[1], Rainer Leupers[1], Gerd Ascheid[1], and Juan Fernando Eusse[2]

[1] RWTH Aachen University, Aachen, Germany
{fuehr,hallawa,leupers,ascheid}@ice.rwth-aachen.de
[2] Silexica GmbH, Cologne, Germany
eusse@silexica.com

Abstract. Increasing the efficiency of parallel software development is one of the key obstacles in taking advantage of heterogeneous multi-core architectures. Efficient and reliable compiler technology is required to identify the trade-off between multiple design goals at once. The most crucial objectives are application performance and processor power consumption. Including memory power into this multi-objective optimisation problem is of utmost importance. Therefore, this paper proposes the heuristic MORAM solving this three-dimensional Pareto front calculation. Furthermore, it is integrated into a commercially available framework to conduct a detailed evaluation and applicability study. MORAM is assessed with representative benchmarks on two different platforms and contrasted with a state-of-the-art evolutionary multi-objective algorithm. On average, MORAM produces 6% better Pareto fronts, while it is at least 18× faster.

Keywords: Power-performance trade-off · Mapping · Heterogeneous · MPSoCs · Multi-objective optimisation · Pareto

1 Introduction

For today's computational requirements of the embedded domain, heterogeneous Multi- and Many-Processor Systems-on-Chip (MPSoCs) provide the best trade-off for power, performance and cost requirements. However, developers writing applications for MPSoCs are forced to consider the increased hardware complexities all at once. Moreover, power management techniques, such as Dynamic Voltage and Frequency Scaling (DVFS), have to be set carefully to handle power budgets efficiently. Especially for high-performance embedded applications, memory power consumption has a share of up to 46% of the entire system power [11,16]. Hence, fast and accurate compiler technology has to ease software development and determine the trade-off between all requirements.

Consequently, it is not a coincidence that the simultaneous optimisation of different goals is the next evolution towards optimised software [6,12,13,15,18].

© Springer Nature Switzerland AG 2020
A. Brinkmann et al. (Eds.): ARCS 2020, LNCS 12155, pp. 56–68, 2020.
https://doi.org/10.1007/978-3-030-52794-5_5

This simultaneous optimisation is essentially a Multi-Objective Optimisation Problem (MOOP), which is known to be NP-hard [25]. The main research focus is still towards application performance and Processing Element (PE) power consumption, neglecting the impact of the memory to the entire power share. Therefore, this paper presents a solution for this three-dimensional MOOP. Compared to single-objective optimisation, an entire set of non-dominated optimal solutions is determined. This set is also known as Pareto front. These precomputed solutions can be used during execution of the application to select the most appropriate configuration dynamically [22,23].

In the literature, there are numerous multi-objective optimisation algorithms, e.g. particle swarm optimisation [31,32]. However, a widely utilised family of algorithms suitable for MOOPs in the context of MPSoC optimisation are Evolutionary Multi-Objective Algorithms (EMOAs) (Sect. 2). EMOAs are preferred as they find close-to-optimal solutions. They are general-purpose search strategies, population-based and inspired by biological evolution. However, EMOAs are performance sensitive to their hyperparameter setup. Also, the deterioration in solution quality is significant when the computational resources are restricted.

Much attention has also been paid to ensuring comprehensive tool flows. Examples are HOPES [14], DAEDALUS [29] or MAPS [19], and SLX [2].

As a consequence, this work proposes the novel heuristic *MORAM* designed to calculate three-dimensional Pareto fronts. The MOOP considers the objectives application performance, PE and memory power consumption for software application mapping on MPSoCs. The solution quality is comparable with a state-of-the-art EMOA implementation, while the computation is much faster. Further, MORAM is integrated into SLX to enable the evaluation of the applicability and quality. The case studies are based on representative benchmarks and two different hardware platforms: ODROID-XU3 [1], and an in-house Heterogeneous Many-core Virtual Platform (HeMVP).

2 Related Work

For single-objective problems, heuristics find satisfactory solutions in a short time frame by extracting and integrating the MPSoC platform and application features [27]. As the MOOP solution space is significantly larger, heuristic approaches are commonly not considered. To mention one example that addresses an MOOP, the authors of [10] present a heuristic which computes the Pareto front for two objectives: application performance and PE power. It achieves comparable solutions but with considerably faster speed than an EMOA.

More popular approaches for MOOPs are machine learning models, getting the best power-performance trade-off. The authors of [6] propose run-time optimisation of task mapping, voltage and frequency selection. A library is generated storing the Pareto optimal system configuration for minimum power and maximum performance. At run time, the most appropriate configuration is selected. In [13], a multinomial logistic regression classification is used to map a set of classifiers offline to Pareto optimal platform configurations. During run-time, these classifiers are invoked to select the most suitable configuration for the current system load. A later approach applies Deep Q-Learning to dynamically control the processor type, their number and frequency [12]. Similar to all these run-time methods, design-time training is necessary. With the heuristic approach of the paper at hand, there is no need to apply a machine learning model. Pareto optimal configurations are available immediately after the execution of the heuristic.

Software mapping optimisation based on EMOAs is presented, e.g. in [18]. Following the divide-and-conquer principle, a decomposition approach avoids handling the entire MOOP at once. The workload balancing for each processor, cluster and communication network is computed independently. A post-optimisation step captures the final Pareto front of this mapping problem. In [15], the two objectives application performance and memory energy consumption are optimised based on EMOAs. The latter comes closest to the approach proposed in this work. The heuristic of this paper optimises for performance, processor power and memory power consumption as a three-dimensional MOOP.

3 System Model

For the exploration and modelling of the mapping problem, SLX requires an application written in C for Process Networks and an MPSoC platform model as input. The tool offers heuristics to optimise for performance, PE power consumption, or solving the MOOP of both objectives [5]. A target-specific code generator translates the parallel code including the output of these heuristics into plain C code that is fed into the MPSoC compiler.

3.1 Application Model

The Kahn Process Network (KPN) model of computation is a well-known approach for modelling parallel behaviour [17]. Processes execute deterministically and sequentially, and communicate via unbounded point-to-point First-In First-Out (FIFO) channels. As a consequence, the mapping problem is reduced to the optimal distribution and mapping of the processes and selection of the appropriate power modes.

KPN applications are described as directed graphs, i.e. $A = \{\mathcal{Z}, \mathcal{C}\}$, where $\mathcal{Z}$ is the set of the application processes and $\mathcal{C}$ is the set of directed FIFO channels. Via the FIFO channel $c_{ij} \in \mathcal{C}$, a process $z_i \in \mathcal{Z}$ can communicate with process $z_j \in \mathcal{Z}$. For the implementation of KPN applications in ANSI-C, a small set of keywords form C for Process Networks (CPN). With this, processes and channels, and the required operations for accessing them are described. As unbounded FIFO channels cannot be realised, the minimum size is chosen that allows deadlock-free execution of the application.

In order to assess the application and generate timing and power information, an event-driven approach simulates a CPN application. The combination of static and dynamic profiling enables the computation of process and total execution time, as well as individual and collective power values. The dynamic profiling collects traces that contain the execution dependent behaviour of the application, such as write accesses to output channels. This timing simulation engine estimates the execution time, including communication within a 20% error margin [4].

3.2 MPSoC Model

The MPSoC platform model specifies, e.g., memory and communication architecture, and type and number of PEs. An MPSoC platform L is modelled as a directed graph: $L = \{R, E\}$, where R is a set of hardware resources present in the platform and E defines a set of connections. In this paper, R contains a set of all PEs $\mathcal{Q}$, all memories $\mathcal{M}$, and all caches $\mathcal{K}$, with $R = \mathcal{Q} \cup \mathcal{M} \cup \mathcal{K}$ and $(\mathcal{Q} \cap \mathcal{M}) \cup (\mathcal{Q} \cap \mathcal{K}) \cup (\mathcal{M} \cap \mathcal{K}) = \emptyset$. The set $M_q = \{m_1, m_2, ...\}$ denotes all memories reachable by $q \in \mathcal{Q}$.

A write Hardware Channel (HWC) is the path from q to a reachable $m \in M_q$ using connections $\{e_1, e_2, ...\} \in E$, crossing caches $\{k_1, k_2, ...\} \in \mathcal{K}$. For read HWCs, the direction is the opposite. FIFO channels are assigned to HWC after the processes $\mathcal{Z}$ are mapped to $\mathcal{Q}$. An HWC consists of a write HWC starting at the source PE q_i and a read HWC ending at sink PE q_j. Both write and read HWC use the same $m \in \{M_{q_i} \cap M_{q_j}\}$. Existing heuristics take care to choose a reachable m that is closest to both PE.

Power information is defined for each PE and memory. Hardware resources connected to the same power supply are part of a common voltage domain. Similarly, all resources connected to the same clock are part of the same frequency domain. The underlying power model consists of the basic CMOS power consumption parts, i.e. leakage power $P^s_{f,i} = I \cdot V_f$ and dynamic power $P^d_{f,i} = C \cdot f \cdot V_f^2$, where i indicates the hardware resource, I denotes the leakage current, V_f is the permitted minimum voltage for frequency f, and C is the switching capacitance and f the operating frequency. In [21], it is shown that with this model, power estimates for PEs including L1 caches are possible with about 9% error on average. The memory power model achieves average estimation errors of 15% (DRAM) and 11% (SRAM).

4   Multi-objective Optimisation

The objective functions are evaluated by simulating the task mapping and platform power configuration. The objective space has 3 values: the execution time of the application t^e, the average power consumed by the PEs $P^{\mathcal{Q}}$ and the average power consumed by the memories $P^{\mathcal{M}}$. The following reasoning explains why it is sufficient to not include memory allocation in the decision space. It only consists of the process mapping and the platform power configuration, i.e. the selection of voltage and frequency.

Due to the principles of KPN, source processes send their data to destination processes via the FIFO channels. This procedure requires writes and reads to the memory because the FIFO buffer is allocated there and contributes to increment the memory power consumption. By changing the process-to-PE mapping, the access behaviour to the underlying memory hierarchy is implicitly influenced.

For single shared main memory systems, the effectiveness of the caches can be exploited with an optimal mapping and thus the memory power reduced. In the case of distributed memories of different size or purposes, i.e. scratchpad or shared, it makes sense to allocate the FIFO buffer always to the most local memory (Sect. 3.2). If the source and destination process are assigned to PEs that do not share a scratchpad, the HWC is, e.g., routed via the main memory. The consequence is higher memory power consumption and slower application execution time.

4.1   Problem Definition

For the formal problem definition, the processes $\mathcal{Z}$ and available PEs $\mathcal{Q}$ are part of the inputs. The platform power configuration set $\mathcal{C}$ is also required and taken from the platform model. $\mathcal{C}$ contains the set of possible frequencies $\mathcal{F}$, the permitted minimum voltage V_f for a selected frequency f, the switching capacitance C and the leakage current I for every hardware resource. The CPN simulation engine computes t^e, $P^{\mathcal{Q}}$ and $P^{\mathcal{M}}$ according to Eq. 1, 2 and 3.

$$t^e = \sum_{q \in \mathcal{Q}} \sum_{z \in \mathcal{Z}} \frac{M_{z,q}}{f_{k,q}} (t^c_{z,q} + t^s_{z,q}) \tag{1}$$

$$P^{\mathcal{Q}} = \sum_{q \in \mathcal{Q}} \sum_{z \in \mathcal{Z}} P^d_{f,q} M_{z,q} + P^s_{f,q} \tag{2}$$

$$P^{\mathcal{M}} = \sum_{m \in \mathcal{M}} P^s_m + P^d_m \cdot u_m \tag{3}$$

The number of cycles used by z scheduled on q are given with $t^c_{z,q}$. The simulated inter-process dependencies and concurrencies are considered with $t^s_{z,q}$, namely the latencies incurred by context switches and FIFO data communication, i.e. delays caused by the HWCs. The utilisation of the memory u_m is calculated using the HWC access activity trace, which is generated by the CPN simulation engine. $M_{z,q} = 1$ indicates that process z is mapped to PE q.

The resulting minimisation problem is given in Eq. 4, where (4b) and (4c) define that each process is mapped on exactly one PE.

$$\min \quad \mathbf{f} = \left(t^e, P^{\mathcal{Q}}, P^{\mathcal{M}} \right) \tag{4a}$$

$$\text{s.t.} \quad \sum_{q \in \mathcal{Q}} M_{z,q} = 1, \ \forall z \in \mathcal{Z} \tag{4b}$$

$$M_{z,q} \in \{0,1\}, \ \forall z \in \mathcal{Z}, \ \forall q \in \mathcal{Q} \tag{4c}$$

4.2 Heuristic: MORAM

MORAM finds a Pareto front approximation for the objectives application exe-
cution time $\mathbf{t}^e$, PE and memory power consumption, $\mathbf{P}^{\mathcal{Q}}$ and $\mathbf{P}^{\mathcal{M}}$. As invoking
the CPN simulation engine is a major bottleneck, and due to the large search
space, a pruning step is necessary. This procedure is taken from [10]. The authors
prove that this reduces the search space effectively and application-independent.
The final Pareto front is generated on the basis of this reduced exploration
space. The heuristic contains further techniques reducing the amount of CPN
simulation engine calls.

Algorithm 1 shows the entire pseudo code of MORAM with the input sets:
PEs $\mathcal{Q}$, the processes $\mathcal{Z}$, and all platform power configurations $\mathcal{C}$. The heuristic
outputs the final Pareto front in form of the objective value vectors $\mathbf{t}^e \in \mathbb{R}^{|PP|}$,
$\mathbf{P}^{\mathcal{Q}} \in \mathbb{R}^{|PP|}$, $\mathbf{P}^{\mathcal{M}} \in \mathbb{R}^{|PP|}$, with $|PP|$ being the number of the final Pareto points.
Further, the corresponding platform power configurations $\mathbf{C} \in \mathbb{R}^{|PP| \times |\mathcal{Q}| \times 2}$ con-
tain the selected frequency and voltage per PE and Pareto point. Also, the pro-
cess mappings $\mathbf{M} \in \{0,1\}^{|PP| \times |\mathcal{Z}| \times |\mathcal{Q}|}$ are part of the output. In the following,
the individual steps of MORAM are discussed.

PruneSearchSpace. First, a pre-pruning phase is necessary if $|\mathcal{C}|$ is very large
to keep the run time of the entire pruning phase acceptable. To formalise this, a
user-defined number N enables a uniform distributed random process, selecting
N platform configurations, as shown in line 6–8. The uniform distribution ensures
a representative selection of all possible $\mathcal{C}$. According to [10], a reasonable choice
of N would be $N = 10^5$.

Second, a classification and selection procedure is performed based on two
qualifiers: Total Nominal Power (TNP) and the Execution Time Indicator (ETI)
(lines 9–11). The TNP value for a $c \in \mathcal{C}$ is computed as given in Eq. 5. The ETI
reflects an execution time approximation, where the processes are assumed to
have all input data available and are ready to execute. Also, the process-to-PE
assignment is not done to remain mapping independent. The execution time is
calculated for every PE type $\mathcal{Q}_{type} \subseteq \mathcal{Q}$. Hence, inter-process dependencies and
concurrencies are not considered in Eq. 6.

$$P_{\mathrm{TNP}} = \sum_{q \in \mathcal{Q}} P_{f,q}^d + P_{f,q}^s \tag{5}$$

$$t_{\mathrm{ETI}} = \sum_{q \in \mathcal{Q}_{type}} \sum_{z \in \mathcal{Z}} t_{z,q}^c / f_q \tag{6}$$

A configuration is considered non-dominated, if no other configurations with
lower P_{TNP} and t_{ETI} are available (line 12). As there are too many remaining con-
figurations $\mathcal{C}'$, only a fraction is selected (lines 13–15), namely every $\lfloor log_2(|\mathcal{C}'|) \rfloor$.
This log_2 based selection size causes an efficient reduction of the solution space,
trading subsequent algorithm run time with potential Pareto front candidates.

Originally designed for two objectives, this pruning procedure provides a
notion of whether $c \in \mathcal{C}$ is a potential candidate for the final Pareto front.

Algortihm 1: Heuristic MORAM

Input: $\mathcal{Q}, \mathcal{Z}, \mathcal{C}$
Output: $\mathbf{M} \in \{0,1\}^{|PP| \times |\mathcal{Z}| \times |\mathcal{Q}|}$, $\mathbf{C} \in \mathbb{R}^{|PP| \times |\mathcal{Q}| \times 2}$, $\mathbf{t}^e \in \mathbb{R}^{|PP|}$, $\mathbf{P}^{\mathcal{Q}} \in \mathbb{R}^{|PP|}$,
$\qquad \mathbf{P}^{\mathcal{M}} \in \mathbb{R}^{|PP|}$, with $|PP|$ being the number of the final Pareto points

1 **Function** *MORAM()*
2 $\quad$ $\mathcal{C}_{\text{pareto}} = $ PruneSearchSpace($\mathcal{Q}, \mathcal{Z}, \mathcal{C}$);
3 $\quad$ $\{\mathbf{M}, \mathbf{C}, \mathbf{t}^e, \mathbf{P}^{\mathcal{Q}}, \mathbf{P}^{\mathcal{M}}\} = $ GetParetoFront($\mathcal{Q}, \mathcal{Z}, \mathcal{C}_{\text{pareto}}$);
4 $\quad$ **return** $\mathbf{M}_{z,q} \forall z \forall q$, $\mathbf{C} \forall q$, $\mathbf{t}^e$, $\mathbf{P}^{\mathcal{Q}}$, $\mathbf{P}^{\mathcal{M}}$;

5 **Function** *PruneSearchSpace($\mathcal{Q}, \mathcal{Z}, \mathcal{C}$)*
6 $\quad$ **if** $|\mathcal{C}| > N$ **then**
7 $\quad\quad$ $\mathcal{C}_{\text{new}} = N$ randomly selected entries of $\mathcal{C}$;
8 $\quad\quad$ $\mathcal{C} = \mathcal{C}_{\text{new}}$;

9 $\quad$ **foreach** $c \in \mathcal{C}$ **do**
10 $\quad\quad$ c.TNP = calculate total nominal power;
11 $\quad\quad$ c.ETI = calculate execution time indicator;

12 $\quad$ $\mathcal{C}' = $ non-dominated $c \in \mathcal{C}$ according to TNP and ETI; sort ascending by ETI;
13 $\quad$ **for** $i = 0; i < |\mathcal{C}'|; i \mathrel{+}= \lfloor log_2(|\mathcal{C}'|) \rfloor$ **do**
14 $\quad\quad$ $\mathcal{C}_{\text{pareto}}$.append($\mathcal{C}'$.at(i));

15 $\quad$ **return** $\mathcal{C}_{\text{pareto}}$

16 **Function** *GetParetoFront($\mathcal{Q}, \mathcal{Z}, \mathcal{C}_{\text{pareto}}$)*
17 $\quad$ **foreach** $c \in \mathcal{C}_{\text{pareto}}$ **do**
18 $\quad\quad$ set c; fsize $= |c.frequencyDomains|$;
19 $\quad\quad$ process mapping to $q \in \mathcal{Q}$ with lowest TNP; calculate $P^{\mathcal{M}}$, $P^{\mathcal{Q}}$ and t^e;
20 $\quad\quad$ **for** $x = 2, i = 0; i < fsize; x\mathrel{+}\mathrel{+}$ **do**
21 $\quad\quad\quad$ i = Fibonacci(x);
22 $\quad\quad\quad$ **if** $i > fsize$ **then**
23 $\quad\quad\quad\quad$ i = fsize;
24 $\quad\quad\quad$ $\mathcal{Q}_i = $ take all $q \in \mathcal{Q}$ within i frequency domains with lowest TNP;
25 $\quad\quad\quad$ process mapping with $minCut(|\mathcal{Q}_i|)$; calculate $P^{\mathcal{M}}$, $P^{\mathcal{Q}}$ and t^e;
26 $\quad\quad\quad$ process mapping with $merge(|\mathcal{Q}_i|)$; calculate $P^{\mathcal{M}}$, $P^{\mathcal{Q}}$ and t^e;

27 $\quad$ **return** all non-dominated $c \in \mathcal{C}_{\text{pareto}}$ AND process mappings according to $P^{\mathcal{M}}$, $P^{\mathcal{Q}}$
$\qquad$ and t^e;

Figure 1 exemplifies that $\mathcal{C}_{\text{pareto}}$ forms already a good approximation, when computing a minCut($|\mathcal{Q}|$) mapping for demonstration purposes. This minCut mapping strategy is explained in the next section.

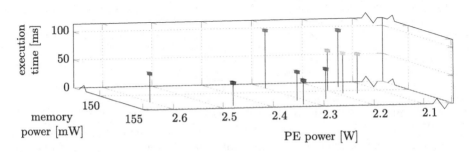

Fig. 1. Process mapping with minCut($|\mathcal{Q}|$) for each $c \in \mathcal{C}_{\text{pareto}}$, *audio filter* and HeMVP

GetParetoFront. MORAM computes three different types of mappings during the Pareto front generation: (i) A graph splitting approach is applied on the basis of minimum cuts, dubbed *minCut*. It focuses on outputting minimum memory power mappings. The KPN graph A of the application is first treated as a single set. After one cut, two sets are produced, which can be mapped to the available PEs. The minimum cut algorithm of [30] is used to keep the FIFO channel communication costs between the new subsets minimised. These cuts are done $|Q|$ times to have as many subsets as PEs available.

(ii) A graph merging approach is chosen to start from the opposite side than minCut, dubbed *merge*. It is chosen to generate mappings with maximum performance. Each node of the KPN graph A is considered as an individual set. Subsets are grouped if they have high FIFO channel communication cost but do not have a high processing load after being merged. These considerations are necessary to achieve optimal performance with low communication cost. Due to the brevity of this paper, the merge procedure cannot be discussed in detail. In brief, the notion of attraction and repulsion forces acting on the subsets is used. The former occurs for high FIFO channel communication and is calculated on the basis of FIFO channel sizes. Repulsion forces between subsets are high if the processing load of the individual subsets is high. It is based on the ETI value.

(iii) Assigning all processes to the PE which has the lowest TNP is done to get a mapping solution with the slowest execution time and lowest power values. In other words, a corner case of the Pareto front is ensured to be included in the final approximation of the non-dominated set.

The entries of C_{pareto} are input to the final Pareto front calculation and considered further (line 17). For each $c \in C_{\text{pareto}}$, mapping type (iii) is computed (line 19). Type (i) and (ii) are evaluated on the granularity of the frequency domains to save run time and iterate more coarse through the added parallel computation options (lines 20–26). Starting with one domain that hosts PEs with minimum TNP, mapping is done utilising only a few PEs to save power. With every added domain, more PEs are considered. With this procedure, the number of idling PEs, which switch to a low power mode, can be maximised in the beginning. Further, distributing the processes among more PEs offers better performance but causes higher PE and memory power consumption.

In case of a high number of frequency domains, it is not necessary to increase the current frequency domain count linearly, due to Amdahl's law. It describes the theoretical speed-up when increasing the PE count for parallel applications. Approximating resulting speed-up curve requires the most samples in the beginning, as the curve levels out. The best approximation is the Fibonacci series because adding a frequency domain results in several added PEs.

In the end, MORAM computes the final Pareto front based on all $c \in C_{\text{pareto}}$ and process mappings that are non-dominated for the three objectives (line 27).

5   Experimental Results

The experimental results consist of two case studies to evaluate the quality and performance. The comparison Pareto front is calculated with the R2-EMOA.

The speed-up of MORAM is computed in relation to the R2-EMOA. The solution quality is indicated with the Hypervolume Indicator (HI) to identify which Pareto front is superior. A non-dominated front is considered better if its solutions are well distributed across the objective space and cover a larger area for each objective value. The HI compresses these conditions, i.e. diversity and dominance into one single value. It is the only method mentioned in the literature that achieves these Pareto-compliant conditions as unary indicator [8].

The comparison Pareto front is calculated with the indicator EMOA presented in [10], dubbed R2-EMOA. It has been chosen because R2 indicator based EMOA are proven to be efficient and less computational expensive in objective domains ≥3 [9]. Two variants are used. The unconstrained R2-EMOA has a population size of 100 and does 6000 evaluations. The constraint variant is limited to a population with 50 individuals and an iteration count of 600.

Execution times and power estimates are solely computed using the CPN simulation engine, due to sufficient accuracies (3.1 and 3.2). A set of representative parallel applications is used [7]. The number of processes is given in brackets: *audio filter* (11), *JPEG* encoder (24), multiple input multiple output orthogonal frequency division multiplexing *MIMO OFDM* transceiver (36), space-time adaptive processing *STAP* (16), and *sobel filter* (5). In-house implementations complement the benchmark set: an LTE uplink receiver physical layer benchmark *LTE* (19) [28], and a Mandelbrot set computation with 16 *Man16* and 150 *Man150* worker processes round off the benchmark set, Discrete Cosine Transformations DCT (8) typically used in video compression.

Table 1. MORAM HI performance relative to constrained R2-EMOA

	ODROID-XU3	HeMVP
Audio filter	−1.1%	++
DCT	−1.6%	++
JPEG	−2.7%	++
LTE	−3.6%	++
Man150	++	++
Man16	+	++
MIMO OFDM	++	++
Sobel filter	−7.9%	−0.1%
STAP	+	++

+: Better than constrained R2-EMOA
++: Better than unconstrained R2-EMOA

5.1   Case Study: ODROID-XU3

The ODROID-XU3 board [1] is built around the Samsung Exynos-5422 processor with ARM big.LITTLE architecture. The frequency ranges from 200 MHz to 1400 MHz (little) and 2000 MHz (big) in steps of 100 MHz per cluster. The ODROID-XU3 supports two levels of coherent caches. Each core has its own set of private L1 instruction and data caches. Per cluster, a shared L2 cache is deployed, which is connected to a 2 GB LPDDR3 DRAM running at 933 MHz. The operating system takes care of automatically setting the most efficient voltage.

The run time of MORAM ranges between 1.5 s and 138 s. Compared to the constrained R2-EMOA, the minimal speed-up is 27× and 200× on average. The run time numbers are shown in Fig. 2. Table 1 gives an overview of the HI mean performance relative to constrained and unconstrained R2-EMOA. MORAM calculates Pareto fronts that are less than 8% worse compared to the constrained R2-EMOA for half of the benchmarks. In four cases, the R2-EMOA is outperformed. Averaging over all cases, the constrained R2-EMOA is 1% better.

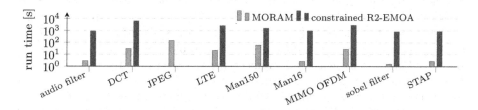

Fig. 2. R2-EMOA and MORAM run times for ODROID-XU3

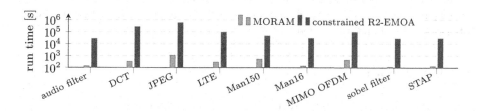

Fig. 3. R2-EMOA and MORAM run times for HeMVP

5.2   Case Study: HeMVP

A SystemC [3] in-house virtual prototype, dubbed HeMVP, models a heterogeneous platform with a hierarchical structure. The platform subsystems consist of either one ARM Cortex-A9 or ADSP Blackfin 609 DSP (BFIN), with private incoherent L1 instruction and data caches. A local memory (1 MB, the same frequency as the PE) is available per subsystem. Four ARM and four BFIN subsystems are combined into a cluster, which also contains a bus and memory (4 MB, 250 MHz). Four clusters are connected globally with a bus, which grants access to shared memory (128 MB, 100 MHz).

The HeMVP has a total of 32 PEs. Two subsystems of same PE type are grouped into a frequency domain, while four share the same voltage domain. The frequency ranges from 200 MHz to 1200 MHz for the ARMs, and from 100 MHz to 500 MHz for the Blackfins. For both, the step size is 100 MHz. This leads to $|\mathcal{C}| = 8.4 \cdot 10^{13}$.

The bare metal runtime environment sets the lowest applicable voltage per voltage domain automatically. Further, it takes care of powering down unused PEs to a clock gated state. Memories that have no data assigned to are powered off entirely. All three memory levels can be used to store the data of FIFO channels. Also, cluster memories host the data structures for synchronisation. The shared memory provides stack, heap and shared code. The memory modelling engine of [24] is used to generate viable power traces. For ARM and BFIN, the power models presented in [20,26] are deployed.

The aforementioned N is set to 10^5 to enable the pre-pruning step, as recommended in [10]. The run times for MORAM and the constrained R2-EMOA are shown in Fig. 3. Due to the larger $|\mathcal{C}|$ and mapping options, MORAM computes between 1.8 min and 18 min. This is at least 88× and on average 278× faster than the constrained R2-EMOA. Further, Table 1 reveals that the heuristic computes Pareto fronts with an HI almost always better than the unconstrained R2-EMOA. On average, MORAM is 4% better.

The reason results from domain knowledge which is explained as follows. The memory assignment of FIFO channel buffers is done implicitly, as explained in Sect. 4. The design of MORAM accounts for the process-to-PE dependent HWC placement. However, the R2-EMOA falls into the category of meta-heuristics. They incorporate none to just a few assumptions about the addressed optimisation problem. This has the advantage that it can be used for a much wider variety of problems. The drawback becomes visible for this MOOP in the form of the missing domain knowledge.

6   Conclusion

This paper proposed a software mapping heuristic approach which solves the three-dimensional optimisation problem of application performance, memory and PE power. Pareto fronts could enable trade-off evaluation and serve as an alternative to established methods for the training of online optimisation algorithms. The applicability and the quality of MORAM were evaluated using two different case studies and a state-of-the-art indicator based EMOA. The heuristic computed Pareto fronts for the ODROID-XU3 and the targeted representative benchmarks at least 80× faster, while having an HI 1% worse compared to the constrained R2-EMOA. Furthermore, testing the heuristic in a highly complex search space scenario, the HeMVP showed a minimum speed-up of 88×. On average, a 4% better HI compared to the unconstrained version was achieved.

References

1. ODROID-XU3. http://odroid.com/dokuwiki/doku.php?id=en:odroid-xu3. Accessed Jan 2020
2. Silexica GmbH. http://silexica.com. Accessed Jan 2020
3. SystemC. http://www.accellera.org/downloads/standards/systemc. Accessed Jan 2020
4. WHITEPAPER - pushing performance: analysis and optimisation of multicore communication with SLX. https://www.silexica.com/resources/#whitepapers-reached. Accessed Jan 2020
5. WHITEPAPER - SLX multi-objective optimisation (MOPT). https://www.silexica.com/resources/#whitepapers-reached. Accessed Jan 2020
6. Aalsaud, A., Shafik, R., Rafiev, A., Xia, F., Yang, S., Yakovlev, A.: Power-aware performance adaptation of concurrent applications in heterogeneous many-core systems. In: Proceedings of ISLPED 2016 (2016)
7. Aguilar, M., Jimenez, R., Leupers, R., Ascheid, G.: Improving performance and productivity for software development on TI multicore DSP platforms. In: EDERC, September 2014
8. Berghammer, R., Friedrich, T., Neumann, F.: Convergence of set-based multi-objective optimization, indicators and deteriorative cycles. Theoret. Comput. Sci. **456**, 2–17 (2012)
9. Brockhoff, D., Wagner, T., Trautmann, H.: 2 indicator-based multiobjective search. Evol. Comput. **23**(3), 369–395 (2015)
10. Führ, G., Hallawa, A., Leupers, R., Ascheid, G., Eusse, J.F.: Multi-objective optimisation of software application mappings on heterogeneous MPSoCs: TONPET versus R2-EMOA. Integration **69**, 50–61 (2019)
11. Ghose, S., Yaglikçi, A.G., Gupta, R., Lee, D., et al.: What your DRAM power models are not telling you: lessons from a detailed experimental study. ACM Meas. Anal. Comput. Syst. **2**(3), 1–41 (2018)
12. Gupta, U., Mandal, S.K., Mao, M., Chakrabarti, C., Ogras, U.Y.: A deep Q-learning approach for dynamic management of heterogeneous processors. IEEE Comput. Archit. Lett. **18**(1), 14–17 (2019)
13. Gupta, U., Patil, C.A., Bhat, G., Mishra, P., Ogras, U.Y.: DyPO: dynamic pareto-optimal configuration selection for heterogeneous MpSoCs. ACM Trans. Embed. Comput. Syst. **16**(5s), 123:1–123:20 (2017)
14. Ha, S., Jung, H.: HOPES: programming platform approach for embedded systems design. In: Ha, S., Teich, J. (eds.) Handbook of Hardware/Software Codesign, pp. 951–981. Springer, Dordrecht (2017). https://doi.org/10.1007/978-94-017-7267-9_1
15. Holzkamp, O.: Memory-aware mapping strategies for heterogeneous MPSoC systems. Ph.D. thesis, Technical University of Dortmund, Germany (2017)
16. Jung, M., Mathew, D.M., Zulian, F., Weis, C., Wehn, N.: A new bank sensitive DRAMPower model for efficient design space exploration. In: Workshop on Power and Timing Modeling, Optimization and Simulation (PATMOS) (2016)
17. Kahn, G.: The semantics of a simple language for parallel programming. In: Proceedings of Information Processing, Stockholm, Sweden, August 1974
18. Kang, S.H., Yang, H., Schor, L., Bacivarov, I., Ha, S., Thiele, L.: Multi-objective mapping optimization via problem decomposition for many-core systems. In: IEEE 10th Symposium on Embedded Systems for Real-time Multimedia, October 2012

19. Leupers, R., Aguilar, M.A., Eusse, J.F., Castrillon, J., Sheng, W.: MAPS: a software development environment for embedded multicore applications. In: Ha, S., Teich, J. (eds.) Handbook of Hardware/Software Codesign, pp. 917–949. Springer, Dordrecht (2017). https://doi.org/10.1007/978-94-017-7267-9_2

20. Onnebrink, G., et al.: Black box power estimation for digital signal processors using virtual platforms. In: RAPIDO 2016 Workshop (2016)

21. Onnebrink, G., et al.: DVFS-enabled power-performance trade-off in MPSoC SW application mapping. In: SAMOS, July 2017

22. Quan, W., Pimentel, A.D.: A hybrid task mapping algorithm for heterogeneous MPSoCs. ACM Trans. Embed. Comput. Syst. **14**, 1–25 (2015)

23. Reddy, B.K., Singh, A.K., Biswas, D., Merrett, G.V., Al-Hashimi, B.M.: Intercluster thread-to-core mapping and DVFS on heterogeneous multi-cores. IEEE Trans. Multi-Scale Comput. Syst. **4**(3), 369–382 (2018)

24. Rudolf, J., Strobel, M., Benz, J., Haubelt, C., Radetzki, M., Bringmann, O.: Automated sensor firmware development - generation, optimization, and analysis. In: Workshop Methoden und Beschreibungssprachen zur Modellierung und Verifikation von Schaltungen und Systemen (MBMV) (2019)

25. Schranzhofer, A., Chen, J.J., Thiele, L.: Dynamic power-aware mapping of applications onto heterogeneous MPSoC platforms. IEEE Trans. Industr. Inf. **6**, 692–707 (2010)

26. Schuermans, S., Leupers, R.: Power Estimation on Electronic System Level using Linear Power Models. Springer, Cham (2019). https://doi.org/10.1007/978-3-030-01875-7

27. Singh, A.K., Shafique, M., Kumar, A., Henkel, J.: Mapping on multi/many-core systems: survey of current and emerging trends. In: Proceedings of Design Automation Conference (DAC) (2013)

28. Själander, M., McKee, S., Brauer, P., Engdal, D., Vajda, A.: An LTE uplink receiver PHY benchmark and subframe-based power management. In: Performance Analysis of Systems and Software (ISPASS) (2012)

29. Stefanov, T., Pimentel, A., Nikolov, H.: DAEDALUS: system-level design methodology for streaming multiprocessor embedded systems on chips. In: Ha, S., Teich, J. (eds.) Handbook of Hardware/Software Codesign, pp. 983–1018. Springer, Dordrecht (2017). https://doi.org/10.1007/978-94-017-7267-9_30

30. Stoer, M., Wagner, F.: A simple min-cut algorithm. J. ACM **44**(4), 585–591 (1997)

31. Zhang, Y., Gong, D.-W., Cheng, J.: Multi-objective particle swarm optimization approach for cost-based feature selection in classification. IEEE/ACM Trans. Comput. Biol. Bioinf. (TCBB) **14**(1), 64–75 (2017)

32. Zhang, Y., Gong, D.-W., Ding, Z.: A bare-bones multi-objective particle swarm optimization algorithm for environmental/economic dispatch. Inf. Sci. **192**, 213–227 (2012)

Towards a Priority-Based Task Distribution Strategy for an Artificial Hormone System

Eric Hutter$^{(\boxtimes)}$ and Uwe Brinkschulte

Goethe University Frankfurt, Frankfurt am Main, Germany
{hutter,brinks}@es.cs.uni-frankfurt.de

Abstract. This paper presents a priority-based task distribution strategy as an extension to the Artificial Hormone System (AHS). The AHS is a distributed middleware based on self-organization principles. It allows to distribute tasks to processing nodes in a self-organizing way while neither having a single-point-of-failure nor requiring external user input. Node failures are detected automatically, resulting in relocation of any affected tasks to operational nodes. This provides self-healing capabilities if sufficient computational resources are available.

Our extension allows tasks to have priorities and enables self-healing by gracefully degrading the system based on the task priorities if the computational resources are not sufficient to completely self-heal the system. We present our extension and analyze its worst-case time bounds for self-configuration as well as self-healing. Quickly degrading the system in overload situations requires a strategy deciding which tasks to stop in such situations. We present a simple strategy and analyze its worst- and average-case self-healing duration.

Keywords: Artificial Hormone System · Organic Computing · Self-organization · Self-healing · Task distribution

1 Introduction

New ways to handle the increasing complexity observed in embedded systems while simultaneously coping with component failures have to be found. One promising approach is to adapt self-organizational principles to computer systems.

The *Artificial Hormone System* (AHS) middleware [14] adapts the natural endocrine system in order to decentrally manage tasks in a distributed system: By exchanging digital messages, called *hormones* after their biological model, via a communication network, tasks can be distributed in the system in a flexible and self-organizing manner, exhibiting properties such as self-configuration and self-healing.

This paper deals with an extension to the AHS middleware that supports task assignment priorities, thus allowing graceful system degradation if the amount of

© Springer Nature Switzerland AG 2020
A. Brinkmann et al. (Eds.): ARCS 2020, LNCS 12155, pp. 69–81, 2020.
https://doi.org/10.1007/978-3-030-52794-5_6

node failures is too big to allow the system to *fully* heal itself. Our contribution is three-fold:

1. We describe a priority-based task-decision strategy for the AHS.
2. We derive hard time bounds for this strategy's self-configuration and self-healing capabilities.
3. We analyze the worst- and average-case time required to degrade a system in an overload situation.

The paper is structured as follows: We first present related work and the general AHS in Sects. 2 and 3. Section 4 describes our priority-based extensions to the AHS. Its worst-case time bounds are derived in Sect. 5. Section 6 proposes a simple degradation strategy to self-heal the system in overload situations and analyzes its worst- and average-case healing times. Finally, Sect. 7 concludes this paper.

2   Related Work

The approach presented in this paper enables a distributed system to recover from hardware failures by dynamically (re)configuring itself. A classical way to improve a system's robustness against such types of failures is the duplication of functional units: By providing each unit with an identical, redundant unit in hot stand-by, a limited number of failures can be compensated. This pattern is frequently used for safety-critical control units in the automotive domain, albeit recent approaches like the AutoKonf project [10] try to reduce costs by sharing a single backup between multiple different control units so that a single failure can be compensated.

In contrast, our approach allows to assign tasks to a distributed system's computing nodes in a self-organizing way, allowing more flexibility. Task priorities allow gradual system degradation after so many node failures have occurred so that the system can no longer fully recover. This flexible mechanism allows to reduce the number of required backup nodes while still being able to tolerate a limited number of node failures.

Our approach is inspired by multiple general research trends: IBM's *Autonomic Computing* initiative [8] introduced *self-x* properties such as self-configuration, selfoptimization or selfhealing. These properties can also be observed in systems based on *Organic Computing* principles [11]: Organic Computing can be characterized as a postponement of various decisions to the system's run-time that were traditionally made at design time [9], allowing the system to dynamically adapt to changed operational conditions [13].

The resulting dynamism distinguishes our concept from approaches like [6] where a (offline) precomputed adaption scenario is applied in case of node failures or overload situations. In contrast, our approach completely postpones the calculation of adaption responses to the run-time and thus allows a more dynamic reaction.

Nevertheless, our concept is by far not the only approach to assign tasks in distributed systems.

Contract Net Protocols [12] can be employed to distribute tasks to agents in a multi-agent system. The approach presented in [17] consists of an improved Contract Net Protocol for task assignment and employs self-healing capabilities as well as task priorities. Yet, contrarily to our approach, it is not completely decentralized and does not guarantee hard real-time bounds.

Contract Net Protocols have also been used for task assignment in Wireless Sensor Networks (WSNs), e.g. in [4]. Other recent research in this domain utilizes self-organization principles [16], game theory [5] or particle swarm optimization [7,15]. Many of these approaches employ some kind of task priority, e.g. deadline-based priorities or number of dependent tasks in a task graph. Additionally, with WSN nodes typically having a limited energy budget, energy-efficiency is one of the main goals of these approaches, rather than guaranteeing real-time behavior as with our approach. In addition, WSNs do not guarantee that any two nodes have a direct communication link as required by our approach, thus needing different methods to distribute the tasks.

To the best of our knowledge, no self-organizing middleware for prioritized task allocation in distributed systems comparable to our approach exists.

3   The Artificial Hormone System

The *Artificial Hormone System (AHS)* is a completely decentralized middleware based on Organic Computing principles that allows the distribution of tasks in a self-organizing way. If a *processing element (PE)* fails, the remaining PEs will compensate this failure by re-configuring themselves.

The AHS works by realizing control loops based on *hormones*, which are short digital messages, on all PEs in the system: They exchange *eager values* for all tasks, indicating their suitability for each task. In every cycle of the hormone control loop (called *hormone cycle*), each PE tries to make a decision upon one task by comparing its own eager value with all received eager values. If it has sent the highest eager value for some task T in the current cycle, it is allowed to start executing T.

Once T has been started, its PE will start sending out a *suppressor* hormone for this task. Upon receiving this suppressor, the other PEs will reduce their eager values for T accordingly, preventing them from taking additional instances of T.

Accelerator hormones act antagonistically to suppressors by increasing a task's eager value: Tasks that cooperate in some way or work on similar problems may be defined as related. When a task T is running on some PE_γ, accelerators for all tasks related to T are spread in the vicinity of PE_γ. This furthers the execution of those tasks on neighboring PEs, forming functional clusters of related tasks.

Figure 1 shows the basic principle of the hormone control loop. It is completely decentralized and thus, the AHS has no single point of failure. In addition, the original AHS (without our priority extension) can guarantee hard time bounds, allowing its use in real-time systems:

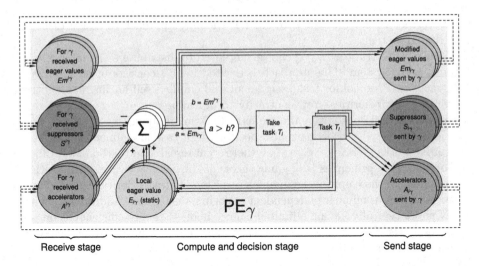

Receive stage   Compute and decision stage   Send stage

Fig. 1. Hormone control loop executed on PE_γ. For each task T_i, a modified eager value $Em_{i\gamma}$ (its static local eager value $E_{i\gamma}$ plus all received accelerators $A^{i\gamma}$ minus all received suppressors $S^{i\gamma}$) is sent to all PEs. If the sent modified eager value is positive and greater than all received modified eager values, T_i may be taken. Thus, suppressors for T_i will be sent to *all* other PEs (preventing infinite assignments of T_i) and accelerators for tasks *related* to T_i will be sent to *neighboring* PEs, forming clusters of related tasks on them.

- The system's initial self-configuration requires at most m hormone cycles, where m is the number of tasks to distribute.
- In case a PE running m_f tasks fails, the AHS will automatically perform a self-healing by reassigning those tasks among the healthy PEs. This takes at most $m_f + a$ hormone cycles where a is the number of hormone cycles required to notice the failure (by missing suppressors for the failed tasks).[1]

The length of each hormone cycle can be chosen arbitrarily, a lower bound is only imposed by the communication bus' latency and bandwidth.

For more detailed information on the AHS, please refer to [1–3,14].

4   A Priority-Based Task Decision Strategy

4.1   Motivation

The AHS' self-healing capabilities are insufficient if the remaining PEs do not have enough computational resources to execute *all* tasks. With many systems consisting of tasks with mixed criticality levels, this may easily lead to situations where low-criticality tasks are running, but high-criticality tasks previously executed on the failed PE cannot be reassigned. In fact, it is undefined which task subset will be running in such situations.

---

[1] In the AHS' current implementation, $a = 2$ hormone cycles holds.

The AHS models system load by means of *load suppressors* a task sends to the PE it is running on, thus limiting the number of tasks the PE can take. If it is fully loaded, it will send an eager value of 0 for all remaining tasks. Therefore, situations of system overload can in principle be recognized by examining the hormones broadcasted in the system.

We thus implemented an AHS extension that allows to give each task a *priority*. This priority is used to (a) control the order in which tasks are assigned during the initial self-configuration and (b) resolve system overload situations by stopping tasks of low priority, freeing capacities for high-priority tasks.

4.2 Conception

Our approach, the priority-based task decision strategy, is an extension of the AHS' so-called *aggressive* task decision strategy [2]: Each PE may take at most one task per hormone cycle. If more than one task were taken per cycle and PE, all tasks could be assigned before accelerators had a chance to become effective, failing to cluster related tasks. Using the aggressive task decision strategy, each PE actively searches for a task it may take in each cycle. This allows at least one PE to take one task per cycle, resulting in the time bound of m hormone cycles to distribute m tasks mentioned in Sect. 3.

Our priority-based task decision strategy has the same operating principle with the following differences: Each task has an integer priority that is known to and equal on *all* PEs in the system. Each PE searches its task list for a task to be taken in the order of *descending* priorities. If the received hormones suggest that another PE has won some task T (and thus *might* take it in this cycle), no task T' having a lower priority than T's may be taken in the current cycle, ensuring a correct order of task assignment. Figure 2a sketches this procedure: The variable *lockPrio* is used to stop deciding on tasks after a higher-priority task has been identified that may be taken on another PE in this cycle. The variable *missingTask* is used to track a high-priority task that is not running in the system because of an overload situation. Both variables are set by the sub-procedure Decide(T) as shown in Fig. 2b.[2]

The decide procedure works by comparing the local eager value sent with all received eager values. There are three possible outcomes of this comparison:

a) No bidders: No PE sent a *positive* modified eager value for T. If suppressors were received for T instead, T is taken somewhere and the decision procedure may continue to the next task. Else, no PE has capacities to take T, so the system is in an overload situation. In this case, lockPrio is set to prevent tasks of lower priority from being taken and *missingTask* is used to track this situation.

b) Loser: The local PE did not send the highest eager value for T. Thus, it sets *lockPrio* to prevent taking any task of lower priority.

---

[2] For the sake of brevity, only a simplified variant of Decide (T) is depicted with some parts omitted, e.g. the offer mechanism belonging to the AHS' self-optimization.

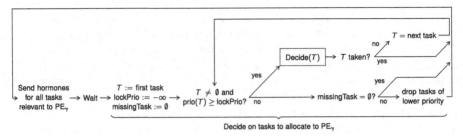

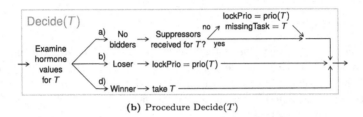

(a) Hormone loop with priority-based task decision strategy

(b) Procedure Decide(T)

Fig. 2. Priority-based task decision strategy

c) Winner: The local PE sent the highest eager value for T. Thus, it takes T (and will send a suppressor for T in the next cycle, preventing the other PEs from taking an additional instance of this task).

The current hormone cycle ends once a task has been taken or a task with lower priority than *lockPrio* has been reached. If, in the latter case, *missingTask* is set, some high-priority task is not running because of an overload situation. In order to resolve this situation, each PE will try to drop tasks of low priority in order to free up resources and send an eager value >0 for this task.

This is, however, based on the following fundamental assumption:

Assumption. *Any task may be (temporarily) stopped at any time in order to free up resources for tasks of higher priority.*

It is up to a *task dropping strategy* to decide on which specific tasks will be stopped in an overload situation; more information on this matter as well as the priority-based task decision's time bounds will be presented in the following sections.

5   Worst-Case Analysis

Our priority-based extension can still guarantee real-time behavior for self-configuration as well as self-healing if the remaining capacities are sufficient to redistribute all failed tasks:

Self-Configuration. It can be shown that it takes at most $2m - 1$ hormone cycles to assign m tasks during the system's initial self-configuration. As our strategy is based on the aggressive strategy, a similar argument to the one given in [2] can be employed: Each PE searches actively for a won task, thus at least one task is taken per cycle in the system. However, after a task T is taken by some PE_α in cycle i, all other PEs will still send out an eager value >0 for T in cycle $i + 1$ before PE_α's suppressor for T finally becomes effective. This introduces one delay cycle in which no task allocation can happen after the last task of each priority level has been assigned. Thus, if all m tasks have different priorities, $m - 1$ delay cycles are introduced and self-configuration takes at most $2m - 1$ hormone cycles.

Self-Healing. If a PE fails, it won't send any more hormones. Thus, it is possible to detect this failure by missing hormones. This takes a constant amount of a hormone cycles.[3] Afterwards, the failed tasks are automatically re-assigned with the time bound for self-configuration applying. If m_f tasks were running on the failed PE and the remaining PEs' resources suffice to take all those tasks, self-healing thus takes at most $2m_f - 1 + a$ hormone cycles.

If, however, the remaining capacities do *not* suffice to take all failed tasks, the system is considered to be in an overload situation. Since a premise of our priority-based task decision is to allow gracefully degrading the system in such situations, the next section will deal with overload situations.

6   Overload Situations

As mentioned in Sect. 4.2, a task dropping strategy is responsible for deciding on which specific tasks to stop in overload situations. However, a model is required to facilitate the analysis of such situations. Thus, let v be the number of PEs that remain operational. Let PE_x denote the failed PE and $PE_1 \ldots PE_v$ denote the remaining PEs. Additionally, we will make the following assumptions:

- All tasks have different priorities.
- All tasks induce equal load to the PEs and each PE may execute any task.
- At the instant PE_x fails, PE_x and $PE_1 \ldots PE_v$ are each completely utilized by executing exactly m tasks.
- No additional PE failure occurs during self-healing.

The resulting model is visualized in Fig. 3.

6.1   Task Dropping Strategy

We now propose the following task dropping strategy to resolve an overload situation:

---

[3] As mentioned before, $a = 2$ holds.

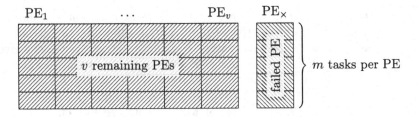

Fig. 3. Overload model used during analysis

Strategy. *Upon noticing an overload situation, each PE shall stop all running tasks that have a priority lower than the priority of the highest-priority task that is currently not running.*

In the context of Fig. 2, this strategy basically stops all tasks having a priority lower than *missing Task*'s priority. After the tasks have been stopped, the system re-configures itself by assigning as many of the highest-priority non-running tasks as possible. Since the system is in overload, not all tasks can be assigned, but no more tasks will be stopped by the next invocation of the task dropping strategy. As this is arguably a very simple strategy, we called it *naive task dropping*. In addition, analyzing its worst-case in the given model is straightforward:

Theorem 1 (Worst-Case Analysis for Overload Situations). *Self-healing in an overload situation takes at most $2mv + a$ hormone cycles when using the naive task dropping strategy.*

Proof. It takes a constant amount a of hormone cycles to notice the failure of $PE_\times$ due to missing suppressors. All v remaining PEs are fully utilized, so the system is in an overload situation.

Thus, in the next cycle, *missing Task* is set to the highest-priority task that was previously running on $PE_\times$ and no task is taken in the system. The strategy will now stop all tasks with a priority lower than *missing Task*'s priority; if *missing Task* is the single-highest priority task, a total of mv tasks will be stopped.

Starting with the following cycle, the mv highest-priority tasks (of all $mv + m$ non-running tasks) will be assigned, taking $2mv - 1$ cycles at most.

As a result, no more than $2mv - 1 + 1 + a = 2mv + a$ hormone cycles are required to complete the self-healing and reach a stable system state again. $\square$

6.2   Average-Case Analysis

In this paper, we additionally want to analyze the time required for self-healing when using this strategy in the *average* case. Although an average-case analysis is not relevant in the context of real-time systems, we decided to nevertheless analyze it in this regard: The expected self-healing duration might especially be of interest for scenarios that don't require *hard* real-time bounds.

Preparations. In order to facilitate this analysis, some arrangements have to be made:

Definition 1. *Let* $n, k \in \mathbb{N}$. *Then, the* rising factorial $n^{\overline{k}}$ *shall be defined as*

$$n^{\overline{k}} := \underbrace{n \cdot (n+1) \cdots (n+k-1)}_{k \text{ factors}} = \prod_{i=n}^{n+k-1} i.$$

Lemma 1. *For* $k, m \in \mathbb{N}$ *with* $k \geq 1$,

$$\sum_{i=1}^{k} i^{\overline{m}} = k \cdot \frac{(k+1)^{\overline{m}}}{1+m} \qquad holds.$$

Proof. Multiplying with $(m!/m!)$ allows to convert the summands to binomial coefficients:

$$\sum_{i=1}^{k} i^{\overline{m}} = m! \cdot \sum_{i=1}^{k} \frac{i^{\overline{m}}}{m!} = m! \cdot \sum_{i=1}^{k} \binom{i+m-1}{m} = m! \cdot \sum_{i=m}^{k+m-1} \binom{i}{m}$$

This sum can now be simplified using the identity $\sum_{i=r}^{n} \binom{i}{r} = \binom{n+1}{r+1}$:

$$= m! \cdot \binom{k+m}{m+1} = m! \cdot \frac{k^{\overline{m+1}}}{(m+1)!} = k \cdot \frac{(k+1)^{\overline{m}}}{1+m}.$$

$\square$

Analysis. We can now analyze the naive task dropping strategy's average case within our overload situation model, assuming all tasks are distributed randomly to the available PEs. For this reason, we quantify the number of tasks stopped on average:

Theorem 2. *Let* X *be a random variable representing the number of tasks stopped by the naive task dropping strategy and* $\mathbf{E}[X]$ *its expected value. Then,* $\mathbf{E}[X] = (m^2 v)/(1+m)$ *holds.*

Proof. We will first calculate the probability distribution of X by assuming that all $(v+1) \cdot m$ tasks are distributed in sequence of descending priorities to mv positions on $\mathrm{PE}_1 \ldots \mathrm{PE}_v$ and mv positions on $\mathrm{PE}_\times$.

Obviously, $0 \leq X \leq mv$ holds: In case the m lowest-priority tasks are running on $\mathrm{PE}_\times$, no tasks have to be stopped. If the highest-priority task is running on $\mathrm{PE}_\times$, *all* tasks on $\mathrm{PE}_1 \ldots \mathrm{PE}_v$ are stopped.

Generalizing this argument yields

- $X = mv \iff$ The highest-priority task is set to one of $\mathrm{PE}_\times$'s m positions.
- $X = mv - 1 \iff$ The second-highest-priority task is the first task to be set to one of $\mathrm{PE}_\times$'s m positions.

$\vdots$

– $X = 0 \iff$ The $(m \cdot (v + 1) - 1)$-highest-priority task (which is the m-lowest-priority task) is the first task to be set to one of $\text{PE}_\times$'s m positions.

Thus, the probability distribution of X is given by

$$\mathbf{P}\,(X = mv) = \frac{m}{m \cdot (v + 1)}$$

$$\mathbf{P}\,(X = mv - 1) = \frac{mv}{m \cdot (v + 1)} \cdot \frac{m}{m \cdot (v + 1) - 1}$$

$$\mathbf{P}\,(X = mv - 2) = \frac{mv}{m \cdot (v + 1)} \cdot \frac{mv - 1}{m \cdot (v + 1) - 1} \cdot \frac{m}{m \cdot (v + 1) - 2}$$

$$\vdots$$

$$\mathbf{P}\,(X = 0) = \underbrace{\frac{mv}{m \cdot (v + 1)} \cdot \frac{mv - 1}{m \cdot (v + 1) - 1} \cdots \frac{1}{m + 1}}_{mv \text{ highest-priority tasks on } \text{PE}_1 \ldots \text{PE}_v} \cdot \frac{m}{m}$$

This is equivalent to

$$\mathbf{P}\,(X = j) = \frac{\prod\limits_{i=j+1}^{mv} i}{\prod\limits_{i=m+j+1}^{mv+m} i} \cdot \frac{m}{m + j} = m \cdot \frac{\prod\limits_{i=j+1}^{mv} i}{\prod\limits_{i=m+j}^{mv+m} i} \tag{1}$$

for all $0 \le j \le mv$. Figure 4 plots the probability distribution as given by this equation for arbitrarily chosen values of m and v.

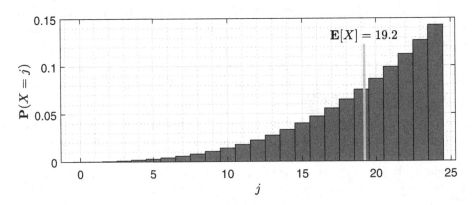

Fig. 4. Probability distribution of number of tasks stopped by naive task dropping strategy for $m = 4$ and $v = 6$

Equation 1 now allows us to calculate $\mathbf{E}\left[X\right]$:

$$\mathbf{E}\left[X\right] = \sum_{j=0}^{mv} j \cdot \mathbf{P}\left(X=j\right) \qquad = \sum_{j=1}^{mv} j \cdot m \cdot \frac{\prod_{i=j+1}^{mv} i}{\prod_{i=m+j}^{mv+m} i}$$

$$= m \cdot \sum_{j=1}^{mv} j \cdot \frac{(mv)!/j!}{(mv+m)!/(m+j-1)!} \qquad = m \cdot \sum_{j=1}^{mv} \frac{(m+j-1)!/(j-1)!}{(mv+m)!/(mv)!}$$

$$= \frac{m}{\frac{mv+m}{\prod_{i=mv+1} i}} \cdot \sum_{j=1}^{mv} \left(\prod_{i=j}^{m+j-1} i\right) \qquad = \frac{m}{(mv+1)^{\overline{m}}} \cdot \sum_{j=1}^{mv} j^{\overline{m}}$$

This expression can be simplified using Lemma 1:

$$= \frac{m}{(mv+1)^{\overline{m}}} \cdot \frac{mv \cdot (mv+1)^{\overline{m}}}{1+m} = \frac{m^2 v}{1+m}.$$

$\square$

Discussion. When examining the number of tasks dropped by the naive task dropping strategy, it becomes obvious that its worst case is not substantially worse than the average case, especially for large values of m:

$$\lim_{m\to\infty} \frac{\text{worst case}}{\text{average case}} = \lim_{m\to\infty} \frac{mv}{\frac{m^2 v}{1+m}} = \lim_{m\to\infty} \left(1 + \frac{1}{m}\right) = 1.$$

As a result, no significant outliers from the average case are to be expected when utilizing this task dropping strategy.

In addition, initial self-*configuration* for mv tasks requires $2mv - 1$ hormone cycles, while self-*healing* in an overload situation takes at most $2mv + a$ hormone cycles: Both bounds are linear in the number of tasks with different (and small) additive constants.

7   Conclusion

This paper described a priority-based extension to the AHS middleware. We analyzed its worst-case time bounds for self-configuration and self-healing. Additionally, a strategy was proposed allowing to degrade the system in case of an overload situation. Its worst and average cases were analyzed. The results show that this strategy does not perform substantially worse in its worst case than it does on average.

Future work will deal with thorough evaluations of our concept as well as further research on degrading the system in overload situations, especially with developing more elaborate task dropping strategies, possibly guaranteeing even better time bounds for self-healing in overload situations.

Additionally, our current analyses assume a reliable communication network. Although empirical experiments suggest that the AHS can handle a limited degree of communication failures quite well, we plan to shift our research focus to guaranteeing time bounds and the system's overall consistency even in the presence of such failures.

References

1. Brinkschulte, U.: Increasing the stability of an Artificial Hormone System for task allocation by accelerator bounds. In: 16th IEEE International Symposium on Object/Component/Service-Oriented Real-Time Distributed Computing (ISORC 2013), pp. 1–10. IEEE, Paderborn, June 2013
2. Brinkschulte, U., Pacher, M.: An aggressive strategy for an artificial hormone system to minimize the task allocation time. In: 2012 IEEE 15th International Symposium on Object/Component/Service-Oriented Real-Time Distributed Computing Workshops, pp. 188–195. IEEE, Shenzhen, April 2012
3. Brinkschulte, U., Pacher, M., von Renteln, A., Betting, B.: Organic real-time middleware. In: Higuera-Toledano, M.T., Brinkschulte, U., Rettberg, A. (eds.) Self-Organization in Embedded Real-Time Systems, pp. 179–208. Springer, New York (2013). https://doi.org/10.1007/978-1-4614-1969-3_9
4. Chen, L., Xue-song, Q., Yang, Y., Gao, Z., Qu, Z.: The contract net based task allocation algorithm for wireless sensor network. In: 2012 IEEE Symposium on Computers and Communications (ISCC), pp. 600–604, July 2012
5. Edalat, N., Tham, C.K., Xiao, W.: An auction-based strategy for distributed task allocation in wireless sensor networks. Comput. Commun. 35(8), 916–928 (2012)
6. Fohler, G., Gala, G., Pérez, D.G., Pagetti, C.: Evaluation of DREAMS resource management solutions on a mixed-critical demonstrator. In: 9th European Congress on Embedded Real Time Software and Systems (ERTS 2018), Toulouse, France, January 2018
7. Guo, W., Li, J., Chen, G., Niu, Y., Chen, C.: A PSO-optimized real-time fault-tolerant task allocation algorithm in wireless sensor networks. IEEE Trans. Parallel Distrib. Syst. 26(12), 3236–3249 (2015)
8. Kephart, J.O., Chess, D.M.: The vision of autonomic computing. Computer 36(1), 41–50 (2003)
9. Müller-Schloer, C., Tomforde, S.: Organic Computing – Technical Systems for Survival in the Real World. AS. Springer, Cham (2017). https://doi.org/10.1007/978-3-319-68477-2
10. Orlov, Sergey, Korte, Matthias, Oszwald, Florian, Vollmer, Pascal: Automatically reconfigurable actuator control for reliable autonomous driving functions (AutoKonf). 10th International Munich Chassis Symposium 2019. Proceedings, pp. 355–368. Springer, Wiesbaden (2020). https://doi.org/10.1007/978-3-658-26435-2_26
11. Schmeck, H.: Organic computing - a new vision for distributed embedded systems. In: Eighth IEEE International Symposium on Object-Oriented Real-Time Distributed Computing (ISORC 2005), pp. 201–203, May 2005
12. Smith, R.G.: The contract net protocol: high-level communication and control in a distributed problem solver. IEEE Trans. Comput. C−29(12), 1104–1113 (1980)
13. Tomforde, S., Sick, B., Müller-Schloer, C.: Organic computing in the spotlight. arXiv:1701.08125 [cs], January 2017. http://arxiv.org/abs/1701.08125
14. von Renteln, A., Brinkschulte, U., Pacher, M.: The artificial hormone system—an organic middleware for self-organising real-time task allocation. In: Müller-Schloer, C., Schmeck, H., Ungerer, T. (eds.) Organic Computing—A Paradigm Shift for Complex Systems, pp. 369–384. Springer, Basel (2011). https://doi.org/10.1007/978-3-0348-0130-0_24
15. Yang, J., Zhang, H., Ling, Y., Pan, C., Sun, W.: Task allocation for wireless sensor network using modified binary particle swarm optimization. IEEE Sens. J. 14(3), 882–892 (2014)

16. Yin, X., Dai, W., Li, B., Chang, L., Li, C.: Cooperative task allocation in heterogeneous wireless sensor networks. Int. J. Distrib. Sens. Netw. **13**(10), 1550147717735747 (2017)
17. Zhang, J., Wang, G., Song, Y.: Task assignment of the improved contract net protocol under a multi-agent system. Algorithms **12**(4), 70 (2019)

He..ro DB: A Concept for Parallel Data Processing on Heterogeneous Hardware

Michael Müller[1], Thomas Leich[2], Thilo Pionteck[3], Gunter Saake[3], Jens Teubner[4], and Olaf Spinczyk[1(✉)]

[1] ESS Group, Institute of Computer Science, Osnabrück University, Osnabrück, Germany
{michael.mueller,olaf.spinczyk}@uos.de
[2] Harz University of Applied Sciences, Wernigerode, Germany
tleich@hs-harz.de
[3] Otto-von-Guericke-University, Magdeburg, Germany
thilo.pionteck@ovgu.de, saake@iti.cs.uni-magdeburg.de
[4] DBIS Group, Department of Computer Science, TU Dortmund University, Dortmund, Germany
jens.teubner@cs.tu-dortmund.de

Abstract. Due to the growing demand on processing power and energy efficiency by today's data-intensive applications developers have to deal with heterogeneous hardware platforms composed of specialized computing resources. These are highly efficient for certain workloads but difficult to handle from the software engineering perspective. Even state-of-the-art database management systems do not exploit *all* heterogeneous hardware components, as their characteristics differ significantly. They are thus hard to integrate within a coherent database architecture.

To address this problem, we propose a design concept that is based on a layered system software architecture: He..ro DB transforms a data-flow graph that describes the data-processing application to a task-based execution plan. Task implementations for the different computing resources and a reasonable degree of parallelism are chosen automatically based on available resources. The concept can cover any hardware configuration and application scenario. It is versatile and offers opportunities for independent optimization on each layer.

Keywords: Heterogeneous many-core systems · Data processing · Databases · Task-parallel programming

1 Introduction

The hardware industry is trying to cope with the growing demand on computational power and energy efficiency of today's data-intensive applications

This work has been carried out in the course of the priority program 2037 *Scalable Data Management for Future Hardware* funded by the German Research Foundation (DFG). The authors would like to thank the DFG for funding and all the project partners for the helpful discussions.

by developing hardware that is inherently parallel and also heterogeneous. For example, the Xilinx Ultrascale+ combines four ARM cores, two ARM Cortex R5 cores and an FPGA fabric on one chip.

Especially data-intensive cyber-physical systems could benefit from the efficiency of these modern hardware platforms. However, we are not aware of any database management system that could make use of *all* heterogeneous resources at once in parallel for boosting its query processing performance. A novel software architecture would be needed. However, for the designers of system software this kind of platform raises a lot of new research questions. In this paper we will address the following:

RQ1: How can the available hardware resources be fairly assigned to isolated **concurrent applications**?

RQ2: Is it possible to **abstract** from individual resource types without losing the ability to exploit a computing resource's specific strengths?

RQ3: With which **execution model** can applications – especially data-intensive programs with high demands on computing power – make use of and benefit from the available heterogeneous resources in a coordinated and parallel manner?

To facilitate system software engineering for heterogeneous platforms that are running data-intensive application, this paper presents a design concept, namely the He..ro-DB architecture and a preliminary evaluation of an early prototypical implementation. By a layered software architecture different concerns become cleanly separated and optimizations are possible on each of these layers independently. The He..ro-DB architecture assumes that data-processing operations can be expressed as a data-flow graph containing logical operators and edges along which data flows from data sources to data sinks, e.g. database tables. We sketch an architecture that is able to transform this high-level description into an optimized execution plan that consists of elementary operations, which we call *tasks*. During this transformation process the most appropriate degree of functional and data parallelism is estimated and the most promising selection of optimized task implementations for the heterogeneous computing resources is made.

The outline of this paper is as follows: To motivate the need for the presented conceptual design framework Sect. 2 will discuss existing approaches to integrate heterogeneous computing resources into data-processing systems. As none of the existing systems is able to exploit all available (heterogeneous) computing resources, we will describe the He..ro DB system software architecture in Sect. 3. The validation of the approach is based on a concrete application scenario. Section 4 will explain how that would be handled in a He..ro-based system software stack. Section 5 will reflect the presented architecture by discussing the design space, the decisions that have been made, and the remaining freedom for concrete implementations. Finally, we will present the results of a performance evaluation that we conducted with the He..ro DB prototype implementation in Sect. 6 and our conclusions in Sect. 7.

2   Related Work

The Utilization of heterogeneous computing resources, such as FPGAs and GPUs, to accelerate database operations has been investigated intensively in the recent years. So all major operators have been realized as FPGA functions or GPU kernels, such as sorting [5,12,16], selection [8,15] and join [5,9,18]. Although significant performance improvement could be achieved, none of them allowed to accelerate a whole query.

To accelerate a whole query, query compilers for accelerators have been investigated. So Sukhwani et al. [17], Glacier [11] and Hawk [3] provide a query compiler for FPGAs (the former) and GPUs. Though these solutions are limited to specialized database machines, as they do not provide an execution model that allows load balancing or dynamic adaptation.

With OmniDB [19] and Ocelot [7], attempts have been made to create a fully heterogeneous DBMS. As both use a hardware-oblivious approach though, they cannot make full use of the special characteristics each accelerator provides. By using a hardware-sensitive approach, though sacrificing portability, CoGaDB [2] and Hype [4] can improve the utlization of accelerator hardware even more, leading to better system performance. However, these solutions do not take concurrently running applications into account and are thus exposed to performance degradation by interference with other applications.

OpenCL[1] has made the notion of a kernel, a closed unit of parallel work, the de-facto standard execution model for heterogeneous programs. It allows the application programmer to offload certain functions (kernels) to an accelerator. Although OpenCL provides a good way of abstracting hardware details while still preserving most of its characteristics, it does not provide any means for multiprogramming or scheduling. FluidiCL [13], StarPU [1] and Harmony [6] try to fill this gap by providing a coherent programming model and runtime for heterogeneous tasks. These runtimes schedule tasks or kernels on a given accelerator depending on the expected load and timing requirements of the application. Though, none of them consider multiprogramming, i.e. the concurrent execution of isolated applications.

So far none of the mentioned solutions provide a holistic approach allowing database applications and other concurrent applications to fully leverage the potential of modern parallel and heterogeneous hardware, while providing abstractions for heterogeneous processors, sophisticated load balancing and isolation of concurrent applications without losing the ability to distribute heterogeneous resources among them. This encourages the motivation for our proposal which addresses all the mentioned challenges.

3   He..ro-DB Architecture

This section describes the proposed architecture in detail. It starts by giving an overview and continues with a discussion of each layer in a bottom-up manner.

---

[1] See https://www.khronos.org/opencl.

3.1 Overview

The He..ro-DB architecture seperate resource management (Layer 0), task scheduling (Layer 1) and query planing (Layer 2) from eachother in their own functional layer. Applications run in isolated resource containers, called cells, having their individual task scheduler and query planer, if needed. This allows maximium flexibility regarding the choice of implementations. So each application may have its own tailored scheduling and query planing. As the management of hardware resources has to be done application-independently Layer 0 exists only once as shared layer for all applications.

3.2 Layer 0: Resource Partitioning

Layer 0 is responsible for assigning the available hardware resources to application cells running concurrently on the same hardware platform.

Provided Functions: For a special-purpose system with only a single application, Layer 0 may have almost no functionality. But most modern systems are more complex and isolation of system components is needed, as for cyperphysical systems where mission-critical control functions shall be isolated from other parts of the system. Below is a list of functions that a Layer 0 Implementation would provide;

Isolation: In order to avoid propagation of errors between application cells and system software components as well as security issues, temporal and spatial isolation are required. A typical way of achieving this is by virtualization of resources, such as CPU and main memory. In today's heterogeneous hardware landscape not all computing resources support virtualization on the hardware level. In this case access can be granted only through a special API, which fully controls resource usage.

Prioritization: Since the criticality of applications in a system may differ, the Resource partitioning shall take priorities into account. So a high-priority application (e.g. an interactive user-application) shall be granted more resources than a low-priority one (e.g. a background task). The resource management shall also withdraw resources from lower priority applications when needed by an application of higher priority. Realtime applications might be supported by static assignment of isolated hardware resources.

Mapping: Software components running within one cell are more likely to interact with each other than components in different cells. Therefore, Layer 0 should optimize the placement of cells with the system. For example, in a Non-Uniform Memory Architecture (NUMA) it would make sense to take locality with NUMA regions into account. The same holds for memory areas and I/O devices used by a cell.

Stabilization: A cell reconfiguration (adding, withdrawing, or replacing resources) is always costly. Therefore, Layer 0 must implement strategies to keep cells as stable as possible. The minimum amount of resources that are assigned to a cell is a certain percentage of all resources and depends on prioritization. However, cells produce load dynamically and it is only necessary to provide these resources if actually needed. In such "full load" situations a cell can be given even more resources if other cells are not under full load at the same time. Here a good balance between reactivity and stabilization must be found. The load situation with the cells must be constantly monitored with low overhead.

The list of functions is not intended to be complete. It motivates the need for a global resource management software layer that simplifies application development by handling several operational concerns transparently.

Interface: Layer 0 shall provide a *Cell Management Interface* (CMI) and a *Resource Introspection Interface* (RII). CMI is needed to start, configure, and stop application cells. RMI can be used by cells to get information about the *physical* resources assigned to them. Changes in resource assignment can be signaled to the affected domain. If resources have to be withdrawn, the affected cell will be granted a reasonable amount of time to stop using the resources. Layer 1 is designed in a manner that allows resources to be released quickly (see next section) and to exploit the specific features of the assigned physical hardware components.

Structure/Implementation: The *Resource Partitioning* layer resembles an exokernel. Both share the same principle that there is almost no abstraction of the underlying hardware, to allow optimizations in the applications running on top. This distinguishes Layer 0 from hypervisors which virtualize a complete computer system, hiding the characteristics of the actual hardware, and also from monolithic and microkernel operating systems which usually only provide an abstract machine.

Although Layer 0 is a kind of exokernel, its resource management strategies differ greatly. The original exokernel was designed for machines with a single or only a few CPUs and with uniform memory access. However, the resource partitioning of He..ro DB is designed for heterogeneous many-core systems with complex memory hierarchies and non-uniform memory access that call for new ways of assigning hardware resources.

3.3   Layer 1: Task-Based Runtime System

The purpose of Layer 1 is to provide a runtime system for each cell with a programming model for arbitrary applications that want to make use of heterogeneous computing, memory, and I/O resources in a coherent and automatically optimized way. Figure 1 shows the components of Layer 1 and its interfaces to Layer 0 and 2.

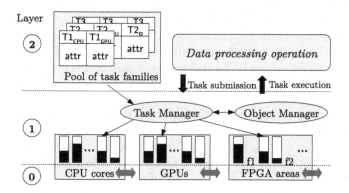

Fig. 1. Structure and interface of the *Task-Based Runtime System*

Provided Functions: The main function provided by Layer 1 is the execution of *tasks* that are submitted by Layer 2 components, such as data processing operations. In this context we define a task as a *finite and non-preemptible* computation on any of the heterogeneous resources of the machine that may read or write data structures in memory (*data objects*) and may have parameters. A task is a member of a *task family* and has a number of *attributes* that describe its usage of resources and interactions with other tasks. Each task in a task family implements a semantically equivalent computation, such as sorting an array of integers or scanning a table for a specific entry, in a different way. The main purpose of this concept is to group variants of data-processing code that is implemented and optimized for different heterogeneous hardware components. In Fig. 1, for instance, the task T1 exists in two variants (family members): One that can execute on a CPU and one GPU implementation. Task families must not be empty, but don't have to be complete.

The *Task Manager* is responsible for a number of scheduling and placement decision needed to execute a task. The *Object Manager* component keeps track of the available memory resources and provides a cost model for memory transfers. During operation the task and object manager have to deal with the following issues:

Load Balancing: If Layer 2 submits a GPU task, but the only assigned GPU is already in use for another task, the task manager may either put the new task into a waiting list or choose another member from the task's family and run the same computation on a different hardware resource. By this mechanism the load on the heterogeneous computing resources can be balanced.

Optimization: Load balancing shall reduce the performance of the system as little as possible. Therefore, the task placement decision must take a cost model into account that considers necessary copying of memory objects and the expected resource usage of the different task family members. The latter information shall be provided by the developer or a dynamic profiler in task attributes.

Synchronization: If tasks have data dependencies or require mutual exclusion while accessing a certain memory object, an elegant way to achieve serialization is to simply insert the tasks in the *same* waiting list. This scheme avoids costs that would otherwise be induced by lock-based synchronization. However, load balancing and optimization might sometimes outweigh the benefits of this kind of task synchronization.

Adaptation: The resource partitioning Layer 0 aims at keeping the assigned resources stable. Nevertheless, Layer 1 must be able to deal with elasticity, i.e. dynamic resource availability. Layer 0 describes the available resources and signals changes by the RII. When a resource is added, Layer 1 can use that from that moment on for the execution of new tasks. Resource withdrawal is more challenging. Layer 1 must make sure that the resource is no longer used within a short period of time. Otherwise, Layer 0 would simply terminate the cell. This is done by resubmitting the tasks that are currently on the waiting list of the resources and waiting for the running task to finish.

Interface: The *Task Execution Interface* (TEI) provides functions for submitting tasks. These are executed asynchronously at a later point in time. For each task there are static attributes, such as the kind of computing resource needed and the expected execution costs. Parameters provided during task submission include references to input and output data objects and synchronization dependencies to other tasks.

Besides this, the *Resource Introspection Interface* (RII) from Layer 0 is also provided as a Layer 1 interface. Thereby, Layer 2 components, such as data-processing operations, can create task execution plans with optimized and well-balanced long-term task-to-resource mappings. As a consequence – if available resources and the load situation are stable and as planned by Layer 2 – Layer 1 will never have to send a task to a different resource than it was intended to run on by Layer 2.

Layer 1 also provides a *Load Introspection Interface* (LII). It describes the current load situation and can be used to inform Layer 2 components if tasks from that component have to be executed often on other computing resources than intended. This allows Layer 2 to create a new execution plan that takes the current resource availability and load situation into account. By this means there is a feedback from Layer 0 up to Layer 2, for instance, when a newly started high-priority application (cell) consumes so many resources that re-planning on all levels becomes necessary.

Structure/Implementation: The *Task-Based Runtime System* can be regarded as a lightweight library operating system or Unikernel [10], because there is one instance per application cell. The runtime system can assume that the application tasks are cooperative. There is no need for user/supervisor-mode separation or other protection means on this level. Traditional operating system features such as file systems or network protocol stacks can be implemented either on top of Layer 1 within an application cell or in a separate global system service cell, which would also make use of the task-based runtime system, as it facilitates the handling of dynamic resource availability.

3.4   Layer 2: Data Processing

The *Data Processing* layer maps the operations of a data-processing application to the task-based execution model of Layer 1.

Provided Functions: For each operation, such as a query on an in-memory database, Layer 2 creates a state machine as shown in Fig. 2. The following functions are involved:

Planning: The first performed step is the step-wise transformation of a data-flow-oriented logical query plan into a physical execution plan that exploits task as well as data parallelism and all available heterogeneous computing and memory resources simultaneously. It also considers the current resource availability and the expected execution costs of the task implementations. An example for this can be found in Sect. 4.

Task Families: During planning a high-level operation must be broken down into primitive operations for which there is a task-based implementation in the pool of task families (see Fig. 1). These implementations are the building blocks of any performed database operation. They are part of Layer 2 and assumed to be known by its planning component.

Execution: When the plan is ready, the respective tasks must be submitted with the *Task Execution Interface* (TEI) of Layer 1. Tasks are represented at runtime by special memory objects called task objects. These memory objects hold the task parameters and all other dynamic task attributes. Layer 2 creates, destroys, and modifies these objects with the help of the Layer 1 object manager.

Dynamic Re-planning: In case that Layer 1 signals a high percentage of tasks that had to be executed on a different computing resource than it was planned, a re-planning will be triggered.

Interface: The logical query plan is provided by the data-processing application as a set of linked memory objects through the *Data Processing Interface* (DPI). The planning and execution steps are triggered by submitting a built-in Layer 2 task that will create further sub-tasks. Hence, planning can also benefit from all heterogeneous computing resources and parallelism. The results of the operation are passed to the applications via memory objects and callback tasks that are triggered when results are ready.

Structure/Implementation: The first and most challenging part of the implementation is the *planning*. High-level operations must be broken down into primitive operations and task families that implement these primitives must be found.

Based on an estimation of data volume, costs per task, costs for memory object transfers, and the available resources, the plan must to transformed into a task graph. Finally, the planned tasks must be executed by passing the respective task family members to Layer 1.

4 Case Study

We validate the presented architecture by explaining how a simple hypothetical data-procession operation would be executed on an exemplary heterogeneous hardware platform. This time we handle the architectural layers from top to bottom.

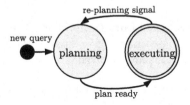

Fig. 2. Per-operation state machine

4.1 Scenario

The hardware platform consists of a multi-core CPU, a GPU that supports multiple independent execution contexts, and an FPGA with two equally-sized re-configurable regions. An in-memory database table R shall be scanned for entries that fulfill the conditions P_1, P_2, and P_3: $\sigma_{P_1 \wedge P_2 \wedge P_3}(R)$. A conventional query optimizer, which only works on the logical level, can turn this relational algebra expression into the data-flow-oriented execution plan shown in Fig. 3 (left part). We regard this as the input for Layer 2.

4.2 Layer 2

Layer 2 is responsible for planning and for submitting tasks as already shown in Fig. 2. Before planning the execution of a new query, Layer 2 gets information on currently available CPU, GPU, and FPGA resources from Layer 1 (LII). If another query is already being executed, it is likely that it uses *all* available cell resources. Therefore, both, the old and the new query execution, must be (re-)planned with an adequate fraction of the resources and considering priorities. Similarly, re-planning is necessary when a query execution terminates and additional resources become available or in situations in which Layer 0 has to resize the cell. In the following, we will focus on planning a single query and its execution.

Planning. During the planning phase the logical data-flow-oriented execution plan (Fig. 3) is searched for structural patterns that would allow a graph transformation. For example, a specific primitive could be replaced by a task node or a number of cooperating tasks. The tasks are chosen from the pool of task families.

It is also possible that a transformation replaces a group of nodes. In our example scenario, the three nodes "Selection σ_{P_2}", "Selection σ_{P_3}", and "Intersection" would be matched and replaced be an efficient FPGA-based implementation of this compound operation.

Eventually, all logical primitives will be replaced by task nodes. It is a complex optimization problem to apply transformations in the right order to minimize the resource consumption during the execution phase. In order solve this problem, Layer 2 needs a cost model so that alternative paths in the search space can be compared. Therefore, estimates for execution costs must be provided by the developer of each task implementation. This metadata is also stored in the pool of task families. Furthermore, costs for transferring data between different memories are provided by the object manager in Layer 1. Based on this, it can be decided to replace the three aforementioned nodes by an FPGA-based selection task and two data transfer tasks as shown on the right-hand side of Fig. 3.

After replacing all primitives with the "cheapest" available task implementations, performance optimizations by exploiting data parallelism would be taken into account. For example, the cheapest implementation of "Selection σ_{P_1}" would in our scenario be a CPU-based task, because the data transfer costs from CPU memory

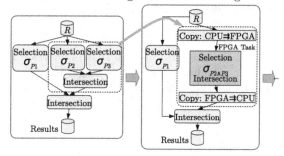

Fig. 3. Execution plan transformation

to GPU memory might be prohibitively high. The planner would consider instantiating multiple parallel CPU tasks that perform the selection after splitting the data into chunks. However, the compound operation on the FPGA can be instantiated only once, because only one FPGA region with the necessary hardware structure is available. The optimal amount of parallel selection tasks on CPU cores depends on the data rate of the FPGA task, because the results of both sides will have to be merged. Both data paths should produce results with the same rate. In our scenario the planner predicts that the FPGA will handle the data faster than the parallel CPU cores. Therefore, it also uses the GPU for a part of the data to further boost the data rate of "Selection σ_{P_1}". Again, nodes for splitting, transferring data, and merging would be added. Figure 4 shows the final execution plan.

Execution. Typically, the plan execution will be performed in a pipelined manner. For example, in our scenario the FPGA has only a small amount of on-chip RAM. It is not possible to copy all the data from R to the FPGA memory at once. As a consequence, the task for selecting rows that match P_2 and P_3 will have to be triggered many times. The execution engine is responsible for allocating the necessary task object, setting up task parameters, and triggering follow-up tasks upon completion. Data dependencies in the execution plan define the order in which tasks must be submitted.

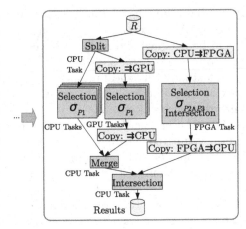

Fig. 4. Final execution plan for the case study

Tasks can use data objects that may reside in any memory region as input or output. The Layer 1 object manager is responsible for copying data from one region to another if necessary. This means that the data transfer nodes in the execution plan can be ignored. They are only needed for cost estimation.

4.3 Layer 1

Layer 1 manages work queues for all computing resources. Besides assigning tasks to these queues the task manager monitors the load. For example, in our scenario the costs calculated by the planner on Layer 2 might have been too imprecise. It might turn out that all CPU cores are overloaded. In this case, Layer 1 would access the pool of task families and replace a CPU task by a GPU task. The object manager would automatically perform the necessary data transfers.

Layer 1 is thus capable of performing short-term load balancing. However, if the rate of these replacements exceeds a threshold, Layer 1 would be informed to trigger re-planning.

The implementation handles all tasks that are submitted within the cell. This means that also other application tasks or tasks submitted by a library operating system contribute to dynamically changing load situations.

4.4 Layer 0

Layer 0 monitors the resource usage of all cells. While the cell is executing the query, it might withdraw resources from other cells that produce a low load. For example, a second cell might have been running with CPU cores at a low clock speed. While the query is running, Layer 0 might decide to withdraw CPU cores from the second cell, increase the clock of the remaining cores, and add the withdrawn cores to the cell that executes the query. A signal mechanism will be used to inform Layer 1 asynchronously.

5   Discussion

This section will reflect on the design decisions that we made and issues that were intentionally not addressed.

Decision: Task abstraction The ability to abstract from arbitrary heterogeneous computing resources requires a universal abstraction. The "task" can model the execution of a function on a CPU, a kernel on a GPU, or the data flow through gates on an FPGA. Tasks are smaller units of computation than threads and it is, thus, easier to annotate data structures used for input and output.

Decision: Layer 0 and 1 support arbitrary tasks It would be unrealistic to assume that the complete hardware platform is always dedicated to data processing. Therefore, we created a functional hierarchy that first handles resource partitioning and global management functions on Layer 0. If these features are not needed, Layer 0 could be reduced to a simple introspection mechanism that describes the available (static) hardware resources to the layers above.

Layer 1 implements the task execution model. If there was only a data-processing application on a dedicated system, this application would still benefit from the functions provided here. Supporting location transparent identification and automatic transfer of data objects simplifies the design of all software layers above.

Decision: Dynamic resources Layer 1 and 2 assume that resources can be withdrawn. This can have multiple reasons: First, Layer 0 might decide to assign some resources to another cell. However, even in systems with only one application, resources might be dynamic. For example, due to thermal issues not all computing resources can always run at full speed. The system software might need to throttle certain hardware components, which makes it necessary to deal with this problem. Furthermore, in future manycore systems, computing resources might permanently fail or be intentionally turned off to control aging.

Assuming dynamic resource availability makes cost calculations for data processing operations unreliable. However, this situation is not new to optimizers in DBMS and can be dealt with by re-planning.

Decision: Task Families We are aware that OpenCL allows developers to program an algorithm that could run on either CPU, GPU, or FPGA. In our opinion this approach is orthogonal to the concept of task families. The members of a task family could be generated from the same source code, e.g. from OpenCL code, or from completely differently code. The only assumption is that the functional behavior (input-to-output transformation for given parameters) is the same. It is not necessary that a task family has members for all computing resources – any subset is sufficient. By not assuming that task family members are created from the same source code there is room for arbitrary implementation optimizations.

Not addressed features: Various system optimizations are possible on Layer 0, which are left to individual implementations. So far our prototype only posseses a task scheduler that schedules a set of tasks in a way that the makespan is minimized. More sophisticated strategies can be implemented on Layer 1 that also consider the memory hierarchy. As query optimization is a research area on its own, we sketched only a few ideas for inspiring developers.

6   Prototype Performance

In a set of early experiments with our prototype implementation we have evaluated the performance of selection operators. Figure 5 shows that combining CPU cores and a GPU actually pays off (right column). The

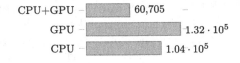

Fig. 5. Makespan for processing units in μs

execution platform was a notebook with Intel Core i7 CPU with eight cores and an integrated GPU[2]. He..ro DB was executed directly on the hardware without any other system software. Our prototype lacks Layer 0. Therefore, Layer 1 is a self-made bare-metal tasking framework.

The test data was a 16 MiB sized table from the TPC-H benchmark [14]. 16 queries of three different kinds were executed randomly. The implementations of the selection operators were provided as a task family: Code for the GPU was written in OpenCL while the code for the CPU was written in C++. The task scheduler could thus decide at runtime where the next task (operator) is to be executed. In the combined CPU/GPU run this decision was based on an execution time estimate, which is contributed by each task itself. With this the scheduler can estimate for each execution unit when the new task would start to be executed, based on the length of the task queue, and when it would be finished. The processor, which would finish the task first, is chosen.

During the experiments it turned out that for the highly memory bound selection operator, the integrated GPU is only three times faster than an i7 CPU core. For compute-intensive tasks we have seen much higher speedups on the same platform. This makes us believe that we follow the right approach, because (A) the combined use of CPU core and accelerators improves the performance and (B) the scheduling decision is non-trivial—meaning that a specialized system software component is needed.

7   Conclusions

This paper addressed the problem of exploiting all available computing resources on a modern heterogeneous hardware platform for data-intensive applications.

---

[2] Only seven CPU cores were used for task execution, as the eighth core was needed for benchmark control and time measurement.

The proposed He..ro DB is a design concept that is based on a layered system software architecture. It can be used as a blueprint for future system designs and supports independent optimizations on all of its layers. Some of the presented ideas have already been implemented in prototype systems by the authors.

References

1. Augonnet, C., Thibault, S., Namyst, R., Wacrenier, P.-A.: StarPU: a unified platform for task scheduling on heterogeneous multicore architectures. CCPE **23**(2), 187–198 (2011)
2. Breß, S.: The design and implementation of CoGaDB: a column-oriented GPU-accelerated DBMS. Datenbank-Spektrum **14**(3), 199–209 (2014). https://doi.org/10.1007/s13222-014-0164-z
3. Breß, S., Köcher, B., Funke, H., Rabl, T., Markl, V.: Generating custom code for efficient query execution on heterogeneous processors. arXiv preprint arXiv:1709.00700 (2017)
4. Breß, S., Saake, G.: Why it is time for a HyPE: a hybrid query processing engine for efficient GPU coprocessing in DBMS. Proc. VLDB Endow. **6**(12), 1398–1403 (2013)
5. Casper, J., Olukotun, K.: Hardware acceleration of database operations. In: Proceedings of the FPGA 2014, pp. 151–160, New York, NY, USA. ACM (2014)
6. Diamos, G.F., Yalamanchili, S.: Harmony: an execution model and runtime for heterogeneous many core systems. In: Proceedings of HPDC 2008, pp. 197–200. ACM (2008)
7. Heimel, M., Saecker, M., Pirk, H., Manegold, S., Markl, V.: Hardware-oblivious parallelism for in-memory column-stores. Proc. VLDB Endow. **6**(9), 709–720 (2013)
8. István, Z., Sidler, D., Alonso, G.: Runtime parameterizable regular expression operators for databases. In: FCCM 2016, pp. 204–211, May 2016
9. Kaldewey, T., Lohman, G., Mueller, R., Volk, P.: GPU join processing revisited. In: 8th International Workshop on DaMoN (DaMoN 2012), pp. 55–62, New York, NY, USA. ACM (2012)
10. Madhavapeddy, A., et al.: Unikernels: library operating systems for the cloud. SIGPLAN Not. **48**(4), 461–472 (2013)
11. Mueller, R., Teubner, J., Alonso, G.: Glacier: a query-to-hardware compiler. In: ACM SIGMOD International Conference on Management of Data (SIGMOD 2010) (2010)
12. Mueller, R., Teubner, J., Alonso, G.: Sorting networks on FPGAs. VLDB J. **21**(1), 1–23 (2012). https://doi.org/10.1007/s00778-011-0232-z
13. Pandit, P., Govindarajan, R.: Fluidic kernels: cooperative execution of OpenCL programs on multiple heterogeneous devices. In: 12th International Symposium on Code Generation and Optimization (CGO 2014), pp. 273:273–273:283, New York, NY, USA. ACM (2014)
14. Poess, M., Floyd, C.: New TPC benchmarks for decision support and web commerce. ACM SIGMOD Rec. **29**(4), 64–71 (2000)
15. Sidhu, R., Prasanna, V.K.: Fast regular expression matching using FPGAs. In: FCCM 2001, pp. 227–238, March 2001
16. Sukhwani, B., et al.: Large payload streaming database sort and projection on FPGAs. In: IEEE International Symposium on Computer Architecture and High Performance Computing, pp. 25–32. IEEE (2013)

17. Sukhwani, B., et al.: A hardware/software approach for database query acceleration with FPGAs. Int. J. Parallel Progr. **43**(6), 1129–1159 (2015). https://doi.org/10. 1007/s10766-014-0327-4
18. Ueda, T., Ito, M., Ohara, M.: A dynamically reconfigurable equi-joiner on FPGA. IBM Tehnical Report RT0969 (2015)
19. Zhang, S., He, J., He, B., Lu, M.: OmniDB: towards portable and efficient query processing on parallel CPU/GPU architectures. Proc. VLDB Endow. **6**(12), 1374–1377 (2013)

Investigating Transactional Memory for High Performance Embedded Systems

Christian Piatka[1]([⊠]), Rico Amslinger[1], Florian Haas[1], Sebastian Weis[2], Sebastian Altmeyer[1], and Theo Ungerer[1]

[1] University of Augsburg, Universitätsstr. 2, 86159 Augsburg, Germany
{piatka,amslinger,haas,altmeyer}@es-augsburg.de,
ungerer@informatik.uni-augsburg.de
[2] TTTech Auto Germany GmbH, Emmy-Noether-Ring 16, 85716 Unterschleißheim, Germany
sebastian.weis@tttech-auto.com

Abstract. We present a Transaction Management Unit (TMU) for Hardware Transactional Memories (HTMs). Our TMU enables three different contention management strategies, which can be applied according to the workload. Additionally, the TMU enables unbounded transactions in terms of size. Our approach tackles two challenges of traditional HTMs: (1) potentially high abort rates, (2) missing support for unbounded transactions. By enhancing a simulator with a transactional memory and our TMU, we demonstrate that our TMU achieves speedups of up to 4.2 and reduces abort rates by a factor of up to 11.6 for some of the STAMP benchmarks.

Keywords: Transactional memory · Contention management · Unbounded transactions · Embedded systems

1 Introduction

To fully utilize multicores, the ability to generate efficient parallel code is essential. Because in-depth parallelization has proven to be very error prone, alternative synchronization mechanisms, such as transactional memories (TM) [12], evolved to be a subject of research.

Implementations of hardware transactional memories were integrated into commercial high performance chips from Intel and IBM. Despite their benefits, current available commercial HTMs (e.g. Intel's TSX) do not meet the high requirements of embedded systems. Commercial HTMs statically implement contention management strategies, which can lead to high abort rates. To meet the high requirements concerning power consumption, embedded systems depend on low abort rates. Another disadvantage of COTS HTMs is that they bound transactions in several ways. The size of a transaction is limited by the capacity and

---

This project received funding by Deutsche Forschungsgemeinschaft (DFG).

A. Brinkmann et al. (Eds.): ARCS 2020, LNCS 12155, pp. 97–108, 2020.
https://doi.org/10.1007/978-3-030-52794-5_8

associativity of the L1 cache. In addition, transactions are aborted by events like interrupts, which limits their duration. This can negatively impact performance and complicates usability, leading to more programming errors, which is unacceptable for embedded systems due to the increasing demands of computational power and the scarce resources provided.

For our work, we developed two challenges: (1) Lowering abort rates by providing effective contention management. (2) Enabling unbounded transactions in terms of size. We want to achieve these goals by implementing a Transaction Management Unit (TMU). The main contributions of this paper are: (1) The design of a flexible TMU, which enables the user to apply different contention management strategies. (2) A solution to enable unbounded transactions, considering their size.

The rest of this paper is structured as follows: After giving an overview on the state of the art of transactional memories, we will describe our TMU. In the following section, our proposal is evaluated. At the end of this paper, we discuss related work and conclude by summing up our results and describing future work.

2   State of the Art

A transaction is a sequence of instructions that is monitored by the transactional memory system. The beginning and the end of a transaction are usually marked by special instructions. To ensure a correct execution of the program, the transactional memory system has to ensure that every transaction fulfills the following three criteria: (1) Transactions have to be executed atomically, which means that they commit or abort as a whole. (2) Transactions have to run isolated, which means that they do not impact each other. (3) The transactional executions have to be serializable, which means that a sequential execution with a matching output exists.

To fulfill these criteria, the transactional memory system has to ensure that values, which are consumed in a transaction, are not modified by another transaction running in parallel. For this purpose, read and write accesses in a transaction are logged at cache line granularity in a read and write set. A conflict occurs whenever a write access of a transaction tries to manipulate a cache line, which is already added to the read or write set of a competing transaction. A conflict also occurs, when a read access tries to read a cache line already contained in the write set of another transaction. To keep track of read and write accesses inside of transactions, HTMs usually utilize the cache coherence protocol.

If a conflict is detected, it has to be resolved by the HTM, by aborting all but one of the conflicting transactions. This involves setting back all the memory modifications performed during the transactions (rollback). Additionally, the read and write sets have to be cleared and the register files have to be restored. Afterwards, the aborted transactions have to be restarted.

Another source of transactional aborts are physical limits of the hardware, or interrupts. Physical restrictions are usually based on the size or associativity of the L1 caches, which are used to store the transactional read and write sets. Most HTM systems do not implement any mechanisms to allow the read or write set to overflow the size or associativity of the cache. This limits the transactions in terms of consumed and modified cache lines. Interrupts limit a transaction concerning its duration. Frequent transaction aborts because of physical limits or interrupts can be critical for the performance, since a significant amount of work has to be discarded.

Due to these physical restrictions, a programmer usually has to provide an alternative path of execution utilizing different synchronization mechanisms, which are not affected by physical hardware boundaries. The fallback path is a weak spot for transactional memory usage. It uses alternative synchronization, which can be error prone and reduce performance, depending on the depth of parallelization. Additionally, it takes away one of the main advantages, which is the easy usability, because the fallback path increases the complexity of the parallel code. Providing an efficient alternative would render transactional memory superfluous.

3   Transaction Management Unit

In this section, we first describe the implementation and the hardware setup of our system. Afterwards, we give a short overview of the selection of contention management strategies we implemented. At the end of this section, we explain how our solution is able to support unbounded transactions concerning their size.

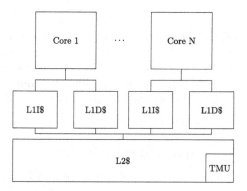

Fig. 1. The multicore system we consider consists of up to 16 cores. Each core has a private L1 instruction cache (L1I$) as well as a private L1 data cache (L1D$). The TMU is integrated into the L2 cache and is able to monitor the messages relevant for the transactional execution.

3.1 Hardware Integration

As depicted in Fig. 1, our TMU is integrated into the shared L2 cache. We consider a multicore system with N cores (we assume $N \leq 16$). The TMU monitors the execution and collects as well as provides data concerning the transactions. To be able to favor a transaction over others, our TMU is able to store priorities. Four ($\log_2 16$) bits are needed at most to be able to save a specific priority for every core. The priority of a transaction can be specified by the programmer at transaction start. The default priorities are the core IDs. In order to store priorities, timestamps, or performance counters, our TMU provides a 64 bit value. The timestamps can be set at different times (e.g. transaction start, transaction commit, etc.) depending on the conditions of the contention management strategy. Performance counters provide information concerning the transactional execution, e.g. the number of committed transactions. To mark whether a transaction runs unbounded, the TMU provides an additional bit per core. The TMU consists of a memory, which stores information, relevant for the transactional execution of each core. The information stored depends on the applied strategy. To resolve a conflict, the TMU takes as inputs (1) the core ID of the core running the transaction, which detected the conflict, and (2) the core IDs of the cores running the conflicting transactions. After comparing the corresponding data, the TMU signals to abort the transaction that detected the conflict, or the conflicting transactions. We optimistically estimate an upper bound for the hardware costs, when considering a 16 core multicore, by:

$$\text{memory} = 2 \times 16 \times 65 \text{ bit} \qquad = 260 \text{ byte} \qquad (1)$$
$$\text{comparators} = 2 \times 16 \times 65 \text{ bit} \qquad = 260 \text{ byte} \qquad (2)$$
$$= 520 \text{ byte}$$

Because we rely on a dual ported memory, we doubled the assumed memory capacity in our estimation (Eq. 1). A comparator works similar to an adder, which is the reason why the hardware costs are approximately double the amount of the bits compared (Eq. (2)). Even if we consider the double amount for additional hardware cost, our approach consumes less than 0.05% of the space provided by a 2 MB L2 cache.

3.2 Contention Management Strategies

Whenever a conflict between two running transactions occurs, the responsibility for resolving the conflict is handed over to the TMU. Depending on the strategy, the priority, a timestamp, or the number of commits are stored in the TMU. After comparing the relevant data, the TMU determines which of the conflicting transactions are aborted. We implemented three strategies:

priority: The transaction with the higher priority is allowed to continue. This strategy allows to enforce an ordered commit of the transaction and a prioritization of a transaction over others. We would like to utilize this strategy in the future to enable various real-time strategies (e.g. mixed criticality).

timestamp [16]: The transaction, that started first can carry on. Taking the timestamp of a transaction into account reduces the indeterminism concerning the aborts and guarantees progress.

commit: The transaction on the core, which committed fewer transactions is able to continue. This strategy leads to a more balanced execution, because cores, which were not able to commit transactions, are favored when conflicts occur.

Unbounded transactions always overrule the contention management strategy.

3.3   Unbounded Transactions

Transactions have to abort whenever a transaction's read or write set exceeds the size or associativity of the L1 cache. Therefore, most HTMs have to provide a fallback mechanism consisting of an alternative execution path. This does not only make it harder for the programmer to write efficient and correct code, it can also be crucial for performance because of the loss of already computed work. The TMU monitors the transactional execution and sets a bit whenever a transaction is forced to run in unbounded mode. Whenever the bit is set, conflicts are resolved favoring the unbounded transaction. Therefore, the transaction will never be aborted, which means it does not have to be rolled back. Since it is guaranteed that the transaction will succeed, the backup version of the cache line is not needed, which allows the transaction to use the entire cache hierarchy. The TMU can only support one unbounded transaction at the time. If another transaction or thread tries to perform a conflicting access, the TMU takes actions to suppress them, e.g. by stalling the core.

4   Evaluation

For the implementation of our approach, we utilized the gem5 simulator [4]. We selected the STAMP benchmark suite [6] to evaluate our approach. In this section we will describe in detail our evaluation methodology followed by the presentation of our results.

4.1   Simulation Methodology

The gem5 [4] is a cycle accurate processor simulator. It offers the possibility to choose an instruction set architecture out of a selection such as ARMv7, x86, etc. Furthermore, the periphery can be configured freely. The configuration of our system is described in Table 1. We chose this configuration, as it models a contemporary embedded multicore. High-performance embedded systems as smartphones exhibit similar specifications.

Due to the long run times entailed by the large input set of the STAMP benchmark suite [6] and the authors' recommendation to use the smaller input configuration for simulators, we chose to do our evaluation with the small input configuration depicted in Table 2.

Table 1. System configuration

Num CPUs	{1,2,4,8,16}
Microarchitecture	ARM Cortex-A15
L1 data cache	32 KB
L1 data cache assoc.	8
L2 cache	2 MB
L2 assoc	16
Cache coherence	Directory-based

Table 2. Benchmark configuration

Benchmark	Parameters
bayes	-v32 -r1024 -n2 -p20 -s0 -i2 -e2
genome	-g256 -s16 -n16384
intruder	-a10 -l4 -n2038 -s1
kmeans	-m40 -n40 -t0.05 -i inputs/random2048-d16-c16.txt
labyrinth	-i inputs/random-x32-y32-z3-n96.txt
ssca2	-s13 -i1.0 -u1.0 -l3 -p3
vacation	-n2 -q90 -u98 -r16384 -t4096
yada	-a20 -i inputs/633.2

4.2 Baseline Transactional Memory System

For our baseline, we implemented a transactional memory system into the ARM-based gem5 simulator [4]. The implementation of the interface is similar to those offered by Intel TSX [13] and the newly announced ARM TME [3]. Our interface allows the programmer to explicitly start and end transactions using the corresponding commands, which are provided by our transactional memory system.

Our baseline HTM detects and resolves conflicts eagerly: Conflicts are detected instantly when the conflicting memory access occurs (in contrast to detecting them at commit time). When a conflict occurs, the transaction, that detects the conflict, aborts to resolve it.

We provide a fallback path with regular POSIX Thread synchronization in our baseline implementation. In our baseline as well as in the runs supported by our TMU, a transaction is executed in the fallback path, if the attempt to execute the transaction failed 100 times. Trying to re-execute a transaction for 100 times makes sense, because the execution of a transaction in the fallback path prohibits the other cores to execute work. Whenever the read or write of a transaction in our baseline exceeds the L1 cache, it is directly executed in the fallback path.

4.3   Analysis

We evaluated the STAMP benchmark suite [6]. Figure 2 depicts the evaluation of the eight STAMP benchmarks *bayes*, *genome*, *intruder*, *kmeans*, *labyrinth*, *vacation*, *ssca2* and *yada*. Each graph depicts three lines. All lines show the absolute speedup compared to the reference execution (one core, no synchronization). We focused on the region of interest, which are the parts executed by transactions, because they can be quite small compared to the entire benchmark, making it difficult to show the effects of our work. We calculated the speedup as shown by Eq. 3.

$$speedup = \frac{reference\ execution\ time}{examined\ execution\ time} \tag{3}$$

The labeling of the lines in Fig. 2 indicates whether the line represents the baseline execution or a contention management strategy combined with unbounded transactions.

In the following, we describe in detail the behavior of the evaluated benchmarks:

bayes: For the benchmark *bayes*, we were able to beat the baseline execution for most executions. Up to 62 unbounded transactions are executed, which shows that it is beneficial to implement unbounded transactions concerning their size. We are able to achieve the best speedup for the execution with four cores and the timestamp strategy. Considering the entire run time of the benchmark, the part in which transactions were executed, is extremely short.

genome: The benchmark *genome* scales quite well. Our system produces the same results as the baseline. The features of the TMU become relevant for the executions with eight and sixteen cores. For these runs, we are able to significantly lower the number of aborted transactions. In these executions, transactions are started, which do not fit in the L1 cache and therefore have to be executed in the fallback path. Because of our TMU, we are prepared for these cases and are able to continue without having to abort them.

intruder: For the benchmark *intruder*, we made similar observations as with the benchmark *genome*. The main difference is that the positive effects of our extensions only take effect for the execution with sixteen cores. For this execution, the baseline contention management strategy performs so poorly, that we are able to lower the abort rate by a factor of 11.6. Within the execution of the benchmark, no transaction faces a capacity problem, which means we achieve the speedup only through better contention management.

kmeans: For the benchmark *kmeans*, we were not able to outperform the baseline. The reason for this is that no transaction, for any execution, faces a capacity problem, which means no unbounded transaction has to be executed. Additionally, the benchmark has hardly any conflicts, which eliminates the grounds of what we can improve.

labyrinth: The baseline execution for the benchmark *labyrinth* is below one, because the benchmark launches fairly big transactions, which do not fit in the L1 cache and cause the transaction to abort and execute in the fallback path. The already achieved computational progress is discarded, which is

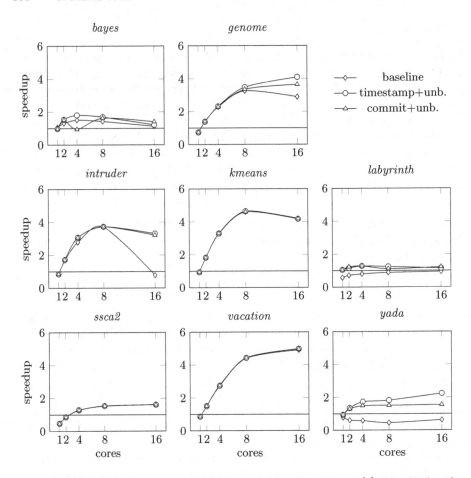

Fig. 2. Results of the execution of the STAMP benchmark suite [6]. For the benchmarks genome, intruder and yada we improved performance compared to the baseline implementation.

why the baseline execution falls below one. For this benchmark, our work is beneficial. We manage to raise the speedup above the baseline execution and one.

ssca2: The benchmark *ssca2* behaves similar to the benchmark *kmeans*. Hardly any of the almost 50000 committed transaction aborts. None of the transactions faces an issue with the capacity of the L1 cache.

vacation: The observations, which can be made for the benchmark *vacation*, are similar to those of the benchmarks *kmeans* and *ssca2*. Of the 4097 committed transactions, a maximum of only about 490 transactions aborts. Additionally, all of the transactions fit into the L1 cache, which is why no unbounded transactions are needed.

yada: The baseline execution for the benchmark *yada* suffers from a lot of conflicts, due to poor contention management. To commit around 4900 transactions, up to 33590 aborts occur. Additionally, some transactions face a problem with the capacity of the L1 cache. Therefore, the TMU handles up to 170 unbounded transactions, which is beneficial to performance and allows us to improve the baseline execution with both strategies. Additionally, we are able to achieve speedups bigger than one.

In Fig. 3, we depicted the number of aborts for every benchmark of the STAMP benchmark suite [6]. The line labeled as baseline depicts the baseline execution. The other lines represent an execution with a contention management strategy. Because we want to show the benefits of the implemented contention management strategies, we disabled the unbounded transactions for this evaluation.

For most of the benchmarks, we are able to lower the number of the aborts. Especially for executions with 8 and 16 cores. For these executions, the contention management strategy of the baseline performs poorly and we are able to reduce the number of aborts significantly for some benchmarks.

For the benchmarks, which already had a low abort rate, our strategies were not beneficial and sometimes even caused more aborts (e.g. *ssca2*). Our strategies perform best, when the contention between the transactions is high.

Our evaluation showed that our work is beneficial to a transactional memory system in terms of performance and abort rates.

5   Related Work

There are some proposals describing how to handle unbounded transactions e.g. [2,7,8,14]. In this section we describe and discuss solutions for similar problems.

The authors of [5] focused on unbounded transactions. They proposed a permissions-only cache, which allows large transactions by only tracking read and write bits without the corresponding data. Once the permissions-only cache overflows, one of two proposed implementations, to handle unbounded transactions, can be utilized. ONE-TM-Serialized only allows one overflowed transaction at a time and stalls the other cores. ONE-TM-Concurrent allows several concurrent transactions to run in parallel, although only one transaction can run in overflowed-mode. Our approach possesses the same runtime characteristics as ONE-TM-Concurrent, the difference between the approaches lies in the management of the unbounded transaction. In contrast to [5], where the authors propose to use per block meta data to ensure the correct execution of the unbounded transaction, we use our TMU to manage and protect the unbounded transaction. Due to a LogTM-style [14] baseline transactional memory system, the authors' proposal is also able to survive interrupting actions performed by the operating system. Contention management strategies were no subject to the authors.

The authors of [9] adapted an HTM for embedded systems, focusing on energy consumption and complexity. In this proposal, the authors evaluate different cache structures and three different contention management schemes (eager, lazy,

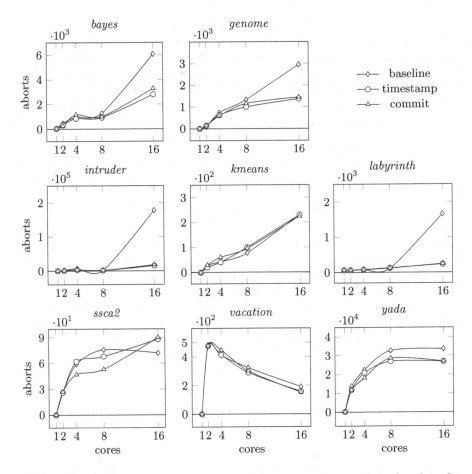

Fig. 3. We were able to reduce the number of aborts for most of the benchmarks. Especially the benchmarks, for which a lot of aborts were saved (*genome*, *intruder*, etc.), achieved significant speedups, which can be observed in Fig. 2.

forced-serial), concerning their complexity and energy consumption. The authors also provide a mechanism to support overflowing transactions (exceeding cache limits) by running them in serial mode. Because the authors are very sensitive for complexity, they only allow a simple execution mode for unbounded transactions. Therefore, running a transaction in serial mode means that all other CPUs get suspended. The overflowed transaction can now run isolated and is able to utilize the complete memory hierarchy. Our approach differs from [9], because we focus on performance and abort rates. Therefore, we provide a more complex execution mode for unbounded transactions. Furthermore, we offer several different and more complex contention-management strategies.

The work describing the most relevant contention management policies focus on software transactional memories (STM) [10,11,16,17]. Later work has applied some of these contention management strategies to HTMs e.g. [15]. In contrast to our work, the authors focused on using HTM as an synchronization primitive for an operating system as well as managing it in the scheduler. This made it necessary to implement a new more complex HTM. The authors focused, concerning the contention management strategies, on finding a well performing policy in most of the cases. This makes sense, since the best working policy is workload dependent, as also mentioned by the authors.

6 Conclusion and Future Work

In our work, we present a TMU, which is located in the shared L2 cache and costs approximately less than 0.05% of the space of a 2 MB L2 cache. We provide three different contention resolution policies and enable unbounded transactions. In our evaluation, we did not consider the contention management strategy, which enables priorities, because in our perspective it would not produce any interesting results concerning its execution time. The priority strategy will be of more focus in our future work. By our evaluation with the gem5 simulator [4] and the STAMP benchmark suite [6], we show that the TMU is beneficial for performance and is able to reduce the number of aborted transactions.

The work we present in this paper is the foundation to employ several other features. To further increase performance, we also would like to enable thread-level speculation, which will utilize the TMU to ensure correct execution. Our research also concerns fault tolerance utilizing transactional memory [1], where we will also consider investigating the use of the TMU. Because safety is a major issue for embedded systems, we want to try to utilize our TMU to enable mixed criticality and real time for hardware transactional memories.

References

1. Amslinger, R., Weis, S., Piatka, C., Haas, F., Ungerer, T.: Redundant execution on heterogeneous multi-cores utilizing transactional memory. In: Berekovic, M., Buchty, R., Hamann, H., Koch, D., Pionteck, T. (eds.) ARCS 2018. LNCS, vol. 10793, pp. 155–167. Springer, Cham (2018). https://doi.org/10.1007/978-3-319-77610-1_12
2. Ananian, C.S., Asanovic, K., Kuszmaul, B.C., Leiserson, C.E., Lie, S.: Unbounded transactional memory. In: 11th International Symposium on High-Performance Computer Architecture, pp. 316–327, February 2005. https://doi.org/10.1109/HPCA.2005.41
3. ARM Ltd.: Transactional memory extension (TME) intrinsics. https://developer.arm.com/docs/101028/0009/transactional-memory-extension-tme-intrinsics. Accessed 13 Jan 2020
4. Binkert, N., et al.: The gem5 simulator. SIGARCH Comput. Archit. News **39**(2), 1–7 (2011). https://doi.org/10.1145/2024716.2024718
5. Blundell, C., Devietti, J., Lewis, E.C., Martin, M.M.K.: Making the fast case common and the uncommon case simple in unbounded transactional memory. SIGARCH Comput. Archit. News **35**(2), 24–34 (2007). https://doi.org/10.1145/1273440.1250667

6. Minh, C.C., Chung, J.W., Kozyrakis, C., Olukotun, K.: STAMP: stanford transactional applications for multi-processing. In: 2008 IEEE International Symposium on Workload Characterization, pp. 35–46, September 2008. https://doi.org/10.1109/IISWC.2008.4636089

7. Chuang, W., et al.: Unbounded page-based transactional memory. SIGARCH Comput. Archit. News **34**(5), 347–358 (2006). https://doi.org/10.1145/1168919.1168901

8. Damron, P., Fedorova, A., Lev, Y., Luchangco, V., Moir, M., Nussbaum, D.: Hybrid transactional memory. In: Proceedings of the 12th International Conference on Architectural Support for Programming Languages and Operating Systems, pp. 336–346 (2006). https://doi.org/10.1145/1168857.1168900

9. Ferri, C., Wood, S., Moreshet, T., Bahar, R.I., Herlihy, M.: Embedded-TM: energy and complexity-effective hardware transactional memory for embedded multicore systems. J. Parallel Distrib. Comput. **70**(10), 1042–1052 (2010). https://doi.org/10.1016/j.jpdc.2010.02.003

10. Guerraoui, R., Herlihy, M., Pochon, B.: Polymorphic contention management. In: Fraigniaud, P. (ed.) DISC 2005. LNCS, vol. 3724, pp. 303–323. Springer, Heidelberg (2005). https://doi.org/10.1007/11561927_23

11. Guerraoui, R., Herlihy, M., Pochon, B.: Toward a theory of transactional contention managers. In: Proceedings of the Twenty-Fourth Annual ACM Symposium on Principles of Distributed Computing, pp. 258–264 (2005). https://doi.org/10.1145/1073814.1073863

12. Herlihy, M., Moss, J.E.B.: Transactional memory: architectural support for lock-free data structures. In: Proceedings of the 20th Annual International Symposium on Computer Architecture, pp. 289–300 (1993). https://doi.org/10.1145/165123.165164

13. Intel Corporation: Intel Transactional Synchronization Extensions (Intel TSX) Overview. https://software.intel.com/en-us/cpp-compiler-developer-guide-and-reference-intel-transactional-synchronization-extensions-intel-tsx-overview. Accessed 23 Jan 2020

14. Moore, K.E., Bobba, J., Moravan, M.J., Hill, M.D., Wood, D.A.: LogTM: log-based transactional memory. In: 2006 The Twelfth International Symposium on High-Performance Computer Architecture, pp. 254–265 (2006). https://doi.org/10.1109/HPCA.2006.1598134

15. Rossbach, C.J., Hofmann, O.S., Porter, D.E., Ramadan, H.E., Aditya, B., Witchel, E.: TxLinux: using and managing hardware transactional memory in an operating system. In: Proceedings of Twenty-First ACM SIGOPS Symposium on Operating Systems Principles, pp. 87–102 (2007). https://doi.org/10.1145/1294261.1294271

16. Scherer, W.N., Scott, M.L.: Contention management in dynamic software transactional memory. In: PODC Workshop on Concurrency and Synchronization in Java Programs, pp. 70–79 (2004)

17. Scherer, W.N., Scott, M.L.: Advanced contention management for dynamic software transactional memory. In: Proceedings of the Twenty-Fourth Annual ACM Symposium on Principles of Distributed Computing, pp. 240–248 (2005). https://doi.org/10.1145/1073814.1073861

X-CEL: A Method to Estimate
Near-Memory Acceleration Potential
in Tile-Based MPSoCs

Sven Rheindt[1]($\boxtimes$), Andreas Fried[2], Oliver Lenke[1], Lars Nolte[1],
Temur Sabirov[1], Tim Twardzik[1], Thomas Wild[1], and Andreas Herkersdorf[1]

[1] Technical University of Munich (TUM), Munich, Germany
sven.rheindt@tum.de
[2] Karlsruhe Institute of Technology (KIT), Karlsruhe, Germany

Abstract. Near-memory acceleration strives to tackle the data-to-task locality issue in MPSoCs in order to obtain higher performance and lower power consumption. However, it is not easy to determine whether the advantages arise from the near-memory integration or the hardware acceleration (versus software execution). We propose *X-CEL*, a method to accurately estimate the potential of near-memory acceleration using an easy-to-integrate *near-memory core*. We showcase *X-CEL's* benefits with three variants of graph copy mechanisms in a tile-based MPSoC. Evaluations reveal that the estimated speedup is in good accordance with the actual speedup achieved by the near-memory accelerator.

Keywords: Data-to-task locality · Near-memory acceleration · Design space exploration · Graph copy · Tile-based MPSoC

1 Introduction

The performance and power consumption of today's MPSoCs are dependent on data-to-task locality more than ever. A significant amount of energy and time is nowadays spent on data transfers between processor cores and the main memory, especially for memory-intensive applications, which are dominated by data access and movement [3,10]. Conventionally, sophisticated cache hierarchies are used to improve data-to-task locality by bringing data closer to the processor cores, thus lowering memory access latencies and the energy footprint. However, their benefit is decreasing due to the emergence of large, irregular and cache-unfriendly datasets, utilized by today's and future applications [10]. The locality challenge becomes worse when shifting towards tile-based manycore architectures, as on these the distance between physically distributed cores and memory grows.

Many recent approaches therefore leverage in- or near-memory computing to bridge the widening gap between processors and memory [1,16,22,25,27]. The majority of them use *near-memory accelerators* (NMAs), which perform

This work was funded by the Deutsche Forschungsgemeinschaft (DFG, German Research Foundation) – project number 146371743 – TRR 89: Invasive Computing.

© Springer Nature Switzerland AG 2020
A. Brinkmann et al. (Eds.): ARCS 2020, LNCS 12155, pp. 109–123, 2020.
https://doi.org/10.1007/978-3-030-52794-5_9

their task both close to memory, as well as in a dedicated hardware module (either near the memory or as a specific accelerator layer in a 3D-stacked circuit). NMAs usually achieve a higher computational density and performance than a software solution while saving energy and resources at the same time. On the other hand, they sacrifice the flexibility of general-purpose computing and every new accelerator requires a significant hardware development effort.

However, it is not always clear which portion of the performance advantage of the NMA originates from the location (i.e., *near-memory* integration) or type of function implementation (i.e. software execution versus hardware *acceleration*). The impact of either one of the two effects is highly dependent on the application and the underlying system architecture. To determine the optimal design, it is therefore essential to analyze the influence of both effects on multiple important user- and case-specific decision criteria, such as: performance, power consumption, resource usage, design effort, flexibility (general- vs. fixed-purpose), system or accelerator utilization, etc. The analysis whether 1. a near-memory integration (near-memory core or near-memory accelerator) is beneficial at all, 2. a dedicated hardware accelerator can outperform a software-programmable core for the given task, or 3. whether only the combination of both achieves a speedup, is crucial to avoid unnecessary and costly development effort. However, it is not trivial to quantitatively predict the effect of the individual optimizations before implementing and measuring them. Further, it has to be determined if a near-memory core or accelerator can handle the workload which is outsourced to it by many cores.

Therefore, a method for speedup estimation which helps the developer to make early yet robust design choices would be of much benefit. Conventionally, a design space exploration (DSE) is mostly performed on a virtual prototype (i.e. simulation-based) or an FPGA-based prototype [8,19]. Both need at least an accurate model or an implementation of the NMA, which already requires a good amount of development effort if the DSE is expected to yield conclusive results. To avoid this effort, we envision an orthogonal approach that could be applied to both virtual and FPGA-based prototyping. We therefore

- propose *X-CEL*, an agile, measurement-based method to estimate the speedup potential of near-memory accelerators in a tile-based MPSoC,
- showcase *X-CEL* with a case study of three graph copy mechanisms (two of them are near-memory),
- and provide an in-depth evaluation of this case study.

This agile development method builds on actual measurements of an intermediate, easy-to-integrate near-memory core implementation. With the intermediate stage, we achieve a better estimation of the target design (near-memory accelerator) because in it the near-memory dimension (i.e. location) has been decoupled from the accelerator dimension (i.e. type of function implementation).

The rest of the paper is organized as follows: Sect. 2 describes the related work. In Sect. 3, we present *X-CEL* followed by the case study in Sect. 4. Section 4 is divided into a description of the showcase scenario (Sect. 4.1 and 4.2) and how we apply *X-CEL* to it (Sect. 4.3). We further perform an in-depth analysis of the evaluation results in Sect. 5, before concluding in Sect. 6.

2   Related Work

Our work is closely related to design space exploration (DSE) of heterogeneous systems. As Sangiovanni-Venticelli et al. strive to do in their *platform-based design* method [23], we place our approach early in the design phase.

During a DSE run, the DSE needs to be able to evaluate the performance of each considered design point. Conventionally, it follows either a *simulation-based* or *analytical* method as defined by Pimentel [19]. When a custom hardware unit is part of the system, both of these methods need a model of that unit to be developed beforehand. Reagen et al. [21] and Altaf et al. [2] demonstrate this approach for the simulation-based and analytical methods, respectively.

There is also the *measurement-based* evaluation method, but Pimentel associates this with a prohibitively high development overhead. This is because instead of a (simplified) model of the custom hardware, the evaluation now needs a full prototype.

Our approach, however, is orthogonal to conventional DSE and allows us to bypass the need to develop a model or prototype beforehand. As we target *near-memory acceleration* (NMA), we extrapolate its performance by leveraging measurements of an easy-to-integrate, software-programmable near-memory core, without the need for the actual accelerator.

Recently, there has been much interest in NMAs for numerical applications [16,25], graph processing [11], and system software [27]. For dealing with object graphs, Maas et al. presented an accelerator (albeit not an NMA) to speed up tracing garbage collection [13]. Rheindt et al. specifically targeted the problem of copying object graphs with an NMA [22], which is also the focus of our paper.

There are also sophisticated software-only approaches to efficiently copy object graphs without costly (de)serialization: Mohr et al. [14] presented Pegasus, which targets embedded MPSoCs, while Skyway by Nguyen et al. [17] optimized object graph transfers over networks.

3   X-CEL

X-CEL is a measurement-based method to estimate and analyze the speedup potential of near-memory accelerators in tile-based manycore architectures. To be able to conquer the complexity of this endeavor, we propose an agile two-stage approach, which separates the near-memory from the hardware accelerator dimension. This decoupling of both effects allows us to make a better estimation.

Our method categorizes the activity of a parallel application scenario running on an MPSoC into three parts: 1. the *task of interest* (TOI), which would benefit from near-memory computing and which is often memory-intensive, 2. all remaining tasks of the application, and 3. idle time of the cores. Figure 2 illustrates this for a parallel application running on N_{cpu} cores. As depicted and defined in Fig. 2, t_{toi} and t_{other} are the accumulated times over all application cores executing the task of interest and the remaining tasks, respectively. The TOI can either be given as a design choice to be explored/analyzed or it can

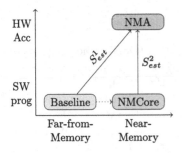

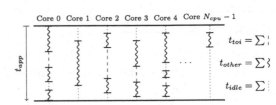

Fig. 1. *X-CEL* reduces the design space exploration complexity by one dimension.

Fig. 2. Example manycore application scenario including definitions of t_{toi}, t_{other}, t_{idle} and t_{app}.

be determined through application profiling, e. g. last-level cache misses indicate which task(s) have the most DRAM accesses.

The idle times arise from sequential parts of the application, limited parallelism, data dependencies, as well as inter-thread communication and synchronization overhead. If there are several different tasks of interest, *X-CEL* could also be individually applied to them to analyze the speedup potential of each. In the following, we assume one task of interest which is executed multiple times throughout the application.

The tile-based manycore architecture we consider (an example is depicted in Fig. 4), contains a main memory, a two level cache hierarchy, many cores and potentially a software-programmable *near-memory core* (NMCore) or dedicated hardware *near-memory accelerator* (NMA). Thus, we can differentiate between three implementation variants: 1. **baseline** (far-from-memory & without accelerator): the task of interest (TOI) and all others tasks are executed parallelized on the *far-from-memory* cores, 2. **NMCore** (near-memory, but without accelerator): the task of interest is executed *near-memory* on the *near-memory core*, while all others tasks remain on the distributed cores, and 3. **NMA** (near-memory & accelerated): similar to NMCore, but the task of interest is offloaded to the *near-memory hardware accelerator*.

Beginning with the existing baseline variant, *X-CEL* introduces and leverages an agile development step via the NMCore variant. The near-memory core serves well as an intermediate step in the two-stage estimation since it has negligible development effort compared to the near-memory accelerator: The existing software algorithm of the TOI just needs to be executed on an additionally instantiated core. This offloading needs to be properly synchronized with the rest of the system. As depicted in Fig. 1, *X-CEL* decouples the near-memory from the hardware acceleration dimension. In contrast, an estimation of the NMA using the baseline measurements would incorporate a change of both dimensions at the same time. This would be a difficult endeavor in such a complex system with many superposed effects of MPSoCs and parallel programming. Therefore, a refined estimation based on the NMCore variant is more promising because the near-memory dimension is fixed due to the same location of the NMCore and the NMA in the architecture.

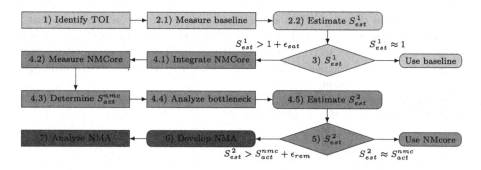

Fig. 3. Flowchart showing the steps of *X-CEL*

Our proposed *X-CEL* method thus follows the steps depicted in Fig. 3:

Step 1. Identify the task of interest (TOI) of the application scenario that could benefit from near-memory acceleration. In case of more than one TOI, apply *X-CEL* either individually or in a combined manner to them.

Step 2.1. Execute the baseline variant and measure the accumulated CPU time of all application cores taken by the task of interest t_{toi}^{base}, all other parts of the program t_{other}^{base}, as well as the overall runtime t_{app}^{base}.

Step 2.2. Determine a first speedup estimate S_{est}^1 of the NMA variant using the baseline measurements. Given that only the TOI is accelerated, while the rest of the application remains untouched, an upper bound estimate is given by:

$$S_{est}^1 = \frac{t_{other}^{base} + t_{toi}^{base}}{t_{other}^{base}} \tag{1}$$

Step 3. If $S_{est}^1 \approx 1$, the TOI has a negligible fraction of the total execution time. There is thus no speedup potential through near-memory computing and the baseline variant can be used. If, however, $S_{est}^1 > 1 + \epsilon_{sat}$, where ϵ_{sat} expresses a user-defined satisfying margin, we consider it worthwhile to speedup the TOI with near-memory computing. However, the confidence of this first stage estimate S_{est}^1 is not very high, as the estimation for the near-memory accelerator is based on the baseline variant which is neither near-memory integrated nor accelerated. Therefore, we refine the estimation in the next steps.

Step 4.1. Integrate the *near-memory core* (NMCore) variant.

Step 4.2. Execute this variant and measure the respective times of the different tasks t_{toi}^{nmc}, t_{other}^{nmc}, as well as the overall runtime t_{app}^{nmc}.

Step 4.3. Determine the actual speedup of the NMCore variant relative to the baseline implementation:

$$S_{act}^{nmc} = \frac{t_{app}^{base}}{t_{app}^{nmc}} \tag{2}$$

Step 4.4. Analyze whether the near-memory core becomes a bottleneck by monitoring its utilization. If $t_{toi}^{nmc} \approx t_{app}^{nmc}$, meaning the NMCore is utilized almost during the whole execution time of the application, the use of a second near-memory core might be an option. However, as commonly known, interleaved accesses of several cores to the same DRAM memory bank can even deteriorate the performance due to row conflicts. We experienced this behavior and hence employ only one near-memory core.

Step 4.5. Based on the NMCore measurements, refine the speedup estimate for the NMA compared to the baseline variant:

$$S_{est}^2 = \frac{t_{other}^{nmc} + t_{toi}^{nmc}}{t_{other}^{nmc}} \cdot S_{act}^{nmc} \tag{3}$$

As the NMCore and the NMA are located in the same position in the architecture, this second stage estimate is invariant to the near-memory dimension. It therefore promises a higher confidence.

Step 5. Compare the actual speedup achieved by the NMCore variant S_{act}^{nmc} (Step 4.3) with S_{est}^2 (Step 4.5), which is the refined estimation for the NMA speedup potential. Both are relative to the baseline variant and thus directly comparable. If $S_{est}^2 \approx S_{act}^{nmc}$, there is no remaining speedup potential for the hardware accelerator and the near-memory core is sufficient. If $S_{est}^2 > S_{act}^{nmc} + \epsilon_{rem}$, where ϵ_{rem} expresses a big enough remaining speedup margin, the near-memory accelerator should be considered. However, the development effort and the required hardware resources of the NMA should not be neglected in this decision.

Step 6. Develop and implement the near-memory accelerator.

Step 7. Finally, measure the NMA variant and perform an analysis of how close both estimates S_{est}^1 and S_{est}^2 approach the NMA variant.

4   X-CEL Case Study

This section presents a case study of *X-CEL* applied to near-memory graph copy. We first motivate the choice of near-memory graph copy as a showcase scenario (Sect. 4.1) and describe the prototype and benchmark setup of our case study (Sect. 4.2), before applying *X-CEL* to it (Sect. 4.3).

4.1   Motivation for Near-Memory Graph Copy

As mentioned in Sect. 1, data-to-task locality and the reduction of data movement is especially challenging on tile-based manycore architectures. Although parallel applications and operating systems help to exploit the increased scalability, they often impose significant overhead for inter-tile communication, data transport and thread synchronization. Common communication patterns of parallel applications, libraries, and operating systems require the transfer of arbitrary data to remote tiles and its subsequent processing there. As tile-based architectures often omit hardware support for inter-tile cache coherence and consistency [4,5,12], inter-tile communication (data transfer and thread synchronization) has to be handled explicitly via e. g. message passing (e. g. MPI [15])

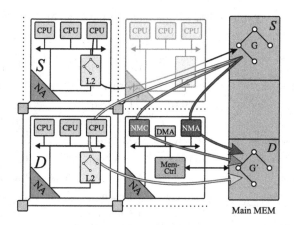

Fig. 4. Tile-based architecture.

or partitioned global address space (PGAS) programming (e.g. X10 [24] or Chapel [7]). These models have in common that they require data transfers between the memory partitions associated with each processor. These architectures therefore normally provide direct memory access (DMA) engines to support efficient transfer of data.

However, if object oriented programming (e.g. Java, X10, Chapel) is used, the data to be copied will be *object graphs* consisting of objects pointing to each other. These pointered data structures cannot be directly copied by a DMA engine since all copied pointers would become invalid. Since it is crucial for the performance of object-oriented applications on such architectures, many approaches optimize the transfer or handling of object graphs [13,14,17,22].

As one of them (Pegasus [14]) uses neither near-memory integration, nor hardware acceleration, it serves well as a baseline implementation in the case study. Another state-of-the art implementation of the same mechanism (NE-MESYS [22]) on the other hand leverages full near-memory acceleration. Both approaches target a MPSoC architecture as well.

4.2 Prototype and Benchmark Setup of the Case Study

We use a tile-based manycore architecture synthesized on a multi-FPGA system consisting of four Xilinx Virtex-7 2000T FPGAs [20]. The 4 × 4 tile MPSoC prototype design consists of up to 15 compute tiles and one memory tile, which is located at grid position (1,1). Figure 4 depicts the top-left-most 2 × 2 part of the whole design.

Each compute tile contains 4 cores (Gaisler SPARC V8 LEON 3 [6,26] processors) with private L1 caches. They are configured in write-through mode and kept intra-tile coherent by a classical bus snooping coherence scheme. The LEON 3 cores further use branch prediction and a floating-point unit. Each compute tile is further equipped with an L2 cache, which caches accesses to the

Table 1. Cache and memory parameters.

Parameter	Value	Parameter	Value
L1-I cache sets	2	LEON 3 freq.	50 MHz
L1-I cache set size	16 kByte	L1 & L2 cache freq.	50 MHz
L1-I cache line size	32 Byte	TLM freq.	50 MHz
L1-D cache sets	2	MEM ctrl freq.	100 MHz
L1-D cache set size	16 kByte	NMCore freq.	50 MHz
L1-D cache line size	16 Byte	NMA freq.	100 MHz
L2 cache sets	4	Local-DMA freq.	100 MHz
L2 cache set size	128 kByte	L1 cache policy	Write-through
L2 cache line size	32 Byte	L1 hit time	1 cycle
L2 cache policy	Write-back	L2 hit time	20 cycles
Tile-local memory (TLM)	8 MByte	L2 miss time	90 cycles
Main MEM	2 GByte	TLM acc. time	20 cycles

remote main memory, and a *tile-local memory* (TLM), which holds the program text, OS data, and temporary user data.

The memory tile is additionally connected to the off-chip DDR-3 main memory and also contains the near-memory core (LEON 3 core with L1 cache) or accelerator (NMA) if present.

A network adapter (NA) connects the tiles to the NoC routers and carries out the remote load-store operations received from the L2 cache back-end. Besides that, the NA can forward remote task invocations and trigger commands to the NMA. Table 1 gives an overview of the core, cache, accelerator and memory configuration parameters.

A distributed operating system [18] which is able to exploit the described hardware features runs on the FPGA prototype. We use the X10 IMSuite benchmarks [9] – a collection of distributed parallel kernels using the PGAS model – in the same configuration as [22].

4.3   X-CEL Applied to Near-Memory Graph Copy

To demonstrate *X-CEL*, we now apply it to the above-mentioned graph copy problem on this tile-based manycore architecture. In this section, we pick one (*MinimumSpanningTree*, MST) out of the twelve IMSuite benchmarks and run it on 15 compute tiles (MST-15) to showcase the different steps of the framework. For a complete study of all twelve benchmarks and different number of compute tiles, refer to the evaluation in Sect. 5.

In **Step 1** of the framework, we identify the memory-intensive graph copy operation as the task of interest (TOI). This task is part of the inter-tile communication routine of the runtime system and therefore occurs during the execution of any kind of parallel application on our system. As outlined in Sect. 3, our goal is to decide whether to perform this graph copy operation on a core in the receiving compute tile, on the near-memory core, or on a near-memory accelerator (see Fig. 4).

In every variant, the sending processor first needs to ensure that the latest version of the object graph G is in main memory. Since our architecture does not provide inter-tile cache coherence, the processor traverses G and explicitly writes back all necessary cache lines. After the write back on sender side and the invalidation on destination side, both the receiving processor and any near-memory processing elements now have a consistent view of G, and the copying operation can begin.

In the baseline variant, the receiving processor itself does the graph copying [14]. Here, the complete object graph needs to be cloned remotely via the cache hierarchy and the NoC from the source memory partition S to the processor and back to the destination memory partition D. The operation is indicated in Fig. 4 with the beige arrow. This limits performance and pollutes the receiver's caches with the source graph. On the other hand, this approach requires no additional hardware and the newly copied data is available in the receiver's cache right away.

Steps 2.1–2.2. We execute the baseline variant, which yields the following measurements:

	t_{toi}^{base}	t_{other}^{base}	t_{app}^{base}	S_{est}^1
MST-15	32.66 s	27.16 s	14.32 s	2.20×

Note, that t_{toi} and t_{other} are accumulated times over all cores, as defined in Fig. 2, while t_{app} is not.

Step 3. As the speedup potential $S_{est}^1 = 2.20\times > 1 + \epsilon_{sat}$ is satisfyingly large, we go on to analyze the near-memory core variant.

Step 4.1. We implement the NMCore variant, where the memory-intensive graph copy is outsourced to the near-memory core. The near-memory core performs the same software graph copy algorithm as the baseline variant. A negligible effort is required to integrate the near-memory core in the system, schedule the existing graph copy software algorithm on it and maintain consistency with it. The near-memory core is assisted by a state-of-the-art DMA engine for copying larger amounts of consecutive, non-pointered data, if existent. Figure 4 shows the existing system architecture including the near-memory core in green.

Steps 4.2–4.4. The execution and measurement of the NMCore variant yielded the following times:

	t_{toi}^{nmc}	t_{other}^{nmc}	t_{app}^{nmc}	S_{act}^{nmc}	S_{est}^2
MST-15	3.09 s	23.00 s	8.94 s	1.60×	1.82×

The actual speedup of the this variant was measured as $S_{act}^{nmc} = 1.60\times$. However, since the NMCore is only utilized during roughly one third ($t_{toi}^{nmc} = 3.09\,s$)

of the total application runtime ($t_{app}^{nmc} = 8.94\,s$), it is far from becoming the bottleneck.

Step 4.5. Based on the measurement results of Step 4.2, we can now do a better estimation of the NMA variant. According to the numbers depicted above, the speedup estimate for the NMA variant compared to the baseline can be calculated to $S_{est}^2 = 1.82\times$.

Step 5. As $S_{est}^2 = 1.82\times > 1.60\times = S_{act}^{nmc}$, we still see potential to achieve a higher speedup by using the near-memory accelerator. However, before this decision is made, all different benchmarks and application scenarios should be evaluated, which is done in Sect. 5. Also the development effort and the required hardware resources (compared to the NMCore) should be considered in this decision.

Step 6. Develop a graph copy NMA as proposed by Rheindt et al. [22]. This implementation uses a near-memory accelerator to perform the graph copy operation which executes the same graph copy functionality as the processor core using a slightly different algorithm that can be performed by a hardware module [22]. The NMA is indicated in purple in Fig. 4. This speeds up the copy operation itself and leaves the processors free for other tasks. However, it requires a tremendous development effort, as well as additional hardware resources of approximately the size of one core. Furthermore, the functionality of the NMA is limited to the graph copy task.

Step 7. The execution and measurement of the NMA variant brought these final results:

	t_{toi}^{NMA}	t_{other}^{NMA}	t_{app}^{NMA}	S_{act}^{NMA}
MST-15	1.65 s	21.38 s	7.69 s	1.86×

The actual measured speedup of the NMA $S_{act}^{NMA} = 1.86\times$ is very close and even slightly larger than the estimate $S_{est}^2 = 1.82\times$. Under the assumption that t_{other} is not effected by the NMA implementation, S_{est}^2 was defined as an upper bound. However, t_{other} decreased to $t_{other}^{NMA} = 21.38\,s$ compared to the baseline implementation's $t_{other}^{base} = 27.16\,s$, which helps to explain the additional improvement compared to the estimate.

5   Evaluation

This section presents the full case study and in-depth analysis for all twelve IMSuite benchmarks and a varying number of compute tiles between one and 15.

We examine the performance predictions of X-CEL in more detail. To this end, we use all benchmarks from the X10-IMSuite, and run them each on differently sized systems (1, 2, 3, 4, 8, 12, and 15 compute tiles). We then compare the two stages of performance predictions made by X-CEL with the actual performance achieved by the NMA.

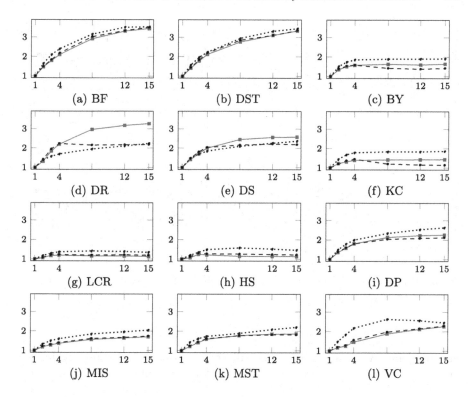

Fig. 5. Individual benchmark speedups of the NMA (—■—) normalized to the baseline for varying number of compute tiles, including $S^1_{est}(\cdots\bullet\cdots)$, $S^2_{est}(\text{-}\bullet\text{-})$: x-axis: number of computes tiles with four cores each, y-axis: relative speedup.

Figure 5 shows the speedups achieved by the NMA in each benchmark with varying system size, relative to the baseline variant of the same system size. The solid line —■— shows the actual speedups, whereas the dashed lines $\cdots\bullet\cdots$ and -$\bullet$- depict S^1_{est} and S^2_{est}, respectively.

For the systems with 3 and 15 compute tiles, we also show the run-times of each variant (Baseline, NMCore, and NMA) in Fig. 6. The dashed lines in these charts represent the run-times predicted by S^1_{est} and S^2_{est}.

The validity of X-CEL rests on two conditions: First, that S^1_{est} gives an indication whether near-memory computing could accelerate the given program at all, and second that S^2_{est} gives an accurate prediction of the run-time achieved by an NMA. We will now examine these two conditions in turn.

We first observe that S^1_{est} usually gives an upper bound on the achievable speedup. That is to say, if S^1_{est} is close to 1, the application will certainly not benefit from near-memory computing.

S^1_{est} only under-estimates the speedup in the DR and DS benchmarks. A closer analysis of the graph copy tasks performed shows a difference to the other benchmarks: DR and DS have many very small graph copy tasks to perform

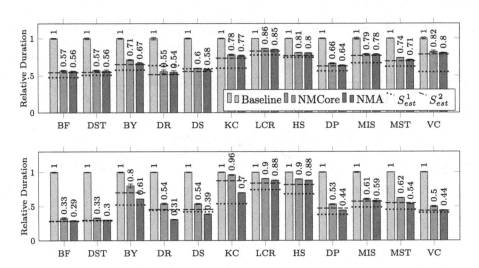

Fig. 6. Runtime measurements of the IMSuite benchmarks with three (Top) and 15 compute tiles (Bottom), respectively.

(e.g., DS transfers a single object of 24 bytes 17 856 times [22]). Thus, the offloading and synchronization overheads come to play a larger role, which our model does not handle as well. Still, we see that S^1_{est} fulfills its function well in most cases.

When examining S^2_{est}, we observe that S^2_{est} approximates the actual speedup well, with a root mean square error of 0.23. Out of all the 84 configurations we evaluated (12 benchmarks × 7 system sizes), in 60 configurations S^2_{est} deviated by less than 5% from the actual speedup.

The other 24 configurations warrant a closer analysis, because too low speedup estimates have a different impact from too high ones: X-CEL uses S^2_{est} as an indication of whether to develop a dedicated hardware accelerator (see Step 5 in Sect. 3). If S^2_{est} turns out to under-estimate the NMA's speedup, this is hardly a problem, because the NMA performs better than expected. On the other hand, if S^2_{est} over-estimates the speedup, the effort spent developing the NMA may have been wasted.

Out of the 24 configuration where S^2_{est} deviates by more than 5 %, it under-estimates the speedup in 14 cases, and over-estimates it in 10. The under-estimates are relatively large in places (up to 32.9 % for DR on 15 compute tiles), but as we have explained, this is not problematic. On the other hand, the over-estimates are at most 10.2 % (HS on 8 compute tiles), and indeed only 5 of the 10 over-estimates are larger than 6 %.

Considering that X-CEL does not need any information about the actual algorithm, the estimates it provides are quite accurate in most cases. Morevoer, if they deviate from the speedup achievable by the NMA, they usually err on the safe side from the developer's point of view.

6   Conclusion

We presented *X-CEL*, a measurement-based method to estimate the potential of near-memory acceleration. It helps to perform an early yet robust estimation whether the development effort of a near-memory accelerator is worthwhile. The two-stage method is based on measurements of an easy-to-integrate near-memory core (near-memory, but no accelerator) variant, which is closer to the target design than the existing baseline implementation (neither near-memory, nor hardware-accelerated). We showcased *X-CEL* with a (near-memory) graph copy problem in a tile-based MPSoC with a set of distributed graph algorithm kernels. An in-depth analysis revealed that the second stage estimate is within 5 % of the actual speedup in 70 % of the configurations. Moreover, it has 36 % higher accuracy than the original estimate.

Future work could refine the estimation model, as well as extend the framework to more case studies.

All in all, we envision *X-CEL* to become an *x-cel*-lent tool in the hand of developers to make sophisticated predictions on the near-memory acceleration potential and thereby avoid unnecessary development effort.

References

1. Ahn, J., Hong, S., Yoo, S., Mutlu, O., Choi, K.: A scalable processing-in-memory accelerator for parallel graph processing. In: Proceedings of the 42nd Annual International Symposium on Computer Architecture, Portland, OR, USA, 13–17 June 2015, pp. 105–117 (2015). https://doi.org/10.1145/2749469.2750386
2. Altaf, M.S.B., Wood, D.A.: LogCA: a high-level performance model for hardware accelerators. In: 2017 ACM/IEEE 44th Annual International Symposium on Computer Architecture (ISCA), pp. 375–388, June 2017. https://doi.org/10.1145/3079856.3080216
3. Arnold, O., Fettweis, G.: Power aware heterogeneous MPSoC with dynamic task scheduling and increased data locality for multiple applications. In: 2010 International Conference on Embedded Computer Systems: Architectures, Modeling and Simulation, pp. 110–117, July 2010. https://doi.org/10.1109/ICSAMOS.2010.5642075
4. Carter, N.P., et al.: Runnemede: an architecture for ubiquitous high-performance computing. In: 2013 IEEE 19th International Symposium on High Performance Computer Architecture (HPCA), pp. 198–209, February 2013. https://doi.org/10.1109/HPCA.2013.6522319
5. Choi, B., et al.: DeNovo: rethinking the memory hierarchy for disciplined parallelism. In: 2011 International Conference on Parallel Architectures and Compilation Techniques (PACT 2011), Galveston, TX, USA, 10–14 October 2011, pp. 155–166 (2011). https://doi.org/10.1109/PACT.2011.21
6. Cobham Gaisler: LEON 3 (2010). http://gaisler.com/index.php/products/processors/leon3
7. Cray Inc.: Chapel language specification (2019). https://chapel-lang.org/docs/_downloads/chapelLanguageSpec.pdf

8. Gries, M.: Methods for evaluating and covering the design space during early design development. Integr. VLSI J. **38**(2), 131–183 (2004). https://doi.org/10.1016/j.vlsi.2004.06.001

9. Gupta, S., Nandivada, V.K.: IMSuite: a benchmark suite for simulating distributed algorithms. J. Parallel Distrib. Comput. **75**, 1–19 (2015). https://doi.org/10.1016/j.jpdc.2014.10.010

10. Kogge, P.: Memory intensive computing, the 3rd wall, and the need for innovation in architecture (2017). https://memsys.io/wp-content/uploads/2017/12/The_Wall.pdf

11. Li, G., Dai, G., Li, S., Wang, Y., Xie, Y.: GraphIA: an in-situ accelerator for large-scale graph processing. In: Proceedings of the International Symposium on Memory Systems (MEMSYS 2018), Old Town Alexandria, VA, USA, 01–04 October 2018, pp. 79–84 (2018). https://doi.org/10.1145/3240302.3240312

12. Lyberis, S., et al.: Formic: cost-efficient and scalable prototyping of manycore architectures. In: 2012 IEEE 20th International Symposium on Field-Programmable Custom Computing Machines, pp. 61–64, April 2012

13. Maas, M., Asanović, K., Kubiatowicz, J.: A hardware accelerator for tracing garbage collection. In: Proceedings of the 45th Annual International Symposium on Computer Architecture (ISCA 2018), pp. 138–151. IEEE Press, Piscataway (2018). https://doi.org/10.1109/ISCA.2018.00022

14. Mohr, M., Tradowsky, C.: Pegasus: efficient data transfers for PGAS languages on non-cache-coherent many-cores. In: Proceedings of the Conference on Design, Automation & Test in Europe, pp. 1785–1790. European Design and Automation Association (2017)

15. MPI Forum: MPI: a message passing interface standard version 3.1 (2015). https://www.mpi-forum.org/docs/mpi-3.1/mpi31-report.pdf

16. Neggaz, M.A., Yantir, H.E., Niar, S., Eltawil, A.M., Kurdahi, F.J.: Rapid in-memory matrix multiplication using associative processor. In: 2018 Design, Automation & Test in Europe Conference & Exhibition (DATE 2018), Dresden, Germany, 19–23 March 2018, pp. 985–990 (2018). https://doi.org/10.23919/DATE.2018.8342152

17. Nguyen, K., Fang, L., Navasca, C., Xu, G., Demsky, B., Lu, S.: Skyway: connecting managed heaps in distributed big data systems. In: ACM SIGPLAN Notices, vol. 53, pp. 56–69. ACM (2018)

18. Oechslein, B., et al.: OctoPOS: a parallel operating system for invasive computing. In: McIlroy, R., Sventek, J., Harris, T., Roscoe, T. (eds.) Proceedings of the International Workshop on Systems for Future Multi-Core Architectures (SFMA). Sixth International ACM/EuroSys European Conference on Computer Systems (EuroSys), vol. USB Proceedings, pp. 9–14. EuroSys (2011)

19. Pimentel, A.D.: Exploring exploration: a tutorial introduction to embedded systems design space exploration. IEEE Des. Test **34**(1), 77–90 (2017). https://doi.org/10.1109/MDAT.2016.2626445

20. PRO DESIGN Electronic GmbH: FPGA module xc7v2000t (2019). https://www.profpga.com/products/fpga-modules-overview/virtex-7-based/profpga-xc7v2000t

21. Reagen, B., Shao, Y.S., Wei, G.Y., Brooks, D.: Quantifying acceleration: power/performance trade-offs of application kernels in hardware. In: International Symposium on Low Power Electronics and Design (ISLPED) (2013)

22. Rheindt, S., Fried, A., Lenke, O., Nolte, L., Wild, T., Herkersdorf, A.: NEMESYS: near-memory graph copy enhanced system-software. In: Proceedings of the International Symposium on Memory Systems (MEMSYS 2019), pp. 3–18. ACM, New York (2019). https://doi.org/10.1145/3357526.3357545

23. Sangiovanni-Vincentelli, A., Martin, G.: Platform-based design and software design methodology for embedded systems. IEEE Des. Test Comput. **18**(6), 23–33 (2001). https://doi.org/10.1109/54.970421
24. Saraswat, V., Bloom, B., Peshansky, I., Tardieu, O., Grove, D.: X10 language specification (2019). http://x10.sourceforge.net/documentation/languagespec/x10-latest.pdf
25. Schuiki, F., Schaffner, M., Gürkaynak, F.K., Benini, L.: A scalable near-memory architecture for training deep neural networks on large in-memory datasets. IEEE Trans. Comput. **68**(4), 484–497 (2019). https://doi.org/10.1109/TC.2018.2876312
26. SPARC Inc.: The SPARC Architecture Manual, Version 8, sav080si9308 edn. (1992)
27. Yitbarek, S.F., Yang, T., Das, R., Austin, T.M.: Exploring specialized near-memory processing for data intensive operations. In: 2016 Design, Automation & Test in Europe Conference & Exhibition (DATE 2016), Dresden, Germany, 14–18 March 2016, pp. 1449–1452 (2016)

Engineering an Optimized Instruction Set Architecture for AMIDAR Processors

Alexander Schwarz[✉] and Christian Hochberger

Technische Universität Darmstadt, Merckstr. 25, 64283 Darmstadt, Germany
{schwarz,hochberger}@rs.tu-darmstadt.de

Abstract. Newly developed instruction set architectures are nowadays typically based on the RISC principle. Yet, more abstract instruction sets also have their advantages. In the AMIDAR project Java Bytecode was used as the instruction set. Instructions are realized as compositions of *micro instructions* that are distributed to specialized functional units. An explicit timing of these micro instructions is not necessary in AMIDAR processors. This simplifies the conversion of compute intense instruction sequences into hardware structures while the system is running. The relatively high abstraction level of the Bytecode facilitates the analysis and synthesis remarkably. Yet, the native execution of the Bytecode comes with a number of drawbacks. In this contribution, we show a new instruction set architecture that preserves the high abstraction level of Bytecode while at the same time avoiding inefficient data transports. We show that on average the new instruction set reduces the number of clock cycles for our benchmark set by a factor of 3.

Keywords: Instruction set architecture · Microarchitecture · Self-timed · Java processor · Online synthesis

1 Introduction

Most new developments in the area of microprocessors use RISC instruction sets. The RISC nature of instruction sets eases decoding and creation of pipelines. On the down side, analyzing such instruction sequences can be very difficult. An instruction set with higher abstraction level will provide more specialized and targeted instructions. Thus, it will be easier to reverse engineer the intention of the programmer.

This is an essential property if we consider dynamic software/hardware migration. In AMIDAR processors, such online synthesis is one major factor for an efficient application execution. Existing AMIDAR processors use Java Bytecode as their instruction set. While we could demonstrate that it is very suitable for an online synthesis into HW structures, we also found that Bytecode makes excessive use of the stack and the local variable memory. Many of these data transports could be avoided.

The motivation to use Java Bytecode as instruction set is twofold: 1) Android based smartphones are programmed with languages that generate Java Bytecode

© Springer Nature Switzerland AG 2020
A. Brinkmann et al. (Eds.): ARCS 2020, LNCS 12155, pp. 124–137, 2020.
https://doi.org/10.1007/978-3-030-52794-5_10

which is then converted into Dalvik executables. Alternatively, a true Java Byte-code processor like an AMIDAR processor could be used in such platforms. 2) Java as programming language has gained a lot of attention for embedded systems due to its inherent safety features. Consequently, real HW implementations of Java Bytecode processors exist and are in commercial use.

In this contribution, we present a novel instruction set architecture (ISA) that preserves the high abstraction level of Java Bytecode, while at the same time reducing the amount of data transports to a minimum. On average, the resulting instruction set can be executed with less than one third of the original AMIDAR clock cycles.

The paper is structured as follows. Section 2 explains the AMIDAR principle. In Sect. 3 we explain the design of the new ISA (requirements, basic concept, code generation and binary format). Section 4 presents challenges together with our solutions for many detail problems with the new ISA. An evaluation of the new ISA is shown in Sect. 5. Finally, a conclusion and an outlook are given.

2   The AMIDAR Principle

AMIDAR [3] processors are composed of multiple functional units (FUs) which work independently of each other. Independence of FUs is a major strength of AMIDAR. It facilitates hardware design and provides opportunities for runtime reconfiguration. Figure 1 illustrates the structure of a Java processor. The Token Machine is a special FU which decodes program instructions into tokens and sends them to FUs using the token distribution network. Tokens contain the information which operations to execute and where to send the results to. Data can be exchanged between FUs using a data interconnect.

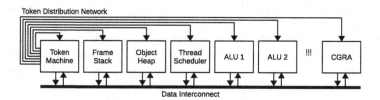

Fig. 1. Structure of the processor

In previous versions of AMIDAR processors, tags are used for synchronizing data with FU operations. Using this technique, every token and data packet contains a tag number. The receiving FU compares the tags of data packet and next token to execute. Only if both tags are equal, the data packet is accepted. Otherwise, the sender has to retry until data transmission is successful. Consequently, no assumptions about the timing of FUs are required and communication between FUs is self-timed.

Apart from its role as instruction decoder, the Token Machine executes all operations which change control flow like branches and method invocations. Furthermore, it provides constants contained in the code. The Frame Stack FU stores for each thread a stack of method frames. Every frame comprises a section for local variables and an operand stack. The Object Heap FU stores objects, arrays and static variables. The Thread Scheduler FU decides which thread to execute and provides thread synchronization using monitors. Several ALUs exist for integer and floating point arithmetic. A coarse grained reconfigurable array (CGRA) is used as flexible hardware accelerator [10].

3   Design of the New ISA

3.1   Motivation

The Frame Stack FU has been identified as bottleneck in previous versions of AMIDAR processors, which use Java Bytecode as their instruction set. Most instructions access the operand stack for reading or writing data. This results in many transfers from and to the Frame Stack FU. Consequently, reducing these data transfers is the main motivation for developing a new ISA.

3.2   Requirements

The processor should run Java programs on a high level of abstraction, like the previous AMIDAR implementation. However, these programs should be executed with higher performance by eliminating unnecessary data transfers. Reconfiguration features like dynamic software/hardware migration should still be supported. This leads to the following requirements.

- Data should be transmitted directly between FUs whenever possible without using intermediate storage. Thereby, execution time and energy consumption are reduced (see Sect. 5).
- Hardware requirements should be moderate. Reducing hardware requirements to an absolute minimum is not the goal. Complex FU operations should still be supported to provide fast execution of programs. On the other hand, complex and energy-consuming techniques for dynamic scheduling and data synchronization should be avoided (see Sects. 4.3 and 4.4).
- Instruction encoding should be compact in order to avoid a bottleneck between code memory and instruction decoder. However, an increased code size in comparison to Java Bytecode can hardly be avoided because small code size is a major strength of Bytecode due to the stack principle (see Sect. 5).
- Arbitrary complex control flow which is expressible in high level languages should be supported (see Sect. 3.3).
- No assumptions about FU timing behavior should be required, neither during code generation nor during token generation (See Sect. 4.3).
- The token generator should have the freedom to assign operations to different FUs as another means for runtime reconfiguration. This assignment should not be fixed by the programmer or code generator (see Sect. 4.5).

3.3   Basic Concept

The basic idea of the new ISA is to specify data flow between instructions explicitly instead of using an operand stack. Each instruction which produces a result specifies another instruction which will receive this result. The four components of an instruction are shown in Fig. 2. Every instruction specifies the operation to execute. Some operations require an additional constant. The *result reference* specifies the instruction which will receive the result. It consists of an instruction offset and a port. The offset is relative to the current instruction in order of execution. A value of 0 references the instruction which is executed next. It is important to note that the static position in the code is not relevant for this offset. Many operations require more than one operand. Therefore, a port number is used in the result reference to specify which of these operands is sent.

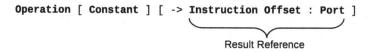

Fig. 2. Assembler representation of one instruction

An example of the resulting code is given in Fig. 3 together with an illustration of control and data flow. The first instruction sends the constant 10 to port 0 of either the add or the sub instruction. The read instruction in line 2 obtains a value from scratch pad memory address 3 and sends it to port 1 of the brg instruction in line 4. The next instruction in line 3 sends a value from scratch pad memory to port 1 of either the add or the sub instruction. The branch instruction in line 4 determines which of both is executed by comparing the received value with zero. Both the add and the sub instructions send their result to port 0 of the mul instruction in line 11. As only one of both is executed, the mul instruction receives exactly one value at its port 0. This value is multiplied with the value read from scratch pad memory address 4. The result is written back to the same address.

This example shows some important features of this kind of data flow description. Every value which is produced by an instruction must have exactly one receiver on every possible path of the program. Furthermore, every instruction must receive exactly one value on each of its ports on every possible path of the program. Every port of an instruction can behave like a ϕ function as known from static single assignment (SSA) forms in compiler engineering. Port 0 of the mul instruction is an example for this. Either the result of the addition or of the subtraction is received depending on the previously executed program path.

3.4   Code Generation

Code for the new ISA can be generated from two types of sources. The first type is assembler code. As the processor operates on a similar level of abstraction as

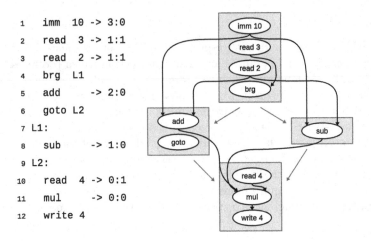

```
1    imm  10 -> 3:0
2    read  3 -> 1:1
3    read  2 -> 1:1
4    brg  L1
5    add      -> 2:0
6    goto L2
7 L1:
8    sub      -> 1:0
9 L2:
10   read  4 -> 0:1
11   mul      -> 0:0
12   write 4
```

Fig. 3. Basic code example (black: data flow, blue: control flow) (Color figure online)

Java Bytecode, meta-information like class structures is part of this code. Bodies of methods are filled with instructions in assembler representation as defined in Fig. 2. An assembler has been engineered which converts a set of assembler files to a single binary named *New AMIDAR Executable* (NAX). This binary contains all information which is required to execute a program on a hardware implementation of the processor.

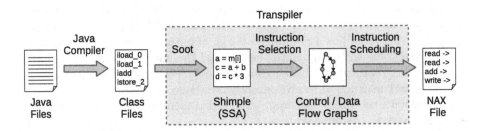

Fig. 4. Code generation from Java source code

The second much more useful type of source code is Java code. The corresponding tool flow is depicted in Fig. 4. A standard Java compiler produces class files from Java source code. A newly developed transpiler converts a set of class files to a NAX file. Figure 4 also shows a simplified version of this transpilation process. The Java analysis and optimization framework Soot is used to convert Bytecode from class files to an SSA form called Shimple [6]. Instruction selection creates a control flow graph for each method of the Shimple representation. Each node of such a control flow graph in turn points to a directed acyclic graph (DAG) defining data dependencies between instructions in the corresponding block. Instruction scheduling orders the instructions in each block to respect dependencies implied by the DAG on the one hand and hardware restrictions on the other hand.

3.5   Binary Format

A binary format for the instructions has already been defined as shown in Fig. 5. Every instruction has a width of 24 bits. This is the smallest multiple of one byte which can store all relevant information and leaves small room for extensions. Code is stored in an external DRAM which is accessed using a 32 bit AXI interface. A sequence of 32 bit words is converted to a sequence of 24 bit instructions in the instruction fetch stage of the Token Machine.

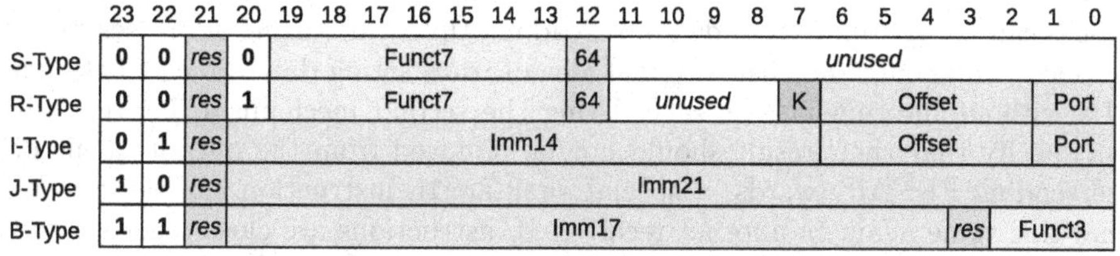

	23	22	21	20	19	18	17	16	15	14	13	12	11	10	9	8	7	6	5	4	3	2	1	0
S-Type	0	0	res	0				Funct7				64					unused							
R-Type	0	0	res	1				Funct7				64		unused			K		Offset				Port	
I-Type	0	1	res					Imm14											Offset				Port	
J-Type	1	0	res							Imm21														
B-Type	1	1	res						Imm17												res	Funct3		

Fig. 5. Binary format of instructions

Five types of instructions exist. The type is encoded in the highest bits. Bit 21 is reserved for future extensions.

- S-type is used for normal instructions which do not produce results. This is typically the case for memory store operations. The *Funct7* field holds the operation. Bit 12 distinguishes between 32 bit and 64 bit operations.
- R-type is used for normal instructions which produce results. This type contains the same fields as S-type plus instruction offset and port for specifying the result reference. Bit 7 is set to 1 if the result should be kept in the output queue as explained in Sect. 4.1.
- I-type is used for sending constant values. Constants up to 14 bits can be stored in the *Imm14* field. Larger constants must either be computed or stored in the constant pool. Special operations exist for loading these constants from the pool.
- J-type is used for unconditional jumps. The *Imm21* field holds the address of the jump target relative to current position in the code.
- B-type is used for conditional branches. The *Imm17* field again holds the relative address of the target. The comparison which decides whether the branch is taken or not is encoded in field *Funct3*. Bit 3 is reserved for future extensions.

4   Challenges

Realization of this ISA has been started by implementing an assembler and a software simulator. Afterwards, the transpilation process has been developed to be able to write programs in Java. All design choices have been taken with possible hardware implementations in mind. This section depicts some of the challenges which have been encountered on this way and their solutions.

4.1   Duplicating Data

As already mentioned in Sect. 3.3 each result must have exactly one receiving instruction. However, one value might be required as operand for multiple operations. Two mechanisms are provided to solve this problem. The first one is a small scratch pad memory, which is implemented as additional functional unit. Values can be written to it and can be read multiple times using addresses. Nevertheless, this contradicts the original idea of transferring data directly between FUs without intermediate storage. Using the second mechanism, instructions can specify that their result should not be removed from the output queue of the sending FU. Afterwards, a special send_again instruction can be used to send this value again to another receiver. If instructions are close together and only few copies are required, the last mechanism is preferred. Otherwise, scratch pad memory is used. The generic structure of an FU is shown in Fig. 6 and is explained in Sect. 4.3.

4.2   Discarding Data

Conversely, it is beneficial in some situations to discard data explicitly. For example, if control flow branches and a value is only required in one branch, the processor must be instructed to discard this value. In register based architectures this is done implicitly by overwriting registers. In this ISA the nop instruction can be used for this purpose. When a result is targeted to such an instruction during execution, the sending FU is informed to remove the value from its output queue without sending it.

4.3   Data Synchronization

The tag mechanism used for data synchronization in the previous AMIDAR implementation has several disadvantages. Firstly, data must be resent frequently in some situations, which results in lost bus cycles. Secondly, concurrency is limited because only data packets are accepted which match the next token to execute. Thirdly, depending on size and topology of the interconnect, tag comparators can be part of a long combinatorial path starting from the sending FU via the comparator of the receiving FU back to the acknowledgment signal of the sending FU.

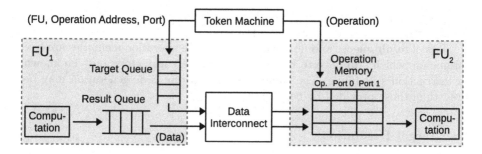

Fig. 6. Hardware components for synchronizing data

Consequently, a new synchronization mechanism has been invented. It uses explicit *operation addresses* to match data and operations. The important hardware components for this mechanism are depicted in Fig. 6. The first thing to note is that tokens are transferred to an FU in two parts. The operation code is sent as soon as the instruction has been decoded. The target information is sent afterwards when the receiving instruction has been decoded.

It is assumed, that an instruction IN_1 has already been decoded which results in operation OP_1 to be executed on FU_1. The result of OP_1 has already been computed and stored in the *result queue* of FU_1. IN_1 references instruction IN_2 as receiver for its result.

Now, the Token Machine decodes IN_2 and sends the corresponding operation OP_2 to the *operation memory* of FU_2. A line of this memory consists of an operation and one data word for each port of FU_2. An operation is stored together with its operands in one line. The address of a line is named *operation address*. Operations are written and read cyclically. Before the next operation can be written to a line, this line must be read and sent to execution. Hence, operation storage has FIFO semantics. Instructions which are mapped to the same FU are executed in the order they are decoded. In contrast, operands can be stored to the memory in any order using operation address and port. An operation can only be sent to execution when all its operands have been stored to the memory.

The Token Machine has an operation counter for FU_2 which is in sync with the operation write address of the operation memory. Therefore, the token machine knows the operation address of OP_2. It sends FU address and operation address of OP_2 together with the result port specified in IN_1 to the *target queue* of FU_1. The token machine sends operations and corresponding target information in the same order. As a consequence, the entries at the front of result queue and target queue belong to each other. They are removed simultaneously and sent via data interconnect to FU_2 where the data word is written to the memory location given by operation address and port.

Decoding is blocked when the target queue is full or no free operation address is available. As an operation is always sent before the target information pointing to this operation, it can be guaranteed that free space is always available in the operation memory when sending a data word. Consequently, no acknowledgment signal is required from the receiver to the sender.

Sizes of result queues and numbers of lines in the operation memories are free parameters which still have to be optimized. These parameters must be known for instruction scheduling. The values assumed during code generation may be lower than those provided by hardware.

4.4   Target Resolution

After the Token Machine has decoded an instruction and has assigned it to an FU, it must resolve the result reference and send this target information to the FU. The required hardware components are illustrated in Fig. 7.

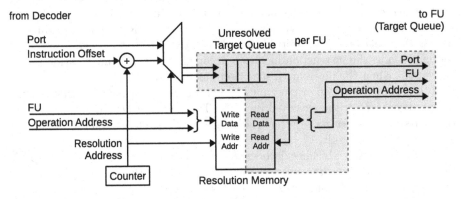

Fig. 7. Hardware components for resolving result references

The main component is the *resolution memory*. It stores FU and operation addresses of the instructions which have been decoded last. The number of addresses in this memory is a free parameter and limits the distance of result references between instructions. A counter generates the *resolution address* for each decoded instruction. It serves as write address for the resolution memory.

Now assume instruction IN_1 has just been decoded and assigned to FU_1 with resolution address RES_1. Its instruction offset points to instruction IN_2, which will be executed by FU_2 with resolution address RES_2. Port and offset are directly extracted from the instruction. Adding RES_1 to the offset yields RES_2, which is stored in the *unresolved target queue* of FU_1 together with the port.

When IN_2 is decoded, its FU and operation addresses are stored to the resolution memory at address RES_2. At the same time, RES_2 is located at the front of the unresolved target queue. As a consequence, the resolution memory is read from this address. The circuit detects when FU and operation addresses of IN_2 are available and sends this information together with the port to the target queue of FU_2. The most significant bit of the resolution address is not

used for addressing the memory but as tag for the memory contents. This allows
to detect when new information has been written.

4.5   Instruction Scheduling

Instruction scheduling is a more complex task in comparison to register based
architectures. Several constraints beyond data and control dependencies between
instructions must be considered to produce executable code.

- Instruction offsets are limited by the binary instruction format and the size
  of the resolution memory in the Token Machine.
- When a result is sent over a branch to different (exclusive) instructions, these
  instructions must have the same distance to the sender because the sender
  can only specify one instruction offset. This can be seen in Fig. 3. If a nop
  would be inserted before the sub instruction, the operands of the subtraction
  would not be received.
- The code must be free of deadlocks. If no care is taken, deadlocks are easily
  produced, which cause the processor to stop. As this constraint is the most
  difficult to handle, it is explained in more detail.

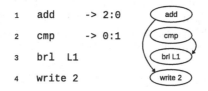

Fig. 8. Deadlock example

Figure 8 shows an example for a deadlock. Inputs of addition and comparison are not shown because they are not relevant for the deadlock. Both addition
and comparison are executed on the same FU. Consequently, the result of the
addition is placed at the front of the output queue, the result of the comparison behind it. However, the receiver of the addition result cannot be resolved
because the branch has not been evaluated yet. Therefore, this result cannot be
removed from the output queue. The branch in turn is waiting for the result
of the comparison, which is blocked by the result of the addition. A cycle of
dependencies is produced, which causes the processor to stop. A simple solution
for this deadlock is to change the order of addition and comparison.

There are many more constellations causing deadlocks. They can be statically
detected by building dependency graphs and searching for cycles in these graphs.
Theoretically, a dependency graph must be constructed for each possible execution path in a program. Calling convention ensures that no deadlocks can appear
across method boundaries. Consequently, methods can be analyzed separately.

Loops still produce an infinite number of paths. However, result references are limited to the current or the next loop iteration. Therefore, no additional deadlocks can appear after analyzing two loop iterations. The number of paths can still grow exponentially. In practice, this problem is solved using a sliding window algorithm. The window slides along the control flow of the method. Whenever the next instruction is added to the window, cycles are searched and removed. Afterwards, instructions which can be proven not to cause new deadlocks are removed from the window. When the algorithm detects that a window position has already been encountered, analysis of this path can be finished. While the problem still has exponential complexity, this algorithm finds all deadlocks in reasonable time even in methods with very complex control flow.

Different actions for removing deadlocks have been implemented. A suitable action is chosen depending on the deadlock constellation. In contrast to finding deadlocks, the problem of removing deadlocks has not been fully solved yet. In some situations, the scheduler fails to produce code free of deadlocks and informs the user about it. Current research investigates different approaches for systematically resolving all deadlocks.

A special `forward` operation is available to facilitate instruction scheduling. It just forwards the received input to another instruction. In hardware, forwarding is done by a separate FU, which helps to fulfill the mentioned constraints.

No new dependencies are introduced if two instructions are executed on distinct FUs instead of on a single FU. Hence, this cannot cause new deadlocks. Consequently, exact assignment of operations to FUs is not required for deadlock analysis. It must only be guaranteed that certain categories of instructions will not be executed on the same FU.

5   Evaluation

The benchmark set used for evaluation comprises 9 encryption algorithms, 7 hash algorithms, and 4 image filters. Additionally, ADPCM encoding/decoding, JPEG encoding, and regular expression matching have been evaluated. Execution times have been determined using simulators which imitate hardware behavior. FU timings of the existing hardware implementation are applied. Each benchmark has been executed once in the simulator for the Bytecode based AMIDAR processor and twice in the simulator for the new ISA. In the last case, benchmarks have been executed with 1 and 2 instructions decoded in parallel. Afterwards, the speedup has been calculated. For the new ISA, the following parameters have been chosen, which seem to be minimal values for reasonable execution.

- Resolution Memory Size: 16
- Operation Memory Size (all FUs): 8
- Output Queue Size (all FUs): 4

Figure 9 illustrates the speedups for all benchmarks. An average speedup of 3.69 is achieved in the single issue case and 4.64 in the dual issue case. Hence, a

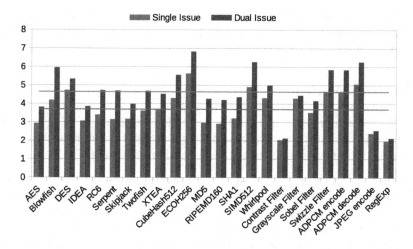

Fig. 9. Speedups achieved in comparison to Bytecode (simulated)

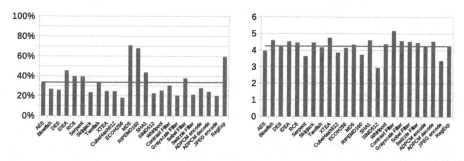

Fig. 10. Data transfers between FUs (left) and code size (right) in comparison to Bytecode

significant speedup in comparison to Java Bytecode can be noted. Furthermore, dual issue is clearly advantageous for this ISA.

However, some benchmarks differ from the average. The first exception is *Contrast Filter*, which uses floating point operations. As these operations are time consuming, speedup achieved by an improved ISA is lower. *JPEG encode* is a complex, data dominated algorithm, which is split across multiple methods. This lowers the speedup to 2.55. *RegExp* is an example for control flow dominated algorithms with many method invocations. It shows a speedup of 2.14.

The main reason for high speedups is the reduced number of data transfers between FUs. They are decreased by a factor of 2.98 in average as shown in Fig. 10. This has been a major design goal as defined in Sect. 3.2. On the other hand, code size grows by a factor of 4.25 in average, which is caused by an increased size and number of instructions.

All benchmarks require less than 10 s for code creation from class files, with the exception of *SIMD512* (40 s) and *RIPEMD160* (15 s). In this benchmark set a substantial number of methods from the Java standard library has to be included in the binary file. Measurement has been carried out on an Intel Core i7-6700 CPU with 16 GB RAM and a Java 1.8 HotSpot JVM on Ubuntu 16.04.

6   Related Work

AMIDAR processors use principles from dataflow machines [4]. Thus, often a comparison is made with such processors. In contrast to such machines, AMIDAR avoids the known issues with typical dataflow machines [7]:

- Broadcasting of tokens is done only for a handful of FUs. Thus, handling of tokens is not a problem.
- In a dataflow machine, the availability of input data must be checked for a huge set of operations concurrently. This is often done using costly content addressable memories. In AMIDAR, the availability of input data needs to be checked only localy inside of a functional unit. Thus, it can be implemented much more efficiently.
- Dataflow machines can suffer from deadlocks, if the program is not composed in a proper way. Such situations are not easy to detect and thus greatly complicate the compiler.

Even if dedicated dataflow processors are not longer researched due to the mentioned problems, dataflow is still used in scientific computing approaches. Maxeler uses a Java-like language to generate dataflow graphs and a compiler maps those graphs onto a set of field programmable gate arrays [2]. The big drawback of this approach is its inability to execute regular code. It is only efficient in high-throughput computing.

In AMIDAR, FUs synchronize with each other by the exchange of data. In a similar manor, Transport Triggered Architectures (TTA) [1] use the transport of data to start new operations. Nevertheless, AMIDAR provides more elasticity, since it allows arbitrary execution time for an FU without the need to adjust the microinstructions. In contrast, TTAs require exact knowledge of the FU timing, since the result of an operation must be moved to its destination at the proper time. Even worse is the problem of the huge code memory of TTAs. In order to provide a high degree of parallelism, TTAs must be able to control as many independent data transports as possible. This results in very wide instructions which in turn need a large code memory. Unfortunately, the majority of the code uses only few of the possible transport slots. Approaches have been published that reduce this memory size by means of compression [5]. AMIDAR avoids the huge code memory in a different way by generating the token sets on the fly from a more abstract instruction set.

Finally, one could think about other instruction set architectures than Java Bytecode. Candidates could be Low Level Bit Code [8] from the LLVM framework, Common Intermediate Language [9] from the .NET framework. They share approximately the same abstraction level. Yet, it turns out that both come with severe drawbacks compared to the Java Bytecode. Compute instructions in CIL and LLVM Bit Code do not contain type information. Thus, the required type of operation (int, float, double) has to be reconstructed from the sources of the data. In the worst case, they need to be combined with type conversions at runtime.

7 Conclusion and Future Work

In this work, a promising novel ISA for AMIDAR processors has been presented. It borrows ideas from data flow architectures and in simulation shows significant speedups compared to Java Bytecode as ISA. Through thorough engineering we were able to fulfill almost all requirements that were defined. Only code size leaves room for improvement. However, we are willing to pay this cost in favor of the provided advantages.

A hardware implementation is already existing for a number of components for this new ISA. The remaining components are currently in progress. The full implementation will then be validated against the simulation. An adaptation of the synthesis process to the new ISA is also currently in progress.

We believe that our transpiler still has some room for improvement. In order to support general purpose applicability of the processor, we will need to add support for multi-threading and for debugging (which both already exist for the Bytecode based AMIDAR processor).

References

1. Corporaal, H.: Microprocessor Architectures: From VLIW to TTA. Wiley, Hoboken (1997)
2. Gan, L., et al.: A highly-efficient and green data flow engine for solving Euler atmospheric equations. In: 2014 24th International Conference on Field Programmable Logic and Applications (FPL), pp. 1–6 (2014)
3. Gatzka, S., Hochberger, C.: The AMIDAR class of reconfigurable processors. J. Supercomput. **32**(2), 163–181 (2005). https://doi.org/10.1007/s11227-005-0290-3
4. Gurd, J.R., Kirkham, C.C., Watson, I.: The Manchester prototype dataflow computer. Commun. ACM **28**(1), 34–52 (1985)
5. Heikkinen, J., Cilio, A., Takala, J., Corporaal, H.: Dictionary-based program compression on transport triggered architectures. In: IEEE International Symposium on Circuits and Systems (ISCAS 2005), pp. 1122–1125 (2005)
6. Lam, P., Bodden, E., Lhotak, O., Hendren, L.: The Soot framework for java program analysis: a retrospective. In: Cetus Users and Compiler Infrastructure Workshop (CETUS 2011), October 2011
7. Lee, B., Hurson, A.: Issues in dataflow computing. In: Yovits, M.C. (ed.) Advances in Computers, vol. 37, pp. 285–333. Elsevier, Amsterdam (1993)
8. LLVM Project: LLVM bitcode file format. https://llvm.org/docs/BitCodeFormat.html
9. Various: Standard ECMA-335 Common Language Infrastructure (CLI). ECMA International, Geneva, Switzerland (2012)
10. Wolf, D.L., Jung, L.J., Ruschke, T., Li, C., Hochberger, C.: AMIDAR project: lessons learned in 15 years of researching adaptive processors. In: 2018 13th International Symposium on Reconfigurable Communication-centric Systems-on-Chip (ReCoSoC), pp. 1–8, July 2018

Scaling Logic Locking Schemes to Multi-module Hardware Designs

Dominik Šišejković[1(✉)], Farhad Merchant[1], Lennart M. Reimann[1],
Rainer Leupers[1], and Sascha Kegreiß[2]

[1] Institute for Communication Technologies and Embedded Systems,
RWTH Aachen University, Aachen, Germany
{sisejkovic,merchantf,reimannl,leupers}@ice.rwth-aachen.de
[2] Hensoldt Cyber GmbH, Ottobrunn, Germany
sascha.kegreiss@hensoldt-cyber.com

Abstract. The involvement of third parties in the integrated circuit design and fabrication flow has introduced severe security concerns, including intellectual property piracy, reverse engineering and the insertion of malicious circuits known as hardware Trojans. Logic locking has emerged as a prominent technique to counter these security threats by protecting the integrity of integrated circuits through functional and structural obfuscation. In recent years, a great number of locking schemes has been introduced, thereby focusing on a variety of security objectives and the resiliency against different attacks. However, several major pitfalls can be identified in the existing proposals: (*i*) the focus on isolated and often small circuit components, (*ii*) the assumption of unrealistic attack models that enable powerful attacks on logic locking and (*iii*) the design of very specific locking schemes targeted towards achieving resilience against specific attacks. These observations strongly impair the practicality of logic locking. Therefore, in this paper we present a holistic framework for scaling logic locking schemes to common multi-module hardware designs, thereby showcasing an industry-ready pathway of applying logic locking in a realistic design flow. The framework represents an enhancement of the previously published Inter-Lock methodology, offering several algorithmic improvements as well as toolflow implementation details to facilitate the applicability of the framework to large multi-module designs. The framework is tested and evaluated on a real-life 64-bit RISC-V core.

Keywords: Hardware security · Processor cores · IC Design integrity · Locking framework · RISC-V

1 Introduction

The Integrated Circuit (IC) design and fabrication flow is nowadays heavily driven by third party Intellectual Property (IP) and outsourcing the fabrication to off-site foundries. This business model reduces the total IC design and fabrication cost, and shortens the time-to-market enabling companies to stay competitive in the semiconductor industry. However, the involvement of untrusted

A. Brinkmann et al. (Eds.): ARCS 2020, LNCS 12155, pp. 138–152, 2020.
https://doi.org/10.1007/978-3-030-52794-5_11

third parties has raised countless security concerns, ranging from IP piracy to the insertion of hardware Trojans [13].

As a reaction to the security threats, various design-for-trust countermeasures have been introduced, including logic locking, IC camouflaging [14], watermarking [7], split manufacturing [2] and IC metering [4]. Logic locking is identified as a premier technique to protect the integrity of IC designs, as it can protect against adversaries located anywhere in the IC supply chain. The core idea of logic locking is the insertion of additional obfuscation logic into a gate-level netlist in order to make the original design functionally dependent on a secret key [15]. Since the key is only known to the IP owner, the design remains concealed while being in hands of external parties.

Motivation: Despite the tremendous amount of proposed logic locking solutions in the past, the ever increasing amount of key-recovery attacks represent a serious challenge to designing practical and resilient locking schemes. Moreover, several major pitfalls can be identified in the existing proposals:

- *Isolation:* Existing proposals mostly focus on isolated and often small circuit components or sequential circuits treated as a single component (e.g., singular gate-level netlist). This has the major drawback that the attack complexity relies on the security of the most vulnerable component. Therefore, all components can be attacked independently.
- *Inflexibility:* Modern designs typically include multiple isolated but functionally interconnected components that we refer to as modules (e.g., controller or decoder in a processor). Treating the complete designs as a single isolated component disables the applicability of expert knowledge about the IP. Often, it is necessary to adapt the security measures for specific components depending on their position, significance or exposure in the design. For example, some components might be more vulnerable to a specific attack, requiring dedicated security enhancements. Moreover, by adapting the overhead of the implied security measure in selected components, the overall power dissipation, chip area or performance can be steered to fulfill the desired customer requirements. If the design is seen as a single isolated unit, the mentioned adaptations become significantly more difficult to implement.
- *Impracticality:* Existing logic locking proposals are focused on thwarting specific attack vectors or achieving particular security objectives [1,15]. This hampers the practicality of logic locking, as its applicability depends on achieving very specific goals, instead of offering a general solution.

Contribution: To address the mentioned pitfalls, in this paper we introduce a holistic framework that enables the applicability of any logic locking scheme to modern multi-module hardware designs. Hereby, the focus of the work is not to design a specific locking scheme, but rather to present a methodology of *scaling logic locking* to multi-module hardware designs in a practical design flow, thereby taking the *complexity* and the *interdependent* nature of modern designs into account. The main contributions of this work include the following:

- Based on the proposed Inter-Lock methodology [10], we present and discuss multiple enhancements of the framework in regard to optimizing the integration of security features into a multi-module design, thereby focusing on the exploitation of existing design interdependencies.
- We showcase the framework in a realistic and industry-ready scenario based on a 64-bit RISC-V processor, thereby discussing the implementation, configuration and realization of the toolflow from a practical point of view.
- We evaluate the security-cost trade-off implied by the framework on the selected real-life case study.

The rest of this article is organized as follows. Section 2 introduces the background on logic locking. The framework improvements, setup and application are presented in Sect. 3. The evaluation results are discussed in Sect. 4. Related work is introduced in Sect. 5. Finally, the paper is concluded in Sect. 6.

2   Preliminaries

2.1   Logic Locking

A major type of logic locking is referred to as *combinational* logic locking. This locking type performs design manipulations of the combinational path of integrated circuits. The core idea is the extension of Boolean functions with redundant logic that is bound to an activation key. If the correct key is provided, the design performs as originally intended. Otherwise, an incorrect key ensures the generation of faulty outputs for at least some input patterns. Combinational logic locking is typically applied to a gate-level netlist representation of a design by inserting different types of key-controlled gates into specific locations in the netlist. These gates are referred to as *key gates*.

As an example, let us consider the random locking scheme known es EPIC [9]. This scheme is based on the insertion of XOR and XNOR (XOR + INV) gates at random locations in the design. An XOR gate buffers the second input when its first input is fixed to 0. Same is true for an XNOR gate and the fixed input value 1. Following this rule, the XOR/XNOR gates can be disseminated in the netlist, thereby preserving the original functionality when a correct key is given. Due to the presence of INV, an adversary has to guess if the INV is part of the locking or original functionality, i.e., removal attacks are mitigated.

In the past years, a great variety of combinational locking schemes has been introduced, including locking strategies based on AND/OR, XOR/XNOR and MUX gates. A comprehensive overview of the historical evolution of combinational locking schemes can be found in [15].

In the current literature, logic locking is also referred to as "logic encryption" or "logic obfuscation". In this work, the term "logic locking" implicitly refers to combinational logic locking.

2.2   Logic Locking in the IC Design Flow

The IC design and fabrication flow including logic locking is presented in Fig. 1. The flow consists of two regimes: the trusted and the untrusted. The trusted regime incorporates the tools and personnel involved in the design of the original IP. This includes the design of the register-transfer level and the initial logic synthesis (not shown in Fig. 1) as well as the application of logic locking to the gate-level netlist. Note that after locking, the netlist typically needs to be resynthesized once more to incorporate the changes. The untrusted regime includes an external design house (for the layout synthesis) and the foundry. Hereby, logic locking protects the integrity of the original IP by binding its functionality to a secret key.

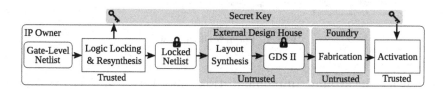

Fig. 1. Logic locking in the IC design flow

Attack Model: Finding the secret key is the first barrier that needs to be overcome by an adversary to successfully unlock and understand the design. Typically, it is assumed that an adversary has the locked netlist as well as an activated IC with oracle I/O access (available from the semiconductor market) at his disposal. This combination enables a great variety of powerful key-recovery attacks [1,11]. However, it has recently been shown that the key storage itself can be compromised by probing attacks or key-extraction hardware Trojans, thereby gaining access to the key without the necessity to formally attack the locking scheme [3,8]. Moreover, most attacks rely on having full access to a scan chain. However, genuine IC vendors typically do not leave a scan chain open (especially in security-critical IPs) or simply use a secured scan chain [5]. Based on these observations, we limit our approach to the following *realistic* attack assumption: the adversary has only access to the locked netlist. Therefore, the locking mechanism is effective only for the first batch of produced ICs before an activated IC with the *identical* locking mechanism and key is available on the market.

3   The Inter-Lock Framework for Processor Cores: A Practical Approach

In this work, we present the practical implementation details of the critical steps of the Inter-Lock [10] flow as well as several algorithmic improvements that enable a targeted applicability of the approach to any hardware design. With the provided details, we bridge the gap between a theoretical locking scheme and its applicability to a large-scale multi-module design.

RISC-V Case Study: All details and improvements are presented through a case study based on the open-source 6-stage in-order Ariane processor [16]. This core implements the 64-bit RISC-V instruction set [12].

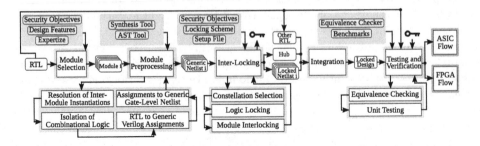

Fig. 2. The inter-lock flow

Framework Setup and Implementation: Inter-Lock is designed to exploit the inherent interdependent nature of common hardware designs; different modules (components) communicate with each other through forward and backward connections (similar to forwarding in pipelined processors). To utilize this existing feature for security purposes in addition to locking, Inter-Lock *adapts* the original functionality of every selected module in a design to generate a subset of the activation key for other modules. This creates a *security dependence* between selected modules; only if one module is correctly activated, its co-dependent modules can be unlocked as well. This functional dependence has the following consequences:

- Since part of each module key is internally derived, an adversary is not able to distinguish between common and key inputs.
- The overall design functionality depends on the correct activation of all components. A single incorrect key in one module creates a chain reaction of functional failures throughout all security-dependent modules.
- To correctly unlock a design, the adversary needs to attack all modules at once. This holds as well in case of attacks that include an activated IC with a closed scan chain.

The complete Inter-Lock flow is presented in Fig. 2. The input is a hardware design description on Register-Transfer Level (RTL). In our case, this is the complete Ariane core available in System Verilog. The output is the same core with the embedded security features. All intermediate steps are described in the following sections in more detail, thereby following the flow in Fig. 2.

3.1   Module Selection

The module selection incorporates the selection of design modules that will be included in the locking procedure. A module defines an enclosed (System) Verilog module. For example, a common processor design typically consists of modules

Table 1. Ariane combinational modules

IC	Abbreviation	#Inputs	#Gates	#Outputs
flush_controller_logic	f_ctrl	145	22	11
csr_buffer_logic	c_buff	222	134	90
instruction_scan	i_scan	32	240	139
instruction_realigner_logic	i_real	183	629	276
compressed_decoder	c_dec	32	848	34
commit_stage	commit	985	1584	417
branch_unit	br_unit	342	1655	328
decoder	decoder	518	2169	362
pc_select	pc_sel	521	3333	128
branch_prediction	br_pred	814	4669	333
alu	alu	206	7412	65

such as a decoder, ALU, controller and others. Any number of modules can be selected for the locking. However, at this stage, it makes sense to only select the modules that are critical in terms of security to mitigate the area/power/delay overhead implied by the locking scheme. For a module to be eligible for further processing, it must not contain further instantiations of other modules or any sequential elements (registers). The reason for these requirements is that logic locking typically works on combinational paths. Therefore, we focus our flow on purely combinational modules. Even though this decision seems fairly limiting, with a few simple adjustments, any module can be transformed to a combinational one, as discussed in the next section. For the purpose of the case study, we selected all Ariane modules shown in Table 1.

3.2   Module Preprocessing

This step prepares a set of selected modules for the locking procedure. The input to this stage is a set of RTL modules, while the output is a set of the same modules in a generic gate-level netlist format. In our case, the generic netlist is represented with simple gate primitives that are defined in the Verilog standard. The preprocessing consists of the following steps: (i) the resolution of inter-module instantiations, (ii) the isolation of combinational logic, (iii) the transformation from RTL to generic Verilog assignments and (iv) the transformation from assignments to a generic gate-level netlist.

Resolution of Inter-Module Instantiations: One module can include multiple instantiations of other modules within its body, especially since we are still operating on RTL at this point. The construct of an instantiation is not compatible with logic locking. Therefore, we need to resolve it. Two viable options are available. The first option includes flattening the module during the process of mapping to a generic library (addressed in the next section). The second one includes temporarily commenting the instantiation while the module proceeds in the framework flow. Afterwards, the instantiation can be re-embedded into the code. In our flow, we proceed with the first option.

Isolation of Combinational Logic: Typically, a single module consists of a combinational path and sequential elements. To simplify the locking procedure that is drafted for combinational logic, we propose the structural isolation by creating internal wrappers for the purely combinational path. An example is shown in Fig. 3 (a). Here, the flush controller logic of the Ariane core is extracted and separated from the sequential part into the module file *flush_controller_logic*. This step is repeated for the following modules as well: *csr_buffer_logic* and *instruction_realigner_logic*.

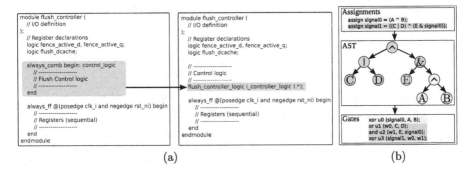

(a)   (b)

Fig. 3. Examples: (a) Isolation of combinational logic and (b) Assignment to gate-level transformation

Transformation from RTL to Generic Verilog Assignments: To enable a smooth transition from RTL to a generic gate-level netlist, we rely on the utilization of an intermediate verilog assignments format. These assignments enable the generation of a generic netlist, thereby decoupling the design from any specific technology. To generate a gate-level netlist, the RTL design must be synthesized according to a technology library. Afterwards, the produced netlist can be processed either as technology dependent or stored in a technology-independent format. The latter has the benefit of remaining independent of any technology or tool specifications, i.e., no specific technology library is necessary. Therefore, the design can proceed with any design flow (e.g., ASIC or FPGA). In our case study, we utilize the Synopsys Design Compiler (DC) to map the RTL to a *generic* library. Afterwards, DC can be instructed to store the generated netlist in a Verilog format that results in simple assignments. In principle, any synthesis tool and technology library can be used for this step.

Transformation from Assignments to Generic Gate-Level Verilog: The final preprocessing step transforms the assignment-level Verilog into a generic gate-level netlist. To perform this task, we utilize the open-source PyVerilog library. This library is able to parse a Verilog file and represent it as an

Abstract Syntax Tree (AST). Through a simple traversal of the AST, we map the assignments to primitive Verilog gates. An example transformation is shown in Fig. 3 (b).

3.3   Inter-Locking

Once the generic gate-level netlists are prepared, the next step includes the setup and execution of the Inter-Lock procedure. The procedure consists of three major parts: (*i*) constellation selection, (*ii*) application of a logic locking scheme and (*iii*) module interlocking (dependence creation). All three steps are described in the following.

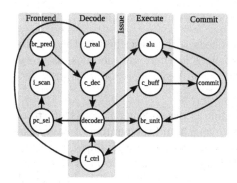

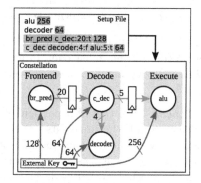

Fig. 4. Example: constellation selection

Fig. 5. Example: constellation setup file

Constellation Selection: The first step defines the security interdependence between modules, i.e., which modules influence the correct activation of other modules in a design. The goal of defining a constellation is to create a cyclic interdependence, meaning that every module depends on the activation of every other module. To understand the principle, we represent all modules as a dependency graph in Fig. 4. A node represents a *single module* and an arc represents a *security dependency*. This dependency is defined by a source and a sink module, *where the activation of the sink depends on the activation of the source.* In other words, once a source module is correctly activated, it generates the correct internal keys for the sink module. The nodes use the abbreviated naming scheme defined in Table 1. Moreover, the nodes in the example are placed according to their position in the processor pipeline. To ensure that an adversary has to consider all modules at once in an attack, all nodes must be included in the dependency graph. This can be done by selecting a constellation in which every node has at least one input and one output arc. If this is achieved, starting from any node, a dependency chain can be traced back, covering all other nodes in the constellation.

Besides the security dependencies, the constellation selection also includes the selection of the external key length for each module. To support a simple setup of a selected constellation, we propose a setup file consisting of multiple entries of the following format:

$< source >$ $[< sink : num\_interlocks : use\_reg >]$ $< key\_len >$, where:

- $< source >$: Name of source module.
- $[< sink : num\_interlocks : use\_reg >]$: Optional list of all sink modules for which the source module generates internal keys (known as interlocks), where:
  - $sink$: Name of sink module.
  - $num\_interlocks$: Number of internal key inputs to be generated.
  - use_reg: Defines if a register should be placed between the source and sink module for every interlock.
- $< key\_len >$: Total external key length for the source module.

Using this format, every selected module needs to be described in the file. In other words, the file must contain as many lines as there are modules, as every module must be listed as a source at least once. A simple example is provided in Fig. 5.

Key Length: Note that if a particular module is dependent on others, its *total* key length equals the sum of its *external* key length and the number of interlocks (internal key) from all other modules it is influenced by. For example, the total key length of *c_dec* is $20 + 64 = 84$ bits. This implies that the total *external* key length of the whole design is, in fact, smaller than the actual key, as the internal keys are hidden through interlocks. Compared to the fixed constellations of the previous work [10], this format enables a more flexible application of the locking mechanisms drafted specifically for a selected architecture. Hereby, the designer can follow a few simple rules while drafting a setup (in this case, biased towards processor designs):

- Create dependencies between modules that are near each other, e.g., at most one pipeline stage apart. This follows the natural implementation of a pipelined core, without raising suspicion.
- Place registers between modules that are naturally divided by a pipeline stage (e.g., between *br_pred* and *c_dec*).
- Register placement is not required if the source and the sink are both in the same pipeline stage and a functional connection already exists; for example, if the output of the source is directly driving the sink in the original design (e.g., between *c_dec* and *decoder*).
- Register placement is not required if the source and the sink are in different pipeline stages where a dependency creates a forwarding path (e.g., between *decoder* and *pc_sel*).

Application of Logic Locking: This step includes the application of a selected locking scheme to all preprocessed input modules. Since the framework itself is independent of the actual locking scheme that is applied, any scheme can be selected at this point. To perform the locking, the toolflow has to calculate the correct total key length for each source module (sum of external and all internally-derived keys). Afterwards, a selected locking scheme is applied using this particular key length, where the key itself can be randomly generated or predefined. Moreover, the process of creating interdependencies (internal keys) does not interfere with the actual locking mechanism, since the locking only cares about the key input itself rather than how the key is derived. A modular implementation enables a simple switching of locking schemes and the targeted application of specific schemes to specific modules. This can especially be useful in the case when a module is more exposed (e.g., to the primary inputs or outputs), thereby being more susceptible to selected attacks. For the case study, we selected the simple random locking scheme described in Sect. 2.1. This scheme is a superset of other XOR-based locking schemes as it disseminates XOR/XNOR gates on random locations, i.e., without making biased decisions. Therefore, it is a valid selection for the cost evaluation.

Module Inter-Locking: Inter-locking is defined as the procedure of adapting the functionality of the source and sink modules to generate the security depen-dencies defined in the selected constellation. The input to this stage is a set of already locked modules. The idea is as follows. A source module must generate correct and constant output keys for all its sink modules once activated. Note that this is true only for a correct key; otherwise, the output keys are changing based on the circuit input. This internal key bits are referred to as *interlocks*. To perform this task, the inter-locking procedure integrates an additional *Inter-Locking Circuitry (ILC)* to the source module. The properties of the ILC can be summarized as follows:

- If the source itself is not correctly activated, the ILC generates incorrect outputs. On the contrary, if the source is activated, the output keys must be correct and constant. This is achieved through a random Boolean function whose output depends on a subset of the key inputs of the source.
- The ILC is indistinguishable from the rest of the source implementation. This is achieved by binding the functionality and structure of the ILC to the original source functionality. More details can be found in [10].

Activation Procedure: An important part of Inter-Lock is the activation proce-dure of the whole design. Compared to the existing work, we introduce several implementation details that enable a smooth design activation in terms of logic locking. As previously, we focus on the Ariane core. For a correct activation of the core, the correct external key must be provided to all locked modules before the execution starts. This is performed by setting the *reset* signal for a given amount of cycles. Afterwards, the reset is lifted and the core starts executing. Depending on how the inter-locking procedure is implemented, the activation can fail if not facilitated with multiple "free" cycles. We propose the following activation sequence strategies:

- Cycle-Preventive Insertion: Let us assume that two modules influence each other, i.e., they both act as source and sink. This constellation can create haz-ardous combinational loops and an unstable activation sequence. The latter can occur if both activations are at all times incomplete because both modules never become fully activated (one is waiting for the other and vice versa). This can be prevented by avoiding the usage of key outputs (interlocks) of the first module in the input cone of the ILC of the second module. On one hand, this cycle-preventive insertion is impairing the unrestricted dissemination of key gates, thereby having a negative impact on the underlying locking scheme. On the other hand, this insertion does not necessarily require register placement as cycles are prevented by design. In both cases, if longer security dependencies exist, the core needs *multiple cycles* until a stable activation is reached. This can be achieved by blocking the core for multiple cycles through the *reset* input or by providing multiple NOP instructions before the actual code execution. This activation sequence mimics a sequential locking mechanism, as the core has to move through different cycles until reaching the correct activated state. Moreover, an interesting observation can be made: it only works if the reset state of the core is *correctly* implemented. We noticed this in different versions of the same Ariane core. One had a faulty reset which led to changed states in the core regardless of the activated reset. Such a behavior impacts the activation procedure as it changes signal values that in turn lead to faulty ILC outputs even if the locking mechanism is correctly implemented. This showcases the tight interleaving of the locking mechanism with the functionality of the core.

– Exclusive Insertion: This insertion adapts the inter-locking procedure by ensuring that the ILC of every module exclusively depends on external keys. If this is the case, the activation of all modules is performed instantly, i.e., within the *first cycle*. The security of this approach is not affected, since we assume that the ILC is indistinguishable by design. So an adversary has no advantage in detecting the ILC even if exclusive insertion is used.

3.4   Integration

Once the inter-locking is performed, the resulting locked modules must be reintegrated into the original design. To facilitate this procedure, the toolflow generates a *hub*; a Verilog module defining the correct wiring based on the selected constellation. The input of this module are all external keys as well as all internal key outputs (interlocks) generated by all source modules. The output consists of all final (internal and external) keys for every module. All these connections might be routed through multiple levels of module instantiations, depending on the location of the locked module. Note that this step also includes the integration of RTL modules that have not been modified by the locking procedure.

3.5   Testing and Verification

The result of the integration is a locked design containing RTL and generic technology-independent Verilog netlists. To verify the correctness of the Inter-Lock flow, we resort to equivalence checking and functional unit testing. The equivalence checking is performed using Synopsys Formality, thereby formally comparing the original RTL to the synthesized core with the correct activation key applied. Note that this step is still performed in-house; therefore, the key is known. The equivalence checker proves that the module preprocessing, inter-locking as well as integration have not introduced functional errors to the core; i.e., with the correct key, the design is functionally equivalent to the original. Functional testing can further be performed to check the desired functionality of the core. Hereby, we applied the open-source RISC-V test suite containing a set of assembly and benchmark tests [16]. Once the design is verified, it can proceed with either the ASIC or FPGA flow since the Inter-Lock toolflow provides technology-independent locking.

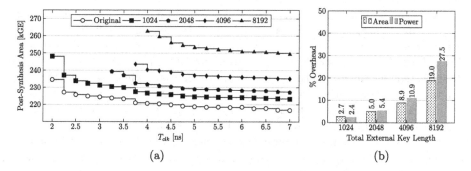

(a)   (b)

Fig. 6. (a) Post-synthesis AT-plot for different total external key lengths and (b) Area and power overhead at $T_{clk} = 4$ ns (250 MHz)

4   Cost Evaluation

4.1   Experimental Setup

The cost evaluation is performed on the Ariane core, including all modules from Table 1. The main objective of this evaluation is to show the cost impact of locking a variety of critical processor modules. Hereby, it becomes difficult to select all necessary Inter-Lock properties (constellation, number of interlocks, key size and others). Therefore, we propose the following setup. We evaluate a set of fixed total external key lengths (1024, 2048, 4096 and 8192). This implies that, e.g., a key of 1024 bits is divided among all selected modules (similar to the example in Fig. 5). For each key length, the constellation is *fixed* to the one shown in Fig. 4. The register insertion is done using exclusive insertion, as discussed in Sect. 3.3. The external key is divided among the modules linearly to the module size (number of gates). As a rule of thumb, we fixed the total number of interlocks generated by a source module to 5% of the amount of its original outputs. In case a source has multiple sink modules, the interlocks are evenly divided among them. Logic synthesis was done with Synopsy DC using the standard-performance cell library for the UMC 90 nm CMOS process operating under typical conditions (1 V, 25 °C). QuestaSim was used for RTL and gate-level simulation. A security analysis of the approach is available in [10].

4.2   Evaluation Results

We performed an Area vs Time (AT) evaluation to compare the influence of various total external key lengths to the original design. The results are presented in the AT-plot in Fig. 6 (a). The area is shown in Gate-Equivalent (GE) and the clock period (T_{clk}) in ns. One GE is the area of one 2-input drive-1 NAND gate. The original design achieves a minimum T_{clk} of 2 ns (500 MHz). As expected, the design area as well as the minimum T_{clk} are increasing with larger keys. The 1024-bit key design is able to achieve $T_{clk} = 2$ ns, resulting in 0% delay overhead. However, the 2048-bit, 4096-bit and 8192-bit key designs achieve $T_{clk} = 3.25$ ns, $T_{clk} = 3.75$ ns and $T_{clk} = 4$ ns respectively. This implies a delay overhead between 62.50% and 100%.

The second evaluation concerns the cost comparison of the locked variants for $T_{clk} = 4$ ns. This clock period is achieved for all key lengths. By fixing the clock period, we can take a closer look at the area and power cost differences, as shown in Fig. 6 (b). The area overhead ranges from 2.7% (1024-bit) to 19% (8192-bit). As expected, the area overhead doubles (approximately) when doubling the key length. The power overhead increases in line with the area (approximated with DC); from 2.4% (1024-bit) to 27.5% (8192-bit). At $T_{clk} = 4$ ns, the original design area is 220.71 kGE, while the total power is 43.37 mW.

The presented results provide us with a closer look at the cost of applying locking schemes to a practical processor design at a larger scale, thereby considering multiple modules, their interdependencies as well as large external keys. Moreover, based on the evaluation, one can choose an appropriate hardware-secured processor design, thereby balancing the area, power and delay overhead against the key length.

5   Related Work

A similar framework-based approach is known as MIRAGE [6]. This framework can be used for design space exploration as well as obfuscation strength analysis. However, the focus of the framework lies within the selection and evaluation of specific logic locking schemes applied to isolated components. In comparison, our approach takes a more abstract view of the locking procedure for multi-module designs, regardless of the specific locking scheme. In that regard, MIRAGE can be used for the dedicated selection of locking schemes for each specific component of the overall design within Inter-Lock. Therefore, in this paper, we do not focus on algorithmic details of prior locking schemes, as our approach is decoupled from any algorithmic specifications. An extensive overview of locking schemes can be found in [15], as well as in the prior work [10].

6   Conclusion

This paper presents the application of Inter-Lock from a practical point of view, thereby addressing an important security challenge; scaling logic locking mechanisms to multi-module designs under the consideration of their complexity and interdependent nature. We presented multiple framework improvements and provided an in-depth overview of the setup and implementation of the underlying toolflow. All framework components were showcased through a practical case study based on a 64-bit RISC-V processor. Furthermore, we evaluated the cost impact of the approach in terms of area, power and delay overhead compared to various key lengths. The insights provided in this paper offer a first look into the procedure and cost of comprehensively locking a modern processor design. In future work, we plan to perform an evaluation on a multi-core environment.

References

1. Azar, K.Z., Kamali, H.M., Homayoun, H., Sasan, A.: Threats on logic locking: a decade later. GLSVLSI **2019**, 471–476 (2019). https://doi.org/10.1145/3299874. 3319495
2. Imeson, F., Emtenan, A., Garg, S., Tripunitara, M.: Securing computer hardware using 3D integrated circuit (IC) technology and split manufacturing for obfuscation. In: 22nd USENIX, pp. 495–510. USENIX, Washington (2013)
3. Jain, A., Zhou, Z., Guin, U.: TAAL: tampering attack on any key-based logic locked circuits. ArXiv abs/1909.07426 (2019)
4. Koushanfar, F.: Provably secure active IC metering techniques for piracy avoidance and digital rights management. IEEE TIFS **7**(1), 51–63 (2012). https://doi.org/ 10.1109/TIFS.2011.2163307
5. Lee, J., Tebranipoor, M., Plusquellic, J.: A low-cost solution for protecting IPs against scan-based side-channel attacks. In: 24th IEEE VTS, pp. 6–99, April 2006. https://doi.org/10.1109/VTS.2006.7
6. Menon, V.V., Kolhe, G., Schmidt, A., Monson, J., French, M., Hu, Y., Beerel, P.A., Nuzzo, P.: System-level framework for logic obfuscation with quantified metrics for evaluation. In: 2019 IEEE SecDev, pp. 89–100, September 2019. https://doi.org/ 10.1109/SecDev.2019.00020
7. Newbould, R.D., Irby, D.L., Carothers, J.D., Rodriguez, J.J., Holman, W.: Watermarking ICs for IP protection. Electron. Lett. **38**(6), 272–274 (2002). https://doi. org/10.1049/el:20020143
8. Rahman, M.T., Tajik, S., Rahman, M.S., Tehranipoor, M., Asadizanjani, N.: The key is left under the mat: on the inappropriate security assumption of logic locking schemes. Cryptology ePrint Archive, Report 2019/719 (2019). https://eprint.iacr. org/2019/719
9. Roy, J.A., Koushanfar, F., Markov, I.L.: EPIC: ending piracy of integrated circuits. In: 2008 DATE, pp. 1069–1074, March 2008. https://doi.org/10.1109/DATE.2008. 4484823
10. Šišejković, D., Merchant, F., Leupers, R., Ascheid, G., Kegreiß, S.: Inter-lock: logic encryption for processor cores beyond module boundaries. In: 2019 IEEE ETS, pp. 1–6, May 2019. https://doi.org/10.1109/ETS.2019.8791528
11. Šišejković, D., Leupers, R., Ascheid, G., Metzner, S.: A unifying logic encryption security metric. In: SAMOS 2018, SAMOS 2018, pp. 179–186. ACM, New York (2018). https://doi.org/10.1145/3229631.3229636
12. Waterman, A., Lee, Y., Patterson, D., Asanovic, K.: The RISC-V instruction set manual. volume I: user-level ISA, version 2.0, Technical report UCB/EECS-2014-54 (2014)

13. Xiao, K., Forte, D., Jin, Y., Karri, R., Bhunia, S., Tehranipoor, M.M.: Hardware trojans: lessons learned after one decade of research. ACM Trans. Design Autom. Electr. Syst. **22**(1), 6:1–6:23 (2016). https://doi.org/10.1145/2906147
14. Yasin, M., Sinanoglu, O.: Transforming between logic locking and IC camouflaging. In: 2015 IDT, pp. 1–4, December 2015. https://doi.org/10.1109/IDT.2015.7396725
15. Yasin, M., Sinanoglu, O.: Evolution of logic locking. In: 2017 IFIP/IEEE VLSI-SoC, pp. 1–6, October 2017. https://doi.org/10.1109/VLSI-SoC.2017.8203496
16. Zaruba, F., Benini, L.: The cost of application-class processing: energy and performance analysis of a Linux-ready 1.7-GHZ 64-bit RISC-V core in 22-NM FDSOI technology. IEEE TVLSI **27**(11), 2629–2640 (2019). https://doi.org/10.1109/TVLSI.2019.2926114

Exploration of Power Domain Partitioning with Concurrent Task Mapping and Scheduling for Application-Specific Multi-core SoCs

Bo Wang[1]($\boxtimes$), Aneek Imtiaz[2], Joachim Falk[1], Michael Glaß[3], and Jürgen Teich[1]

[1] Friedrich-Alexander-Universität Erlangen-Nürnberg (FAU), Erlangen, Germany
bo.wang1102@gmail.com, {joachim.falk,juergen.teich}@fau.de
[2] Technische Universität München, Munich, Germany
aneekimtiaz@gmail.com
[3] Universität Ulm, Ulm, Germany
michael.glass@uni-ulm.de

Abstract. This paper proposes a novel approach to explore the design space of Power Domain (PD) partitioning in the architecture definition phase of heterogeneous SoCs. By formulating an Integer Linear Program (ILP), task mapping and scheduling is determined concurrently while considering power-off dependencies among cores in the same PD and the power-gating break-even time. Compared to state-of-the-art approaches aiming at design phases where task mapping and scheduling has been frozen, our proposed approach shifts joint exploration into earlier design phases, creates more power-gating opportunities for PD partitions, and thus identifies better trade-offs in terms of energy consumption and design costs.

Keywords: Power domain partition · Task mapping and scheduling · Evolutionary algorithm · Integer linear programming

1 Introduction

Power gating is an effective technique to reduce static power consumption of System-on-Chips (SoCs), like 5G New Radio modems in which dozens of heterogeneous cores are often adopted to achieve Gbits/s uplink and downlink speed. An SoC is divided into multiple Power Domains (PDs), which can be switched off individually when all cores and Hardware (HW) IPs in the same PD are idle, a so-called common idle interval. Power-gating control is more flexible when finer-grained power domains are partitioned. However, this would indeed result in a huge design, verification, and layout effort, even increase area and degrade power consumption and timing closure [13]. On the other hand, due to

---

This research work was funded by Intel Deutschland GmbH.

A. Brinkmann et al. (Eds.): ARCS 2020, LNCS 12155, pp. 153–167, 2020.
https://doi.org/10.1007/978-3-030-52794-5_12

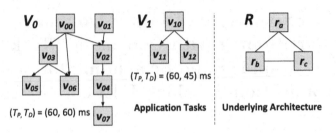

Fig. 1. Task graphs for given applications V_0 and V_1 with the same period T_P but different deadline T_D, as well as underlying heterogeneous architecture R.

parallelism among tasks, merging HW resources which are active simultaneously into the same power domain may reduce design complexity without sacrificing power efficiency.

Some researchers have started investigating methodologies for exploration of PD partitioning to trade off energy consumption and the number of PDs. In [13], PD partitioning is explored by using a Multi-Objective Evolutionary Algorithm (MOEA), but it aims at the design phases in which task mapping and scheduling has been accomplished already, and determines the idle intervals of each HW resource rather than optimizing them. During subsequent PD partitioning, common idle intervals are post-processed for each PD, as well as power-gating break-even times. Power gating is exploited only for common idle intervals longer than a break-even time. After that, energy consumption is evaluated for partition candidates. Finally, trade-off fronts are obtained by the MOEA in terms of energy consumption and the number of used power domains. However, this approach does not explore the influence of task mapping and scheduling. We illustrate the lost potential through a motivating example in the following.

1.1 Motivating Example

Figure 1 shows two periodic applications with the same period generated by TGFF [5], as well as a HW architecture consisting of three fully connected heterogeneous processors. Power consumption of each processor is modeled by three power states [14], i.e., P_{run}, P_{idle}, and P_{off}, where the state RUN denotes the resource actively executing a program task, $IDLE$ denoting being powered on with no task in execution, and OFF denoting the power-gated mode. First, task mapping and scheduling is performed to minimize energy consumption, where only two states – RUN and $IDLE$ – and transition energy between them are assumed for processors. After that, PD partitions are explored using the approach in [13]. The found trade-off fronts are presented in Fig. 2. Take the trade-off front with 2 PDs as an example shown in Fig. 3(a). Although r_b is idle from 0 ms to 23 ms, PD_1 cannot be powered off because r_a is still executing. If the task mapping and scheduling would consider the power-off dependency between r_a and r_b, it may re-allocate the tasks and align the execution in the same PD.

Unfortunately, scheduling before PD partitioning does not have such knowledge and, thus, misses optimization potential.

Based on this observation, we propose a methodology to explore power domain partitioning with concurrent task mapping and scheduling. For each candidate explored during PD partitioning, task mapping and scheduling is performed with additional constraints for the power domain dependency and power-gating break-even time. As a result, more and longer common idle intervals in each PD may be created by properly mapping and aligning task execution on processors, as shown for v_{03} in Fig. 3. Power consumption is thus reduced due to longer power-gated state as shown in Fig. 3(b) and Fig. 2. More important, system architects may even prefer the 2-PD option identified by our approach to reduce design cost if it already meets the power target. The proposed approach actually expands the exploration space of PD partitioning.

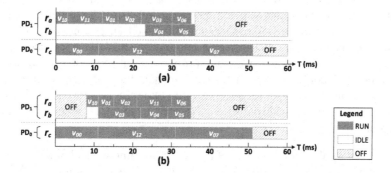

Fig. 2. Power domain partitioning and task mapping & scheduling for the trade-off front with 2 PDs for the motivating example: (a) PD partitioning performed after task mapping and scheduling; (b) PD partitioning with concurrent task mapping and scheduling as proposed in this work.

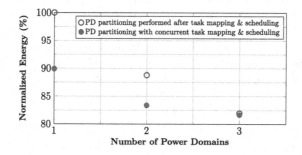

Fig. 3. Trade-off fronts for normalized energy (to energy of 1-PD trade-off front obtained by partitioning PDs after task mapping and scheduling) vs. number of power domains (design complexity).

1.2   Contribution

State-of-the-art approaches for PD partitioning exploration consider power vs. design cost for heterogeneous multi-core SoCs where task mapping and scheduling has been already frozen at design time, e.g., assuming multiple subsystems are re-used and integrated in an SoC. This paper discusses the further optimizations applicable to SoCs when task mapping and scheduling can be combined with PD partitioning and jointly optimized. Our major contributions are summarized as follows:

- Tasks are mapped and scheduled specifically for each PD partition candidate, concurrently with PD partitioning exploration by a Multi-Objective Evolutionary Algorithm (MOEA). This aligns task execution and creates more common idle intervals for power gating.
- Task mapping and scheduling is formulated as an Integer Linear Programming (ILP), in particular integrating: 1) power-on/off dependencies introduced by PD partitioning among HW resources in the same PD; 2) constraints of power-gating break-even time due to transition energy and latency overhead.
- Experimental results show that our proposed joint exploration can identify much better trade-off fronts with significantly reduced design costs but without scarifying the power target. E.g., one experiment shows that the same power target can be achieved by 2 PDs, instead of 8 PDs when applying the approach in [13].

The aimed application domains of this work are time-critical or safety-critical [3] application specific embedded systems, such as wireless communications and electric vehicles [10]. There, most application tasks and use cases are known at design time, and static scheduling is also more favorable due to its determinism.

2   Related Work

Several research works exist on how to partition power domains at circuit level. In [2], Finite State Machine with Datapath (FSMD) circuits are decomposed into loosely coupled domains which may be power or clock gated. But, the workload characteristics are not considered. In [1], an approach leveraging rule-based design is proposed to automatically partition combinational logic into multiple PDs while considering usage characteristics. However, all of these studies [1,2] focus on micro-architecture level and RTL design phases. In [13], PD partitioning is explored at the Electronic System Level (ESL), thus for SoC architecture definition phases, but after task mapping and scheduling has been accomplished. As motivated earlier, this may hinder the maximization of idle intervals to reduce power or to allow to lower the number of power domains. In [7], a relevant task mapping and scheduling problem is discussed to Maximize Common Idle Interval (MCIT) among all cores, though the objective is to reduce active time and power consumption of a shared memory. The ILP formulation of common idle intervals is based on a discrete time axis. In [6], the idle interval of each core is modeled at a continuous time axis. But the approach does not formulate common idle intervals. In both [7] and [6], homogeneous multi-core systems are considered. However, these are different from the power optimization of a heterogeneous architecture. Allocating tasks to more energy efficient cores may lead to lower power than merely pursuing MCIT. Moreover, both works do not investigate PD partitioning problem, but assume each core in an individual power domain.

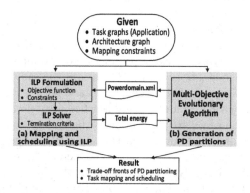

Fig. 4. The proposed design flow for exploration of power domain partitioning with concurrent task mapping and scheduling.

Some other works address voltage-frequency islands partitioning at system level [9,12], to reduce dynamic power. But the problem formulation is different. PD partitioning has to model power-off states, on/off dependencies within power domains, and power-off break-even times. This is difficult to model together with the problem of task mapping and scheduling. And, [12] does not consider task mapping and scheduling while [9] considers scheduling but not mapping.

3 Overview of the Methodology

An overview of our methodology is presented in Fig. 4.

Given

– Periodic applications, each of which can be modeled as a directed acyclic task graph $G(V, E, T_P, T_D)$, in which a task v belongs to the set of tasks V, E denotes data dependencies among tasks, an arbitrary period T_P and deadline T_D.
– An SoC architecture consisting of a set of HW resources denoted as R, power model of any resource $r \in R$ in different power states, e.g., $P_{run,r}$, $P_{off,r}$, $P_{idle,r}$, power-gating transition latency $T_{tr\_off}(r)$ and energy $E_{tr\_off,r}$, as well as wake-up transition latency $T_{tr\_on,r}$ and energy $E_{tr\_on,r}$ from power-off state.

– Mapping constraints that represent which task can be realized on which resource and the execution time of each task $D_{v,r}$ for a given resource.

Objective and Solution

The objective is to explore trade-off fronts in terms of energy consumption and the number of power domains (representing a measure of design complexity) for the problem of power domain partitioning including task mapping and scheduling.

An MOEA in [11] is used to explore the space of PD partitionings. Physical design or floorplan constraints can be added to prune the exploration space, if they can be forecast from previous products. For example, two resources far away in floorplan make less sense to be placed into the same PD.

For each PD partition, an ILP is generated and solved to determine a mapping and schedule for each task and a suitable schedule of power mode transitions for each PD, with the objective to minimize the energy consumption. Power-on/off dependencies of HW resources in the same PD, power-gating transition energy and break-even time are all considered here. The energy consumption value derived by the ILP solver is fed back to the MOEA as one evaluated objective of each PD partition. The state-based power modeling approach as in [14] is chosen because it achieves sufficient accuracy at system level and early design phases. The power models can be refined along the design cycle, e.g., consider different active power $P_{run,r}$ for different types of tasks running on a resource.

This work considers only static scheduling at design time. In principle, it may inspire the solution that considers the impact of run-time task migration. For example, add online scheduling algorithms after the ILP solver, and then evaluate the power consumption of each PD partition. However, it would take significantly longer exploration time, because the simulation is required to evaluate the power consumption. This is not the target application domain of this work.

4 ILP Formulation

The time is assumed to be discrete, divided into unit time intervals $[t, t + 1)$, for $t = 0, 1, \ldots$, which we call *time slots* [7]. We refer to $[t, t + 1)$ as *time slot* t, or even as *time* t. Tasks are assigned to time slots and $D_{v,r}$ is an integer. The continuous-time version of the same problem can be approximated as a discrete-time version.

In this work, multiple independent periodic applications, e.g., $[V_0, \ldots, V_L]$, with arbitrary deadlines and periods, can be considered together in a single ILP. This applies to the architecture which supports multiple applications simultaneously. A hyper-period of all applications, denoted as M, is chosen to map and schedule tasks from all applications within this hyper-period. Moreover, when the deadline of an application is longer than the period, a pipelined schedule is performed, i.e., a task graph is divided into several pipeline stages so the current iteration of the task can overlap in execution with previous iterations [15]. However, our methodology is not limited to any specific pipeline approach, which is also not the focus of this paper. The following formulations are elaborated by using only one application with multiple periods for ease of explanation. But experiments in this work were done for problems containing multiple applications.

Table 1 defines ILP constants which are determined for each PD partitioning candidate by the MOEA. Table 2 explains the introduced ILP binary variables prior to introducing the ILP mapping and scheduling model.

Table 1. Constants in ILP formulation related to power gating and PD partitioning, and determined by the MOEA.

Symbols	Description
pd	A power domain from power domain set PD
$pd(r)$	The power domain containing resource r
$R(pd)$	Set of all resources in power domain pd
$T_{be,pd}$	Break-even time of power domain pd
$T_{tr\_on,pd}$	Off-on transition time of power domain pd
$T_{tr\_off,pd}$	On-off transition time of power domain pd
$E_{tr\_on,pd}$	Off-on transition energy of power domain pd
$E_{tr\_off,pd}$	On-off transition energy of power domain pd

Table 2. Binary variables in ILP formulation related to power gating and PD partitioning.

Symbols	Description
$X_{k,v,r}$	1 iff task v is mapped to resource r in period k
$S_{k,v,t}$	1 iff task v in period k is starting at time t
$B_{r,t}$	1 iff resource r is busy at time t
$C_{pd,t}$	1 iff all resources in power domain pd are mutually idle at time t
$I_{pd,t}$	1 iff all resources in power domain pd are mutually idle from time t to time $t + T_{be,pd} - 1$
$O_{pd,t}$	1 iff power domain pd is in off state at time t
$Z_{pd,t}$	1 iff power domain pd has either on-off or off-on transition at time t

4.1   Objective Function

An application with N periods is to be scheduled on a heterogeneous architecture. The interval of time slots is denoted as $T = [0 \dots M - 1]$, where the hyper-period $M = NT_P$ in case of only one application. The objective function of the ILP is to minimize the total energy consumption according to Eqs. (1)–(8), including energy consumption of each resource in power states $RUN, IDLE$ and OFF, denoted as $E_{run,r}$, $E_{idle,r}$ and $E_{off,r}$, as well as total on-off and off-on transition energies of each power domain, denoted as $E_{tot\_tr,pd}$.

$$\text{minimize:} \sum_{r \in R} \left(E_{run,r} + E_{idle,r} + E_{off,r} \right) + \sum_{pd \in PD} E_{tot\_tr,pd} \tag{1}$$

$$E_{run,r} = \sum_{t \in T} B_{r,t} * P_{run,r}, \quad \forall r \in R \tag{2}$$

$$E_{idle,r} = \left(\sum_{t \in T} \left(1 - B_{r,t}\right) - \sum_{t \in T} O_{pd(r),t} \right) * P_{idle,r}, \quad \forall r \in R \tag{3}$$

$$E_{off,r} = \left(\sum_{t \in T} O_{pd(r),t} - \frac{1}{2} * J_{pd(r)} \right.$$
$$\left. * \left(T_{tr\_off,pd(r)} + T_{tr\_on,pd(r)} \right) \right) * P_{off,r}, \quad \forall r \in R \tag{4}$$

Transition energy of a power domain is calculated by Eqs. (5)–(8). J_{pd} denotes total number of transitions (both on-off and off-on) in power domain pd. The PD transition latency is determined by the resource with the longest latency in this PD. During power-off and power-on transitions, other resources are assumed to be in OFF state and $IDLE$ state after its own transition, respectively. The related energies are modeled as part of the PD transition energy, as calculated by

$$E_{tr\_off,pd} = \sum_{r \in R(pd)} \left(E_{tr\_off,r} + \left(T_{tr\_off,pd} - T_{tr\_off,r} \right) * P_{off,r} \right), \forall pd \in PD \tag{5}$$

$$E_{tr\_on,pd} = \sum_{r \in R(pd)} \left(E_{tr\_on,r} + \left(T_{tr\_on,pd} - T_{tr\_on,r} \right) * P_{idle,r} \right), \forall pd \in PD \tag{6}$$

$$E_{tr,pd} = E_{tr\_off,pd} + E_{tr\_on,pd}, \quad \forall pd \in PD \tag{7}$$

$$E_{tot\_tr,pd} = \frac{1}{2} * J_{pd} * E_{tr,pd}, \quad \forall pd \in PD \tag{8}$$

4.2   Constraints

Here, we focus on explanation of ILP formulation related to power gating and PD partitioning. Other ILP constraints for basic task mapping and scheduling are not elaborated, since they are very well-known and not novel, e.g. task mapping constraints, task dependency constraints, deadline constraints, and so on [8].

Unique Start Time Constraint: Each task must start exactly once, thus in one time slot.

$$\sum_{t \in T} S_{k,v,t} = 1, \quad \forall k \in [1 \dots N], \forall v \in V \tag{9}$$

Resource Busy Time Constraint: The number of busy slots of a resource should be equal to the total execution time of all tasks mapped on it. Moreover, from the start time slot of a task, it should be consecutive 1's assigned to the busy vector of a resource on which the task is mapped.

$$\sum_{t \in T} B_{r,t} = \sum_{k=1}^{N} \sum_{v \in V} X_{k,v,r} * D_{v,r}, \quad \forall r \in R \tag{10}$$

$$\sum_{i=t}^{t+D_{v,r}-1} B_{r,i} \geq D_{v,r} * \left(S_{k,v,t} + X_{k,v,r} - 1\right),$$

$$\forall v \in V, \forall r \in R, \forall k \in [1 \dots N], \forall t \in [0 \dots M - D_{v,r}] \tag{11}$$

Common Idle Time Constraint: A power domain is idle only when all resources in that domain are idle. This can be modeled by performing a logical NOR operation among the busy vectors of all resources in that domain:

$$C_{pd,t} = \neg\left(\vee_{r \in R(pd)} B_{r,t}\right), \quad \forall t \in T, \forall pd \in PD \tag{12}$$

The NOR operation is nonlinear, but the Boolean logic operation can be transformed to linear constraints. Let $N_R(pd)$ denote the number of resources in power domain pd. Equation (12) is transformed as below.

$$\sum_{r \in R(pd)} \left(1 - B_{r,t}\right) - N_R(pd) * C_{pd,t} \geq 0, \quad \forall t \in T, \forall pd \in PD \tag{13}$$

$$\sum_{r \in R(pd)} \left(1 - B_{r,t}\right) - N_R(pd) * C_{pd,t} \leq N_R(pd) - 1, \quad \forall t \in T, \forall pd \in PD \tag{14}$$

Off State Time Constraint: A power domain should be switched off only when its common idle interval is longer than its power-gating break-even time which can be modeled as Eqs. (15)–(17), and rounded to the nearest greater integer.

$$T_{tr,pd} = T_{tr\_off,pd} + T_{tr\_on,pd} \tag{15}$$

$$T_{be\_p,pd} = \frac{E_{tr,pd} - T_{tr,pd} \sum_{r \in R(pd)} P_{off,r}}{\sum_{r \in R(pd)} \left(P_{idle,r} - P_{off,r} \right)} \tag{16}$$

$$T_{be,pd} = \lceil \max \{ T_{tr,pd}, T_{be\_p,pd} \} \rceil \tag{17}$$

To derive off-state slot vectors, an auxiliary variable $I_{pd,t} = 1$ is introduced to represent $T_{be,pd}$ adjacent slots of a pd from slot t to slot $t + T_{be,pd} - 1$ are all idle. This can be done by a logical AND operation:

$$I_{pd,t} = \wedge_{i=t}^{t+T_{be,pd}-1} C_{pd,i}, \ \forall t \in [0 \dots M - T_{be,pd}], \forall pd \in PD \tag{18}$$

And, $T_{be,pd} - 1$ zeros have to be padded at the beginning and the end of vector $I_{pd,t}$ using Eq. (19).

$$I_{pd,t} = 0, \quad \forall pd \in PD, \ \forall t \in \{ [1 - T_{be,pd} \dots - 1],$$
$$[M - T_{be,pd} + 1 \dots M - 1] \} \tag{19}$$

Now, the final off state time slot vector $O_{pd,t}$ can be derived from Eq. (20). The off state slot $O_{pd,t} = 1$ if any of $I_{pd,t} = 1$ from slot $t - T_{be,pd} + 1$ to slot t. It can be performed by a logical OR operation. Equations (18) and (20) are non-linear, but they can be transformed into linear inequalities in a similar way as shown in Eq. (12). The details are not shown here.

$$O_{pd,t} = \vee_{i=t-T_{be,pd}+1}^{t} I_{pd,i}, \quad \forall t \in T, \forall pd \in PD \tag{20}$$

Transition State Time Constraint: On-off and off-on transition states are formulated by taking logical XOR operation of the current and previous one slot in the off state vector, as given in Eqs. (21). Similarly, it can be transformed into linear inequalities as well. The number of power domain transitions, i.e., J_{pd}, includes both off-on and on-off.

$$Z_{pd,t} = O_{pd,t-1} \oplus O_{pd,t}, \quad \forall t \in [1 \dots M - 1], \forall pd \in PD \tag{21}$$

$$J_{pd} = \sum_{t \in [1 \dots M-1]} Z_{pd,t}, \quad \forall pd \in PD \tag{22}$$

5   Experimental Results

The proposed approach has been experimented on different benchmarks. The first set of benchmarks is from a public benchmark suite E3S [4], while the second one consists of synthetic benchmarks generated using the tool TGFF [5]. The main program of the flow was implemented using Python, but the MOEA was implemented using Java [11]. All of programs have been executed on a laptop with an i5-5300U CPU @ 2.3 GHz (2 cores, 4 threads) and 12 GB DDR memory.

For comparison, the same experiments were performed by applying the approach [13] performing PD partitioning after task mapping and scheduling. We called it as the reference approach in the following. Here, various task mapping and scheduling algorithms can be applied before PD partitioning with desired optimization objectives, like execution time or power. They lead to different energy consumption after PD partitioning and power gating. Since our work focuses on energy optimization, as a fair comparison, we performed an energy-aware task mapping and scheduling also using the approach of ILP. But in this ILP formulation, processors are assumed to be only in RUN or $IDLE$ states without OFF states. PD partitioning and power-gating related constraints are not applied during this step. Therefore, in the objective function, $E_{off,r}$ and $E_{tot\_tr,pd}$ in Eq. (1) become zero, and $\sum_{t \in T} O_{pd(r),t}$ in Eq. (3) are zero too.

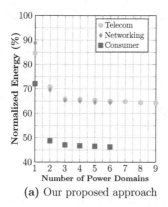

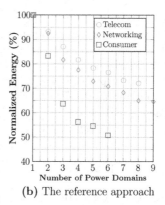

(a) Our proposed approach   (b) The reference approach

Fig. 5. Trade-off fronts for E3S benchmarks with normalized energy (to energy of 1-PD partition obtained by the reference approach [13], i.e., PD partitioning performed after mapping and scheduling) vs. hardware complexity (number of power domains).

5.1   Benchmark Applications from E3S

Three benchmarks are selected from E3S [4], i.e., Networking, Telecom and Consumer. They are scheduled onto a heterogeneous architecture consisting of a 2-D 3×3 mesh of processors whose power consumption is also specified in E3S. The transition latency in Table 1 varied in the range of 10–50 us, and the task execution times ranged in the interval of 0.5–1 ms. The transition energies $E_{tr\_off,r}$ and $E_{tr\_on,r}$ in Eqs. (5)–(6) were assumed zero in the following. Therefore, the power-gating break-even time $T_{be,pd}$ was determined by the transition latency $T_{tr,pd}$ according to Eqs. (16)–(17).

The MOEA has been configured to use 20 generations with 10 individuals per generation. For each number of power domains, the solutions with the lowest normalized energy according to Eqs. (1)–(8) are shown in Fig. 5.

It can be noticed that for each number of power domains, the trade-off point using our approach has a lower energy. This is because our concurrent mapping and scheduling of tasks with PD partitioning is able to create more common idle intervals specific for each PD partition to allow more power-off opportunities. Therefore, better power savings can be achieved even with fewer power domains. For example, in the benchmark of Telecom, a lower power consumption can be achieved even with 2-PD partition, in comparison to a trade-off point for an 8-PD partition in the reference approach [13]. Much better PD partitioning trade-off points can be identified to meet the power target at significantly reduced design cost.

The exploration took 8–9 h in which we set the timelimit of the ILP solver to 3 min. Notably, this is longer than the approach [13] which took about 1–2 h This is expected, because our approach has to perform task mapping and scheduling in addition. Still, limiting the ILP solver to 3 min has two impacts: 1) the currently best found solution by the ILP may not be the optimal one in terms of energy consumption, but has a relative optimality gap of 10–20%, reported by the solver; 2) the ILP solver even may not find any feasible solution as the problem size increases, though it never happened in our benchmarks. Nevertheless, our approach was always able to find lower energy consumption points for each number of PD partitions. If more exploration time is acceptable, our approach would be able to probably find even better results. This is a trade-off that system architects can decide during system-level exploration.

Table 3. Three use cases generated by TGFF.

Use case	Application	Period	Deadline	Hyper-period	Iterations
1	V_0	9 ms	9 ms	18 ms	2
	V_1	18 ms	18 ms		1
2	V_0	7.5 ms	6 ms	15 ms	2
	V_1	15 ms	12 ms		1
	V_2	7.5 ms	6 ms		2
3	V_0	5 ms	10 ms	10 ms	2
	V_1	10 ms	15 ms		1
	V_2	10 ms	12 ms		1

5.2   Benchmarks Generated by TGFF

Three benchmarks have been generated by TGFF [5], with different tightness of deadline, i.e., the deadline is equal to, shorter, or longer than the period, as shown in Table 3. Each use case has multiple applications to be scheduled over their hyper-period. When the deadline is longer than the period, e.g., in use case 3, or a multimedia streaming application, different iterations of applications can overlap. Therefore, we partitioned the task set and performed scheduling for steady state in one hyper-period [15]. All three use cases have size in the range of 40–50 tasks whereas the heterogeneous architecture consists of a 2D mesh with 3 × 3 processors. The power data, transition time, and energy for these processors were obtained from an in-house design. The EA parameters for the exploration are the same as for the E3S benchmarks. As shown in Fig. 6, our proposed approach also identifies better trade-off fronts than the reference approach [13].

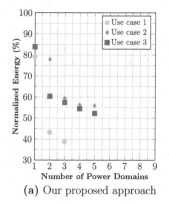
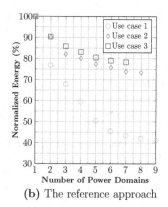

(a) Our proposed approach   (b) The reference approach

Fig. 6. Trade-off fronts for TGFF benchmarks with normalized energy (to energy of 1-PD partition obtained by the reference approach [13], i.e., PD partitioning performed after mapping and scheduling) vs. hardware complexity (number of power domains).

5.3   Scalability Analysis

The total exploration time depends on two parts: 1) EA parameters, mainly the number of generations and individuals per generation (PD partition options), which typically increases with the higher complexity of the hardware architecture; 2) execution time of ILP solver for each PD partition option, which scales non-linearly with the size of hardware architecture, the size of task graph, and most importantly, with the time scale of the schedule. Therefore, our approach is not easily scalable for bigger problems. We experimented the execution time of the ILP solver, given an architecture of a mesh network with 6 processors. When increasing the number of tasks to 80 and set the relative optimality gap of the ILP solver to 20%, a feasible schedule cannot be found within 2 h though it is preferred in the range of minutes as a part of whole flow. Alternative models for scheduling might be the key to reduce the number of binary variables and thus search space of the ILP formulation to improve scalability.

Although our performed experiments were solvable for real-world benchmarks in still an acceptable amount of time, we envision to investigate scalability in future work.

6 Conclusion

In this paper, an exploration approach is proposed to systematically explore PD partitioning for heterogeneous multi-core SoCs, jointly with task mapping and scheduling. An ILP-based task mapping and scheduling is performed for each PD partition candidates while partitioning PDs by a Multi-Objective Evolutionary Algorithm. The ILP formulation considers the constraints of power-off dependencies among hardware resources belonging to the same PD and the power-gating break-even time. For a given PD partition, it creates more and longer common idle intervals of PDs which can be switched off more often to save power. Compared to state-of-the-art approaches performed after task mapping and scheduling frozen, our approach offers significantly larger optimization opportunities for system architects. It has been shown that better trade-off fronts in terms of energy consumption and number of PDs and thus hardware costs may be found by shifting exploration to earlier design phases.

Acknowledgments. This research work was funded by Intel Deutschland GmbH, and finished before Bo Wang and Aneek Imtiaz left Intel. We would like to acknowledge Dr. Yang Xu and Dr. Ralph Hasholzner at Intel, and also Dr. Thomas Wild and Prof. Andreas Herkersdorf at Technische Universität München, for valuable discussions.

References

1. Agarwal, A., Arvind, A.: Leveraging rule-based designs for automatic power domain partitioning. In: ICCAD, November 2013
2. Agarwal, N., et al.: FSMD partitioning for low power using simulated annealing. In: ISCAS, May 2008
3. Baruah, S., Fohler, G.: Certification-cognizant time-triggered scheduling of mixed-criticality systems. In: RTSS, November 2011
4. Dick, R.: Embedded system synthesis benchmarks suites (E3S) (2017). http://ziyang.eecs.umich.edu/~dickrp/e3s/
5. Dick, R., Rhodes, D., Wolf, W.: TGFF: task graphs for free. In: CODES/CASHE, March 1998
6. Esmaili, A., Nazemi, M., Pedram, M.: Modeling processor idle times in MPSoC platforms to enable integrated DPM, DVFS, and task scheduling subject to a hard deadline. In: ASPDAC, January 2019
7. Fu, C., Zhao, Y., Li, M., Xue, C.J.: Maximizing common idle time on multicore processors with shared memory. In: IEEE Transactions on Very Large Scale Integration (VLSI) Systems (2017)

8. Glaß, M., Teich, J., Lukasiewycz, M., Reimann, F.: Hybrid optimization techniques for system-level design space exploration. In: Ha, S., Teich, J. (eds.) Handbook of Hardware/Software Codesign. Springer, Dordrecht (2017). https://doi.org/10.1007/978-94-017-7267-9_8

9. Liu, Y., Yang, Y., Hu, J.: Clustering-based simultaneous task and voltage scheduling for NoC systems. In: ICCAD, November 2010

10. Lukasiewycz, M., et al.: Cyber-physical systems design for electric vehicles. In: DSD, September 2012

11. Lukasiewycz, M., Glaß, M., Reimann, F., Teich, J.: Opt4J-a modular framework for meta-heuristic optimization. In: GECCO, July 2011

12. Ogras, U.Y., Marculescu, R., Choudhary, P., Marculescu, D.: Voltage-frequency island partitioning for GALS-based networks-on-chip. In: DAC, June 2007

13. Wang, B., et al.: Exploration of power domain partitioning for application-specific SoCs in system-level design. In: GI/ITG/GMM Workshop Methoden und Beschreibungssprachen zur Modellierung und Verifikation von Schaltungen und Systemen, MBMV, March 2016

14. Xu, Y., et al.: A very fast and quasi-accurate power-state-based system-level power modeling methodology. In: Herkersdorf, A., Römer, K., Brinkschulte, U. (eds.) ARCS 2012. LNCS, vol. 7179, pp. 37–49. Springer, Heidelberg (2012). https://doi.org/10.1007/978-3-642-28293-5_4

15. Yang, H., Ha, S.: Pipelined data parallel task mapping/scheduling technique for MPSoC. In: DATE, April 2009

FORMUS^{3}IC Workshop

Scalable, Decentralized Battery Management System Based on Self-organizing Nodes

Andrea Reindl$^{(\boxtimes)}$ ⓘ, Hans Meier$^{(\boxtimes)}$ ⓘ, and Michael Niemetz$^{(\boxtimes)}$ ⓘ

Faculty of Electrical Engineering and Information Technology, Ostbayerische
Technische Hochschule Regensburg, Regensburg, Germany
`andrea.reindl@st.oth-regensburg.de`,
{`hans.meier,michael.niemetz`}`@oth-regensburg.de`
`https://www.oth-regensburg.de`

Abstract. Due to the transition to renewable energy sources and the increasing share of electric vehicles and smart grids, batteries are gaining in importance. Battery management systems (BMSs) are required for optimal, reliable operation. In this paper, existing BMS topologies are presented and evaluated in terms of reliability, scalability and flexibility. The decentralisation of BMSs and associated advantages are shown. A scalable, reconfigurable BMS based on a distributed architecture of self-organized, locally controlled nodes is proposed. For distributed system control, producers, batteries and consumers each are equipped with a local microcontroller based control unit, which monitors and controls the local parameters with its own computing and communication resources. Features, advantages and challenges to overcome of the proposed approach are described.

Keywords: Renewable energy sources · Battery management systems · Multi-microcomputer system · Topology · Scalability · Reconfigurable architectures · Availability · Decentralized control · Fault tolerant control · Controller Area Network · Distributed management

1 Introduction

With an increasing share of renewable energy sources and electric vehicles, batteries are one of the most utilized energy storage media [1]. Battery use is essential for maintaining the energy balance and for improving the quality as well as the reliability of power supply in renewable energy systems [2]. A critical challenge facing the widespread adoption of battery technology is to ensure uninterrupted, fail-safe power supply and safe, optimal battery operation to extend battery life. Battery Management Systems (BMSs) are used for these purposes and provide the interfaces between energy producers, consumers and batteries (Fig. 1). They administer system control and management with regard to

ⓒ Springer Nature Switzerland AG 2020
A. Brinkmann et al. (Eds.): ARCS 2020, LNCS 12155, pp. 171–184, 2020.
https://doi.org/10.1007/978-3-030-52794-5_13

energy storage and transmission. Main functions of the BMS include charge and discharge control, balancing, input/output current and voltage monitoring, temperature control, battery protection, fault diagnosis and evaluation [3].

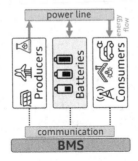

Fig. 1. Principle architecture of a BMS indicating participants, communication and power flow

For this purpose, the following functional requirements are relevant for a BMS:

– Current, voltage and temperature measurement
– State of charge (SOC) and state of health (SOH) determination
– Communication
– Robustness against electromagnetic interference (EMI)
– Redundancy of the system in terms of functional safety
– Electrical isolation of the functional systems
– Balancing [4,5]

Besides the BMS unit, which includes data acquisition, status monitoring and control, the topology of the BMS is crucial for large-scale battery management. The topology covers the electrical connection of the individual batteries or battery cells, the control structure and the communication architecture. It directly influences costs, ease of installation, maintenance, measurement accuracy and above all the reliability of the system.

This paper first describes existing BMS topologies together with relevant literature and outlines their benefits and limitations. The proposed classification divides the BMS topologies into

– centralized,
– modularized,
– distributed and
– decentralized.

The identified trend towards the decentralization of BMSs is shown: Centralized BMSs with a single control unit [6–8] are increasingly replaced by a decentralized management, whereby sensor, control and computing resources are distributed [9–13]. The characteristics of the control strategies are therefore analysed and compared.

An approach for a fully decentralized, distributed BMS based on autonomous, locally operating units is proposed. The characteristics and advantages of the proposed approach are described. The requirements, particularly in terms of system control and management, are analysed and challenges to be overcome are identified. The aim is to provide a holistic overview of the features of the proposed BMS and the resulting system requirements.

2   Battery Management System Topologies

2.1   Centralized

In centralized BMSs, the entire functionality is integrated into a single module, which is connected to the batteries or battery cells via several wires (see Fig. 2) [14]. The centralized BMS provides single cell voltage, string current and temperature measurement.

A centralized BMS is described in [15] based on a single chip. The protective function is divided into two stages. The first stage monitors voltage, current, temperature and coordinates the balancing function. Another approach for a centralized BMS is provided in [16]. Advantages of centralized BMS include cost-effectiveness as well as maintenance and repair. If only a single integrated circuit is used, costs are reduced and errors are easily detected. Another advantage is the accuracy, as centralized BMS use the same offsets for all cells. The clearly defined coordination structure provides effective system control.

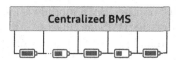

Fig. 2. Reduced block diagram of a BMS based on centralized topology

Disadvantages include the large number of long cable connections, which considerably increase the risk of short circuits. Furthermore, inputs can easily be mixed up and incorrectly connected and connections can become loose, which increases the susceptibility to errors.

Another disadvantage is the lack of scalability and flexibility of the system architecture. In central master-slave BMSs, the maximum number of batteries is strictly predefined. During system development, the number of actively used batteries is fixed and can usually only be changed afterwards by changing the wiring. Adding additional cells is not possible at all if all input connectors are used or vice versa, some inputs might remain unused. In addition, only predefined, mostly single battery technologies are supported and combinations thereof are not feasible.

Furthermore, the master controller is a single point of failure. The entire system control depends on the error-free function of the master controller. In case of failure or malfunction of the master controller, the entire system operation is endangered. This is a significant disadvantage, especially with regard to a reliable, uninterruptible power supply.

2.2   Modularized

Modularized BMSs are characterized by several identical modules, which are connected to the individual batteries or battery cells via cables, similar to centralized BMS (Fig. 3). The BMS modules provide data acquisition (single cell voltage, current, temperature) and communication interfaces to the other BMS modules. Often one of the modules is assigned to the role of master or a separate module serves as master. The master module controls the entire battery pack and communicates with the rest of the system, while the other modules merely record the measured data and transmit it to the master.

A modularized BMS with the aim of improving the performance of BMS to provide a safe, reliable and cost-efficient solution for smart grids and electric vehicles is proposed in [3]. The modularized BMS for electric vehicles presented in [17] focuses on effective single cell monitoring and balancing for a large number of battery cells with comparatively small size and complexity. An advantage of modularized BMSs is the improved manageability. The modules are placed close to the batteries, which avoids long cables. To improve functional safety, the function of the BMS can be easily replicated on the individual modules. The scalability is also increased compared to centralized BMSs. If the battery pack is extended by further cells, another BMS module is simply appended.

The number of inputs of the BMS modules is still fixed and under certain circumstances, inputs may remain unused. In addition, the costs of modularized BMSs are higher. Compared to centralized BMS, the failure of one BMS module does not endanger the entire battery operation. Defective battery cells or batteries are simply removed from the system, reducing capacity but maintaining operation.

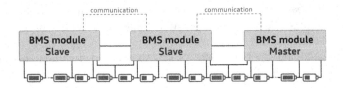

Fig. 3. Block diagram of a BMS based on a modular topology

2.3   Distributed

In distributed BMSs, each cell string or cell is equipped with its own BMS module. The Cell BMS modules provide measurement of operating parameters, balancing and communication. The BMS controller handles the calculation and communication (Fig. 4).

A distributed BMS divided into a master and several battery modules for real-time monitoring and reporting of battery operating conditions is proposed in [18]. This approach combines central control management and distributed data collection. In order to reduce costs and time-to-market and to increase flexibility, scalability and adaptability, a distributed BMS with smart battery cell monitoring is presented in [19]. The smart battery cell monitoring consists of electronics for monitoring and a data transmission interface for bidirectional communication with the superordinate BMS. The BMS functions as the master and controls energy storage at system level.

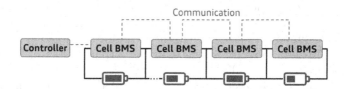

Fig. 4. Block diagram of a BMS based on a distributed topology

The distributed BMS simultaneously offers a high level of reliability and robustness as well as a cost-efficient development process, allowing a significant reduction in the cost of the final battery pack. The advantages of distributed BMSs compared to centralized and modularized topologies are scalability and flexibility. No maximum number of inputs is defined and cells can be added or removed even after installation. This allows easy hardware integration for homogeneous modules. Scaling the battery pack to the size required for different applications does not require any changes to the hardware or software of the modules–only additional battery cell modules have to be assembled or removed. Furthermore, the single point of failure of centralized approaches is avoided. Local control of each cell additionally increases safety. Sensor information only needs to be processed for the local cell and mandatory actions can be triggered immediately. A further advantage is the high measurement accuracy, which is achieved by the specialization of the battery cell module. Furthermore, shorter connecting wires enable more accurate voltage measurement and better interference immunity. Maintenance or replacement of defective parts is facilitated by the modular, distributed architecture.

Disadvantageous are the increased costs for the BMS, as a separate BMS module is required for each cell and for most applications also an additional master module.

2.4 Decentralized

The decentralization of BMSs is a possible solution to overcome the disadvantages of central control structures. Decentralized BMSs consist of several equal units, which provide the entire functionality locally and autonomously. Each of the individual BMS units is able to operate independently of the remaining ones. Communication lines between the units enable information exchange and task coordination between the units. They are used in several decentralized BMS (Fig. 5). While this architecture offers advantages like scalability, minimal integration effort and increased functional safety, the development requires new methods. Decentralized BMSs are further subdivided into communication-less, wireless and wired communication based topologies. A decentralized BMS without communication requirements is proposed in [20]. The smart cells work locally and autonomously, which increases safety and reliability.

A decentralized BMS based on the droop control for a series connection of battery cells is presented in [21]. Droop control is applied to ensure power sharing among connected components. Droop characteristics are used for the power distribution, which correspond to V-I characteristics in voltage droop control. They determine the required output/input current according to the actual voltage deviation. Physically the droop control behaves like an output resistance. Therefore the droop characteristic is also called virtual resistance. [22,23] Droop control offers high reliability due to the decentralized architecture and the communication-less control. A drawback of the droop-based control is the imprecise control [24]. With the consideration of line resistance in a droop-controlled system, the output voltage of each converter cannot be exactly the same. Therefore, the output current sharing accuracy is affected. In addition, the voltage deviation increases with the load due to the droop characteristic [25].

Due to the possibility of cable breaks in wired communication systems like CAN or I^{2}C, BMS approaches based on wireless communication are developed [26]. As a possible solution, [26] proposes a distributed and decentralized wireless BMS based on an Internet of Things (IoT) network.

In [27], a fully decentralized BMS is proposed, whereby the entire BMS functionality is integrated into the cell management units. One cell management unit per cell is used, providing local sensing and management capabilities autonomously and system-level functionality by coordination via communication. A CAN bus is used for wired communication, which enables broadcast communication between the cells. The major advantage of decentralized BMSs is the absence of a central control unit, on which error-free function the entire operation depends. Furthermore, the scalability and flexibility are advantageous. The number of inputs is not fixed and can be extended/reduced even after installation.

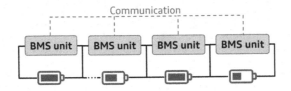

Fig. 5. Block diagram of a decentralized BMS

A challenging feature is the distributed system control based on the equal, parallel-operating and autonomous nodes. In addition, it has to be ensured that the single point of failure is not only shifted but eliminated. For a reliable system, a holistic approach is required.

2.5 Overview and Evaluation of the Battery Management System Topologies

The decentralization of the BMS topology results in functionality distributed to several individual units. The functional units are closer to the battery/battery cell and more elaborately equipped to work independently. Operation is becoming increasingly independent of a central coordination unit and the failure of individual functional units has a minor impact on the system function. As a result, the reliability of the system is improved. The scalability increases with rising decentralisation. The number of batteries/battery cells is not limited by pre-defined inputs but is variable even after the initial layout. Individual batteries/battery cells can be added or removed. A variable number of batteries results in enhanced flexibility. The BMS is adaptable to the requirements of a wide range of applications.

Table 1 summarizes the evaluation of existing BMS topologies in terms of reliability, scalability and flexibility. Compliance with the criteria is evaluated, where ++ means full compliance, + partial compliance, 0 neutral, − partially not satisfied, and − − not satisfied at all.

Table 1. Evaluation of existing BMS topologies in terms of reliability, scalability and flexibility

BMS topology	Reliability	Scalability	Flexibility
Centralized	− −	− −	− −
Modularized	0	−	−
Distributed	+	+	+
Decentralized	++	++	++

3 Decentralized Battery Management System Based on Self-Organizing Nodes

The proposed system is fully decentralized and consists, in contrary to the proposed approaches, of three types of modules: renewable energy producers, batteries and consumers. All components are connected together with a common power line and at least one global communication bus (Fig. 6).

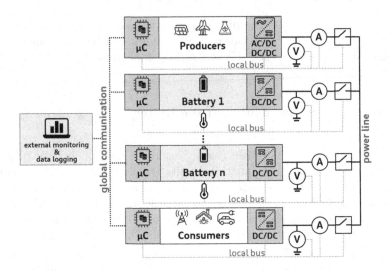

Fig. 6. Block diagram of the decentralized BMS

3.1   Distributed Control

For distributed, autonomous control, each battery, producer and consumer is equipped with its own local control unit (LCU). The LCU includes:

- Current, voltage and temperature measurement to record actual operating parameters,
- a communication interface for data exchange between the components.
- a microcontroller for calculation, data management and evaluation,
- a DC/DC converter with target current and target voltage values which are adjustable during operation, and
- a relay which is opened in case of failures to avoid safety critical voltage levels or for maintenance purposes.

Producers and consumers use the LCU to provide their operating parameters for load/generation forecasts and for voltage control. Batteries provide the ability to absorb excess power or deliver missing power and thus are able to control the system. Therefore, additional algorithms for system control and leader election are implemented on the LCUs of the batteries.

The implemented software for system control manages both the actual operating data such as current, voltage and temperature and the system states resulting from previous measurements. The SOC and the SOH are determined. In addition, the battery fitness (BF) is defined. The BF is a numerical value based primarily on SOC, SOH, number of charge cycles, time of last charge/discharge, the system-wide normalized capacity and the actual operating parameters. Taking into account the optimum operating range of the respective battery technology, the battery condition is evaluated. The criteria, e.g. SOC or temperature, are weighted. The criteria weighting can be adjusted depending on the battery technology and the system status. The adjustment of the weighting provides the basis for system optimization according to various criteria such as cost minimization, maximum safety or availability. The BF enables a system-wide definite evaluation of different battery technologies. In turn, this enables the combination of different battery technologies in a single system. The combination of different battery technologies offers advantages including optimization of the system control, extending battery life and increasing system reliability [28]. Additionally, it offers a second life application to a wide range of batteries [29,30].

The BF is also a decision criterion for the leader election. The participating nodes work autonomously and locally and control the system in a collaborative manner. Highly parallel computer systems exist for solving complicated mathematical problems. In contrast, the challenging task in the context of the proposed approach is to structure, intelligently equip and network the nodes to such an extent that the overall system and its control interact harmoniously. The LCUs are interacting in the physical domain in their control task while communication latency for negotiations is high compared to the control requirements. In addition, in reality the nodes do not work perfectly synchronized but asynchronously [31]. Therefore, the development of a system control consisting of decentralized, autonomous, distributed, asynchronous nodes is a non-trivial, challenging task. The target of the decentralized control structure is to make the system independent of the error-free function of a component. This can be achieved if the role of the central control unit is not permanently assigned to a single component.

Therefore, instead of the decentralized system control being distributed to all nodes, the approach of the system control coordinated by a temporary master which gets reassigned on a regular basis was chosen. One LCU of the batteries is chosen as the temporary central control unit applying a leader election algorithm. The temporary central control unit determines the required charge/discharge power of the remaining battery nodes, taking into account their BF. In case of failure, malfunction or changes in control capability, one of the battery nodes is selected as the new central control unit. As a result, the single point of failure of existing centralised approaches is avoided.

3.2 Communication

Communication between the peer nodes is the key to the autonomous, local control of the decentralized BMS. For autonomous decision making and system control, the nodes communicate their operating parameters and work on a system-wide consistent database. A suitable communication methodology is required to enable fast and energy-efficient communication between the nodes. Furthermore, a robust communication architecture is required to withstand the harsh environments of e.g. automotive applications. In addition, establishing a secure communication protocol between the individual nodes is essential for the safe operation of the BMS. Therefore a well-proven, robust, noise-free, fast and reliable communication technology is required. To achieve a minimum of integration effort, an architecture with minimal wiring harness is required for the distributed topology.

A bus-based communication architecture achieves higher bandwidth and enables broadcast communication between the nodes, which is advantageous for the leader election and system control. Controller Area Network (CAN) is a robust bus-based broadcast communication technology. It is particularly suitable for applications with a small amount of information to be exchanged. Furthermore, CAN is a message-based network and each node is equipped with a filtering mechanism that filters messages based on their identifiers. Thus, only messages relevant to the node are considered. Due to its characteristics CAN is chosen as communication technology for the decentralized BMS. For first implementations a communication based on a single CAN bus is used. For future developments dual CAN, CAN in combination with optical data transmission via polymer optical fiber (POF) and CAN combined with Ethernet are conceivable approaches providing diverse redundancy to increase system reliability and availability.

3.3   Suitability for Active Balancing

The decentralized BMS is able to support active balancing. On the one hand, weaker batteries are protected by taking the BF and thus also the SOC into account when setting the target value for individual energy delivery. In addition, batteries with higher SOC are set to higher target currents during discharge while those with lower SOC absorb higher charging currents. On the other hand, the controllable relays allow individual batteries to be disconnected from the power line. An additional power line between the batteries could additionally enable effective, active balancing by connecting the batteries to be balanced (Fig. 7). This architecture enables one-to-one, one-to-many and manyto-many balancing at a voltage level controlled by the DC/DC converter [32]. Taking into account the BF, the system–wide standardised nominal capacity and the SOC, the more powerful batteries supply the weaker ones.

3.4   Scalability and Integration

The number of inputs and thus of participants is not fixed in the proposed decentralized BMS. A minimum of two batteries is recommended for a reliable supply. Adding and removing nodes is possible after installation and during operation. Both hardware and software are designed for effective integration [33]. The variable number of participants, which can be adjusted and changed during operation, allows the system to be adapted to requirements changing over its lifetime. Optimizations in terms of e.g. cost efficiency, safety or maximum service life can be implemented or changed. The reconfigurable architecture increases reliability, performance and flexibility of the proposed BMS [34].

3.5   Flexibility

The variable number of participants and the possibility to use and combine different battery technologies increases the flexibility of the system. Existing

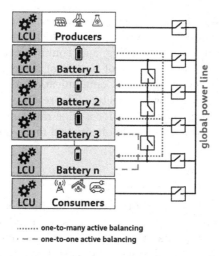

········ one-to-many active balancing
· ─ ─ one-to-one active balancing

Fig. 7. Additional lines and individually controllable relays enable one-to-one, one-to-many and many-to-many active balancing

approaches tend to specialize in a single battery technology [35,36]. In order to improve the performance and energy density, new battery technologies are constantly being developed [37–39]. The BMS is flexible and effective in adapting to changing conditions for optimal and safe battery operation. The software is effectively expandable and software updates during operation support the effective integration and potentially necessary software adjustments supporting new battery technologies [40].

3.6 Fields of Application

The flexible, scalable, reconfigurable architecture opens up various fields of application including uninterruptible power supply, electric vehicles, (islanded) dc microgrids, grid support for peak load shaving or load management. The applications result in different requirements for the BMS. For electric vehicles, for instance, high availability, safety and energy density with minimum size and weight are required. For islanded micro grids, the relevant criteria include effective service lifetime, cost efficiency, reliability and resistance to environmental effects. In addition, various battery technologies and combinations thereof are supported. The combination of different battery technologies improves the system control as well as the battery life of various applications [41]. Furthermore, second life and second use applications are possible for a large number of batteries [30].

4   Conclusion

In this paper, existing BMS topologies were presented and discussed in terms of scalability, flexibility and reliability (cf. Table 1). A decentralized, distributed

BMS based on self-organized and locally operating nodes was proposed. The system control is distributed among the LCUs, which record operating parameters and provide their own computing and communication capacities. Possible approaches for the coordination of a control system based on a many-microcomputer system were suggested. Communication requirements were analysed and suitable technologies were selected. The resulting flexible architecture allows optimized system configurations for a wide range of applications, adaptability to newly developed battery technologies and multi-criteria optimizations.

5   Outlook

Future developments will further optimize the reliability and fault tolerance of the system. Several communication technologies are combined to achieve various redundancies. As a fallback strategy in case of communication failure, the implementation of a droop-based control is planed. It is avoided to move only the single point of failure. The goal is to avoid a single point of failure holistically on the system. Additionally a strategy for active charge balancing during operation under consideration of the BF, which does not require additional hardware, will be developed.

Acknowledgement. The authors thank N. Balbierer and M. Farmbauer for helpful discussions and T. Singer for developing a test environment to validate DC/DC converters.

References

1. Coppez, G., Chowdhury, S., Chowdhury, S.P.: The importance of energy storage in renewable power generation: a review. In: IEEE 45th International Universities Power Engineering Conference, pp. 1–5 (2010)
2. Coppez, G., Chowdhury, S., Chowdhury, S.P.: Review of battery storage optimization in distributed generation. In: Proceedings of IEEE Joint International Conference on Power Electronics, Drives and Energy Systems, pp. 1–6 (2010)
3. Eichi, H.R., et al.: Battery management system: an overview of its application in the smart grid and electric vehicles. IEEE Ind. Electron. Mag. **7**(2), 4–15 (2013)
4. Lelie, M., et al.: Battery management system hardware concepts: an overview. Elsevier Appl. Sci. **8**, 534 (2018)
5. Xiong, R.: Battery Management Algorithm for Electric Vehicles. Springer, Singapore (2020). https://doi.org/10.1007/978-981-15-0248-4
6. Bonfiglio, C., Roessler, W.: A cost optimized battery management system with active cell balancing for lithium ion battery stacks. In: IEEE Vehicle Power and Propulsion Conference, pp. 304–309 (2009)
7. Zhang, A., et al.: Research of battery management system for integrated power supply. In: IEEE Chinese Automation Congress (CAC), pp. 3178–3181 (2017)
8. Bowkett, M., et al.: Design and implementation of an optimal battery management system for hybrid electric vehicles. In: IEEE 19th International Conference on Automation and Computing, pp. 1–5 (2013)

9. Stuart, T.A., Zhu, W.: Modularized battery management for large lithium ion cells. Elsevier J. Power Sources **196**, 458–464 (2009)
10. Pavić, I., et al.: Decentralized master-slave communication and control architecture of a battery swapping station. In: IEEE International Conference on Environment and Electrical Engineering and IEEE Industrial and Commercial Power Systems Europe (EEEIC/I&CPS Europe), pp. 1–6 (2018)
11. Čermák, K., Bartl, M.: Decentralized battery management system. In: 15th International Scientific Conference on Electric Power Engineering (EPE), pp. 599–603 (2014)
12. Karavas, C.-S., et al.: A multi-agent decentralized energy management system based on distributed intelligence for the design and control of autonomous polygeneration microgrids. Elsevier Energy Convers. Manage. **103**, 166–179 (2015)
13. Mahmood, H., Michaelson, D., Jiang, J.: Decentralized power management of a PV/battery hybrid unit in a droop-controlled islanded microgrid. IEEE Trans. Power Electron. **30**, 7215–7229 (2015)
14. Andrea, D.: Battery Management Systems for Large Lithium-Ion Battery Packs, pp. 44–49. Artech House, Boston (2010)
15. Xiao-feng, W., Jian-ping, W., Hai-lin, H.: The smart Battery management system. In: IEEE International Conference on Test, pp. 29–32 (2009)
16. Texas Instruments. Multicell 36-V to 48-V Battery Management System Reference Design, Datasheet (2017). http://www.ti.com/lit/ug/tiducn1/tiducn1.pdf. Accessed 11 Mar 2020
17. Kim, C.H., Kim, M.Y., Moon, G.W.: A modularized charge equalizer using a battery monitoring IC for series-connected Li-Ion battery strings in electric vehicles. IEEE Trans. Power Electron. **28**, 3779–3787 (2013)
18. Linlin, L., et al.: Research on dynamic equalization for lithium battery management system. In: IEEE 29th Chinese Control And Decision Conference (CCDC), pp. 6884–6888 (2017)
19. Lorentz, V., et al.: Smart battery cell monitoring with contactless data transmission. In: Meyer, G. (ed.) Advanced Microsystems for Automotive Applications 2012, pp. 15–26. Springer, Heidelberg (2012). https://doi.org/10.1007/978-3-642-29673-4_2
20. Frost, D.F., Howey, D.A.: Completely decentralized active balancing battery management system. IEEE Trans. Power Electron. **33**, 729–738 (2018)
21. Chowdhury, S.M., et al.: A novel battery management system using a duality of the adaptive droop control theory. In: IEEE Energy Conversion Congress and Exposition, pp. 5164–5169 (2017)
22. Yaoqin, J., Dingkun, L., Shengkui, P.: Improved droop control of parallel inverter system in standalone microgrid. In: 8th International Conference on Power Electronics - ECCE Asia, Jeju, pp. 1506–1513 (2011)
23. Haileselassie, T.M., Uhlen, K.: Impact of DC line voltage drops on power flow of MTDC using droop control. IEEE Trans. Power Systems **27**(3), 1441–1449 (2012)
24. Augustine, S., Mishra, M.K., Lakshminarasamma, N.: Adaptive droop control strategy for load sharing and circulating current minimization in low-voltage standalone DC microgrid. IEEE Trans. Sustain. Energy **6**, 132–141 (2015)
25. Lu, X., et al.: An improved droop control method for DC microgrids based on low bandwidth communication with DC bus voltage restoration and enhanced current sharing accuracy. IEEE Trans. Power Electron. **29**, 1800–1812 (2014)
26. Faika, T., Kim, T., Khan, M.: An Internet of Things (IoT)-based network for dispersed and decentralized wireless battery management systems. In: IEEE Transportation Electrification Conference and Expo, pp. 1060–1064 (2018)

27. Steinhorst, S., Lukasiewycz, M., Narayanaswamy, S., et al.: Smart cells for embedded battery management. In: IEEE International Conference on Cyber-Physical Systems, Networks, and Applications, pp. 59–64 (2014)

28. Merei, G., et al.: Optimization of an off-grid hybrid power supply system based on battery aging models for different battery technologies. In: IEEE 36th International Telecommunications Energy Conference (INTELEC), pp. 1–6 (2014)

29. Alharbi, T., Bhattacharya, K., Kazerani, M.: Planning and operation of isolated microgrids based on repurposed electric vehicle batteries. IEEE Trans. Ind. Inform. **15**, 4319–4331 (2019)

30. Reinhardt, R., Christodoulou, I., García, B.A., et al.: Sustainable business model archetypes for the electric vehicle battery second use industry: towards a conceptual framework. Elsevier J. Clean. Prod. **254**, 119994 (2020)

31. Al-Nayeem, A., et al.: A formal architecture pattern for real-time distributed systems. In: IEEE Real-Time Systems Symposium, pp. 161–170 (2009)

32. Steinhorst, S., et al.: Distributed reconfigurable battery system management architectures. In: IEEE 21st Asia and South Pacific Design Automation Conference, pp. 429–434 (2016)

33. Reindl, A., Meier, H., Niemetz, M.: Software framework for the simulation of a decentralized battery management system consisting of intelligent battery cells. In: 2019 IEEE Student Conference on Research and Development, pp. 75–80 (2019)

34. Rahman, M.A., de Craemer, K., Büscher, J., et al.: Comparative analysis of reconfiguration assisted management of battery storage systems. In: IECON 2019–45th Annual Conference of the IEEE Industrial Electronics Society, pp. 5921–5926 (2019)

35. Zhu, F., et al.: Battery management system for Li-ion battery. IEEE J. Eng. **2017**(13), 1437–1440 (2017)

36. Zhu, W., Shi, Y., Lei, B.: Functional safety analysis and design of BMS for Lithium-Ion battery energy storage system. Energy Storage Sci. Technol. **9**, 271–278 (2020)

37. Pu, X., et al.: Recent progress in rechargeable Sodium-Ion batteries: toward high-power applications. Small **15**, 1805427 (2019)

38. Du, H., et al.: Advanced Li-Se$_x$S$_y$ battery system: electrodes and electrolytes. Elsevier J. Mater. Sci. Technol. (2020)

39. Gentil, S., Reynard, D., Girault, H.H.: Aqueous organic and redox-mediated redox flow batteries: a review. Elsevier Curr. Opinion Electrochem. **21**, 7–13 (2020)

40. Reindl, A., Schneider, V., Meier, H., Niemetz, M.: Software update of a decentralized, intelligent battery management system based on multi-microcomputers. In: Symposium Elektronik und Systemintegration (ESI) (2020)

41. Aneke, M., Wang, M.: Energy storage technologies and real life applications - a state of the art review. Elsevier Appl. Energy **179**, 350–377 (2016)

Security Improvements by Separating the Cryptographic Protocol from the Network Stack onto a Multi-MCU Architecture

Tobias Frauenschläger[✉], Sebastian Renner, and Jürgen Mottok

Laboratory for Safe and Secure Systems (LaS³), Technical University of Applied Sciences Regensburg, 93053 Regensburg, Germany
{tobias.frauenschlaeger,sebastian1.renner,
juergen.mottok}@oth-regensburg.de

Abstract. The number of IoT devices in SCADA and ICS systems is rising quickly, especially in the domain of critical infrastructures. But these kinds of systems are performing mission critical tasks like controlling devices in industrial facilities or substations in the smart grid. Therefore, they are subject to a lot of regulatory standards. Yet, to provide remote access over the internet, special architectures are developed to integrate a network interface into these devices without inferring with the actual functionality. However, these architectures either lack security measures against cyber-attacks or do not offer the necessary performance for time-critical communication interfaces. To solve that, an architecture consisting of three units is introduced in this paper to provide a network interface with extensive security measures and a high performance. The main feature is the isolation of the cryptographic functionality onto an additional MCU. After proposing the basic concept, the paper presents many implementation details. Based on the current state of implementation, a concept validation of the realized architecture is described.

Keywords: Cyber-security · Functional safety · Network security · Industrial Internet of Things · Industrial Control System · Supervisory Control and Data Acquisition System · Multi microcontroller setup · Dos prevention · Critical infrastructures

1 Introduction

With the tremendous growth of the Internet-of-Things (IoT), nowadays nearly everything is connected to the internet, which greatly improves the functionality of many different device categories and even enables new use-cases. By now, this trend reached the industrial sector and critical infrastructures in the form of Industrial IoT (IIoT). Supervisory Control and Data Acquisition Systems (SCADA), e.g. the power grid or water supply, or Industrial Control Systems (ICS) like production facilities are connected to the internet to provide an interface to an external instance. This enables new possibilities regarding supervision, maintenance, control and automation.

© Springer Nature Switzerland AG 2020
A. Brinkmann et al. (Eds.): ARCS 2020, LNCS 12155, pp. 185–199, 2020.
https://doi.org/10.1007/978-3-030-52794-5_14

Most of these systems feature a single point-to-point connection between an end-device in the field and the control unit of the operator. This end-device can be a single PLC (Programmable Logic Controller) or a gateway concentrating local data traffic. Due to the importance of error-free functionality of these systems, intense safety measures are applied to all components.

Unlike functional safety, cyber-security has rather been neglected in the past. For a long time, hardly any security measures were applied to these networks providing a huge attack surface for an adversary to cause serious damage. To prevent a scenario like that, new standards were issued prescribing minimal requirements for cyber-security measures. In order to comply with these new standards, a device has to meet new additional requirements. This turns out to be a non-trivial task, as extensive measures are necessary. Therefore, a comprehensive solution must be developed.

In the research project *Energy Safe and Secure System Module* (ES³M), such a solution is developed at the moment [10]. Currently focused on the power grid, a module consisting of four Microcontroller Units (MCUs) is developed to secure the communication between a substation and the controlling station of an energy provider. However, the created system architecture can easily be ported to any other SCADA, ICS or automotive system. The key characteristic of this architecture is the separation of the cryptographic functionality from the network communication onto two independent MCUs. This separation with its characteristics and implementation details will be further presented in this paper.

1.1 Contribution

Building upon existing work, the paper contributes the following points to the topic of secure communication architectures.

- Higher security confidence: Complete isolation of the cryptographically sensitive data from the network communication onto two separate MCUs
- Small size: The reduction of complexity and code size results in more testable and maintainable software for each MCU
- Transparent functionality: No influence on the actual task of the system
- Efficiency: Performance guarantees are given

1.2 Structure

The paper is structured as follows. In Sect. 2, the background and the context of the paper is presented. Based on this, Sect. 3 evaluates related work. Section 4 describes the basic concept of the architecture, while in Sect. 5 the concrete implementation is introduced. As the implementation isn't completely finished at the time of writing, Sect. 6 only presents basic performance characteristics of the system and mainly depicts the concepts we plan for a comprehensive validation of the architecture in the future. Section 7 concludes the paper with an outlook to future work.

2   Background

2.1   Regulatory Context

Within the current research context, in [2] the regulatory security measures are outlined that must be applied to communication interfaces inside the power grid. In this standard, the usage of the *Transport Layer Security* (TLS) protocol is prescribed for all TCP/IP based connections. This results in the application of both symmetric and asymmetric cryptography as well as X.509 certificates for securing the communication channel. Because most of the application specific protocols running on top of the communication interface assume a persistent connection, the maximum TLS session time is set to 24 h in the standard. This is a trade-off between the lifetime of the secure channel and the time in between new connection setups.

Next to the security related prescriptions, the field of application within critical infrastructures or industrial facilities results in extensive functional safety requirements. In [1], the definition of so called *Safety Integrity Levels* (SIL) can be found. Based on this classification, specific measures can be derived that must be implemented by a device. In the given context, many of the devices in question can be classified to be SIL3, which implies a device availability of $\geq 99.99999\%$ and an error-rate of $\leq 10^{-7}$. To reach such numbers, both a periodic self-test of each MCU and additional monitoring by an independent instance is necessary.

2.2   Attack Vectors

Based on analyses of cyber-attacks on SCADA systems [5] and on IoT smart-world critical infrastructures [6], two different attack vectors can be identified. Firstly, due to a lack of proper security measures regarding confidentiality, integrity and authenticity, the communication can easily be eavesdropped or even modified by an adversary. On the one hand, this can reveal sensitive data, but on the other hand, the attacker can also harm both communication parties in various ways. Through modifications of the data traffic, the operation of a device or the whole system can be manipulated in a malicious way, so the actual functionality is not executed correctly. This could stop the system or even cause serious physical damage. Also, modified data may result in wrong status information about the system leading to incorrect operation or maintenance steps. The second attack vector is a *Denial-of-Service* (DoS) attack. In this scenario, the communication interface is flooded with data, so proper communication is not possible anymore. This, again, may cause the system to fail in its actual task and prevent surveillance or control functionality.

The usage of TLS in the communication channel will prevent all possible attacks of the first attack vector. Because a DoS attack is very hard to prevent, it must be ensured that such attacks will not interfere with the actual task, causing malfunction in the device functionality. Also, the network interface of the device must be fully operational as soon as the DoS attack is over. In order to assure that, the internal functionality and also the functional safety measures must be well prepared for this kind of situation.

3   Related Work

To overcome the possible attacks while conforming to the regulatory context described in Sect. 2, an extensive security solution is necessary. Niedermaier et al. proposed a Dual-MCU architecture that secures a device in an ICS system from a DoS attack [8]. Instead of putting both the control and the network functionality onto a single MCU, the features are split onto two MCUs. One handles all the network communication, in the following referred to as *NW-MCU*, while the second one performs the actual control job relevant to the overall system, further named *IO-MCU*. The communication between the two is done over a SPI (Serial Peripheral Interface) connection in a timely deterministic fashion. In the case of a DoS attack, all additional processing is done on the NW-MCU without influencing the IO-MCU. The result is an unaltered behavior regarding the control functionality during and also after a DoS attack. An additional benefit of this split architecture is the reduction in complexity and code size on each MCU. This simplifies software testing, reduces bugs and enables an easier certification.

This proposed architecture is a proper security solution for the second attack vector, but it lacks cryptographic measures against eavesdropping or manipulating the data traffic described in the first attack scenario. Therefore, adequate measures must be integrated, namely in the form of inserting TLS into the protocol stack. This could be done directly on either the NW-MCU or the IO-MCU, keeping the proposed architecture as is. However, this would on the one hand lead to cryptographically sensitive data being stored in memory that is directly accessible over the network interface. Due to bugs and vulnerabilities in the software in use, this sensitive data, e.g. certificates or private keys, can be obtained by an adversary. In high-class processors, this problem is normally addressed by hardware additions called *Trust Zones* [7] that isolate memory regions from unauthorized processes. But within this research context, only simple MCUs in the form of System-on-Chip modules are used that do not provide such functionality. On the other hand, adding TLS to the IO-MCU would increase the workload and the complexity of its software, resulting in the need for a more powerful MCU. However, this should be avoided, as it would create other challenges related to the regulatory context and certification efforts.

A Possible Solution for that are *Secure Elements*. In 2016, Pascal Urien presented so called security modules based on secure elements that include complete TLS/DTLS protocol functionality for the application in IoT devices [11]. These modules are low power and low priced external chips with their own CPU and, most importantly, tamper-proof memory. The communication between the module and a main MCU is done using the ISO 7816 communication interface [3]. To provide TLS functionality to the application, a software bridge runs on the main MCU. It receives the cipher text from the network stack and sends it to the secure element for processing. After decryption, the plain text is sent back to the MCU, where the software bridge forwards the data to the actual application software. A transmission of plain text over the secure channel works accordingly in the opposite direction. This enables a secure communication using TLS without storing cryptographically sensitive data on the main MCU.

The combination of both approaches, namely the addition of a NW-MCU and a secure element implementing TLS, could address all in Sect. 2.2 described attacks. However, this solution would still have problems. Firstly, when connecting the secure element to the NW-MCU, the decrypted plain text sent back from the secure element is stored on the NW-MCU until it is forwarded to the IO-MCU. Thus, it would still be possible for an adversary to read or modify the plain text due to vulnerabilities in the software. Connecting the secure element to the IO-MCU would prevent that issue, but in this case the workload and complexity of the IO-MCU would again be increased, as it would have to communicate with two parties at the same time. Secondly, the ISO 7816 based communication between a MCU and the secure element and the CPU inside the secure element itself are both very slow, causing a large delay of up to several hundred milliseconds in the processing of the data [11]. In case of high traffic, this may quickly become a bottleneck, no matter to which MCU the secure element would be connected.

Based on this work, in the next section we introduce an extended architecture to resolve the issues in current designs. This architecture introduces an additional MCU to further isolate the TLS functionality from the network stack without increasing the load of the MCU running the actual application.

4   Basic Concept

Building on the introduced architecture from Sect. 3, another split of functionality is performed. Providing a clear and consistent naming scheme, the name *NW-MCU* is kept for the existing MCU handling all the network related functionality. The MCU running the actual application, named IO-MCU in [8], is now called *APP-MCU*, as the application is not limited to I/O control in the context of this paper. In addition to these two MCUs, a new MCU is added implementing the TLS functionality, named *Crypto-MCU*. It is inserted in between the NW-MCU and the APP-MCU, keeping the functionality of both unchanged. The resulting architecture is shown in Fig. 1.

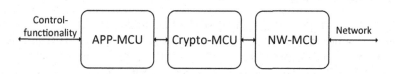

Fig. 1. New architecture with the additional Crypto-MCU

As can be seen in Fig. 1, the NW-MCU still handles all network related functionality including the protection against DoS attacks. The raw TCP payload received over the network interface is forwarded to the Crypto-MCU without any processing. This payload contains the TLS records, which are then processed on the Crypto-MCU. Thereafter, the decrypted plain text is sent to the APP-MCU, which is finally using and interpreting it. Data sent from the APP-MCU to the network is processed in the opposite direction through all three MCUs. The communication between the MCUs is based on SPI with additional hardware flow control for timely determinism and improved robustness.

With this architecture, the cryptographically sensitive data, like keys, certificates and the decrypted plain text, are completely isolated from the network interface and therefore not accessible from the outside. Even if an adversary gains access to the NW-MCU due to a software vulnerability, he cannot obtain or even modify the sensitive data because of the physical separation onto two different MCUs.

To further increase the security of the architecture, two additional components are added. On the one hand, a dedicated *Random Number Generator* (RNG) is placed on the printed circuit board (PCB), generating high entropy random numbers. The selected device is certified in the strongest class PTG.3 [9], which is suitable for any cryptographic application. With it, proper ephemeral keys can be generated. On the other hand, a secure element, as already mentioned in Sect. 3, is added to the system, connected to the Crypto-MCU. However, it is not used to implement the complete TLS functionality, but merely for authentication during the TLS handshake. Certified to Common Criteria EAL 5+ [4], it provides a tamper-proof storage for certificates and private keys, and even features an on-device key generation, resulting in the private keys never leaving the secure element. This ensures maximum security. All in all, the proposed architecture builds an extensive security solution that can protect a device, meaning the APP-MCU in this context, from both attack vectors described in Sect. 2.

5   Implementation

To prove the security improvements of our proposed architecture, we created a prototype containing all of the described components. The details of specific implementations are presented in this section.

5.1   Hardware Setup

The created prototype with all the described components can be seen in Fig. 2. It shows three boards, each containing one MCU. The green board in the middle is a custom PCB containing the Crypto-MCU, the secure element and the dedicated RNG. The boards on the left and the right side are off-the-shelf development boards from STMicroeletronics[1], representing the APP-MCU and the NW-MCU. For easy development, all three MCUs are of the same type in this setup. The two development boards contain the MCU STM32H743ZIT[2] that is

---

[1] https://www.st.com/en/evaluation-tools/nucleo-h743zi.html.

[2] https://www.st.com/en/microcontrollers-microprocessors/stm32h743-753.html.

based on an ARM Cortex-M7 core with a 480 MHz clock frequency. The Crypto-MCU is of the type STM32H753ZIT, which offers the same features as noted above, except for additional hardware accelerators for the Advanced Encryption Standard (AES) algorithm. The MCU type has been chosen due to the high performance while still being a System-on-Chip design, the huge amount of communication interfaces for potential future evaluations and the extensive options for hardware-based network packet filtering.

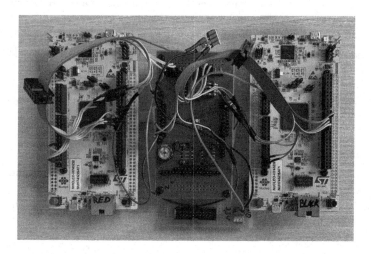

Fig. 2. Current hardware setup with the separation onto three controllers

5.2   Communication Between the MCUs

Before we dive into the specific software details of each MCU, the communication interface between the MCUs is presented. As already mentioned, the communication is based on SPI. However, not the default master-slave topology is used, but a more flexible multi-master system is deployed. This way, a communication with equally distributed access rights is possible, enabling both MCUs to initiate a data transmission whenever they want to. To achieve this, both participants can act as either master or slave depending on the transmission direction. This is configured in software using a flow control based on additional I/O lines. By sharing the SPI lines between the two participants, only half-duplex transmission is possible. For the current prototype, we use this interface for both communications between the three MCUs. But in case of another, maybe simpler APP-MCU, the interface between it and the Crypto-MCU can be changed to a different connection type, e.g. standard SPI or UART (Universal Asynchronous Receiver Transmitter).

For the message transmission over this interface, a proprietary protocol consisting of a *Header* and optional *Payload* has been defined. The header contains the type of the message, the length of the optionally following payload and a

CRC (Cyclic Redundancy Check) field, each occupying 2 bytes. Currently, there are five different message types defined, further described in Table 1.

Table 1. Message Types and their Meaning

Message type	Meaning
Connection_Start	Command to start a new network connection. This can either mean actively connecting to a server or listening for incoming connections
Connection_Established	Notification that a new connection has been established
Connection_Stop	Command to stop the current network activity. This can either mean to close an active connection or to stop listening for incoming connections
Connection_Closed	Notification that all network activities are stopped
Payload	Transmission of network payload

The first four message types are used for controlling and synchronizing the state machines on the different MCUs. Messages with the 'Payload' type are then used to actually exchange payload data between the MCUs. Based on these messages, the cooperation of the MCUs with their distinct functionality is managed.

5.3   Software of the Crypto-MCU

To reduce the amount of additional work for the critical APP-MCU, the Crypto-MCU is considered to be the master of the system related to network functionality. This means that it controls the NW-MCU with its functionality, while simultaneously exchanging the plain text network data with the APP-MCU. In order to provide a clear and scalable architecture, the software is written in the C++ programming language (Version 2014). This enables bundling functionality inside classes with a properly abstracted interface. This way, a loose coupling of the different software components is possible. Additionally, the *FreeRTOS*[3] kernel (Version 10.3.1) is integrated to provide a runtime environment. This real-time operating system is well-suited for MCUs and built with an emphasis on reliability and ease of use. The main functionality of the Crypto-MCU is modeled in three functional units called *PayloadProcessor*, *PayloadTransceiver* and *InterControllerConnection*, each represented by a single class. The PayloadTransceiver and InterControllerConnection classes are used for the payload exchange between the Crypto-MCU and the NW-MCU as well as the APP-MCU. This leads to a double instantiation of both classes. The PayloadProcessor class isolates the actual TLS functionality from the remaining code. The overall structure is shown in Fig. 3, with each unit and other implementation related details explained in more detail in the following sections.

---

[3] https://www.freertos.org/.

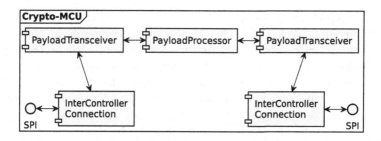

Fig. 3. Structure of the functional units inside the Crypto-MCU software

PayloadProcessor. This class forms the core of the Crypto-MCU software. Here, all the TLS related functionality is isolated from the rest of the software. The program execution is based on an *Event-driven architecture*. At startup, a task is created to handle all incoming events. These events are created in the PayloadTransceiver objects and are sent to the PayloadProcessor over an asynchronous event-queue. There are two categories of events: state-change events and payload-processing events. A state-change event either contains the command to start a new or stop a currently active network connection, or indicates the establishment or termination of a connection. A payload-processing event either means encryption or decryption of actual payload with subsequent forwarding of the processed data.

For the TLS capabilities, the open-source *mbedTLS*[4] library is used. It offers a simple API and is widely used in the embedded community. The code is slightly modified in some places to enable the usage of the RNG, the secure element and the AES hardware accelerators of the MCU. Due to the isolation of TLS and therefore all cryptographically sensitive data into a single task with a defined communication interface using the event-queue, the sensitive data can easily be protected with a *Memory Protection Unit* (MPU). This, in combination with the additional usage of the secure element for storing private keys and certificates, greatly improves the security of the whole system.

PayloadTransceiver. In this class, the state of a single external MCU is managed. Therefore, this class is instantiated twice, both for the NW-MCU and the APP-MCU (see Fig. 3). Internally, this class works in a very similar way as the PayloadProcessor class. It also features an Event-driven architecture with an event-queue that stores events for sequential processing. In this case, there are, again, two categories of events: Either there is an external message available from the other MCU or a message from the PayloadProcessor has received. These messages can either contain payload to forward to the other MCU or are used to change the state of the network connection. In case of an external message, the header is parsed and proper events for the PayloadProcessor are created and added to its event-queue.

---

[4] https://tls.mbed.org/.

The fact that there are three event-queues in total on the Crypto-MCU may seem overly complicated at first, but this architecture results in many advantages. The most important one is the independence of each processing unit. This results in improved timely behavior compared to an otherwise single bigger event-driven system that provides the same functionality, because each task can process the events at its own pace without slowing down the others. Furthermore, the CPU load is reduced by a heavy usage of *Direct Memory Access* controllers (DMAs) for the communication interfaces and the hardware accelerators. The free CPU resources can then be used for processing the remaining event-queues. Another positive aspect of the different event-queues is the possibility to overcome temporary bottlenecks in the processing pipeline, for example caused by a faster reception of incoming data from the NW-MCU compared to the actual decryption, due to the storing capacity of the queues. Lastly, this separation simplifies the usage of a MPU to further secure the decrypted payload from unauthorized access.

InterControllerConnection. The last of the three classes handles the actual communication with the other MCU, as described in Sect. 5.2. This way, the physical communication interface is independent from the logic implemented in the PayloadTransceiver class. As shown in Fig. 3, there are two objects of this class, each one connected to one MCU via SPI and to one of the Payload-Transceiver objects. Furthermore, this abstraction enables a simple replacement of the communication interface, which can benefit future developments. Internally, the transmission and the reception of messages is split. The reception is handled in a distinct task, while the transmission is done from within the PayloadTransceiver task in a blocking manner. The synchronization between the two is done using a mutex.

All in all, the modularity of the Crypto-MCU software with the three event-queues enables responsive and efficient data processing in both directions. Moreover, by splitting the functionality, additional security measures in the form of a MPU can be applied. Finally, the use of FreeRTOS allows scalability for future software additions.

5.4   Software of the NW-MCU

Following the concepts of the Crypto-MCU software, the NW-MCU software also features an event-driven architecture. To ease the development efforts and to minimize the written code, as much code as possible is shared between the MCUs. The result of this effort is the structure shown in Fig. 4.

Compared to the software structure of the Crypto-MCU, there are only a few differences observable in Fig. 4. Mainly, the PayloadProcessor object is gone. As there is no TLS functionality needed on this controller, we do not need an object of this class. Additionally, there is only one PayloadTransceiver object, because we only have to handle one state machine on this controller. The last difference is the replacement of one InterControllerConnection object with an object of the

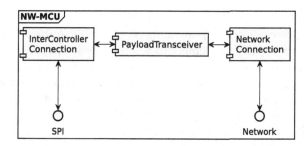

Fig. 4. Structure of the functional units inside the NW-MCU software

class *NetworkConnection*. With the presence of an event-queue on the NW-MCU, this software has the same advantages as described for the Crypto-MCU software. Also, the complete fundamental software framework including the FreeRTOS kernel is shared between the MCUs.

The NetworkConnection class mimics the interface of the InterController-Connection class in order to work with the existing PayloadTransceiver object. However, the implementation is very different. Inside this class, the actual network connection is handled, using the *Lightweight IP*[5] stack (LWIP). This open-source library provides a complete TCP/IP network stack with support for many additional features.

Based on the already described functionality of the data processing and the different messages that are exchanged between the MCUs, a state machine has been created and implemented on the NW-MCU. It is shown in Fig. 5.

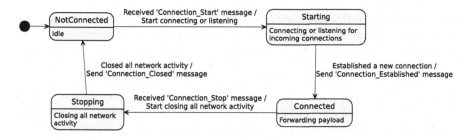

Fig. 5. State machine implemented in the NW-MCU software

As you can see in Fig. 5, there are four different states defined: *NotConnected, Connected, Starting* and *Stopping*. The first two states are the persistent ones, in which an active connection is established or not. In the *NotConnected* state, the NW-MCU is idle. This is also the default state after system startup. In the *Connected* state, the NW-MCU actively forwards payload both from the Crypto-MCU to the network endpoint and vice versa. The latter two states are more

---

[5] https://savannah.nongnu.org/projects/lwip/.

of a temporary kind. The *Starting* state indicates that the NW-MCU is trying to establish a new connection. Depending on the configuration, this can either mean that it actively tries to connect to a remote host or that it is acting as a host listening for an incoming connection on a given port. The *Stopping* state is the counterpiece to this, meaning that currently all network activity is being terminated. This again can imply closing an active connection to a host or to stop listening for an incoming connection. In the current setup, the NW-MCU is able to handle only a single connection at a time. However, this limitation can easily be removed in future developments.

The state transitions are also shown in Fig. 5. There are two types of transitions: Commands from the Crypto-MCU and events from the network stack. The two message types *Connection_Start* and *Connection_Stop*, already shown in Table 1, trigger transitions to the *Starting* and *Stopping* states respectively. As soon as the network stack indicates a successfully established connection or that all network activity is terminated, the state changes to *Connected* or *NotConnected*. In either case, a message of the type *Connection_Established* or *Connection_Closed* is sent to the Crypto-MCU announcing the state transition (see Table 1). Not shown in Fig. 5 are the state transitions caused by errors. If such a situation is encountered, either the *Stopping* or the *NotConnected* state is entered, depending on the current state and the actual error.

With the presented state machine and the code shared with the Crypto-MCU, a flexible, responsive and robust software handling the network connection is created. In cooperation with the Crpyto-MCU, both attack vectors described in Sect. 2.2 are addressed.

5.5   Software of the APP-MCU

The last MCU in the proposed architecture is the APP-MCU. It runs the actual application, to which a secure network interface, implemented by the Crypto-MCU and the NW-MCU, is provided. With the presented architecture, no restriction is given related to the application running on the APP-MCU. It can be anything from a real-time I/O control to a more complex gateway device. Independent from the main functionality, the software of the APP-MCU has to run the already known functional units consisting of a slightly modified *PayloadTransceiver* object and an *InterControllerCommunication* object. This is necessary for the APP-MCU to communicate with the Crypto-MCU. The modified PayloadTransceiver provides an interface for the actual application to send and receive data over the secured network connection.

Within the current research project, the application running on the prototype's APP-MCU is not the endpoint of the network data, but rather acts as a network gateway forwarding the payload to another network host. This way, the prototype represents a gateway device that provides a secured network channel using TLS. For the software of the APP-MCU, this means that the structure is almost identical to the one of the NW-MCU aside from an inverted network behavior. This enables sharing most of the code between the NW-MCU and the APP-MCU.

6   Concept for Validation

The current prototype, with the APP-MCU mirroring the functionality of the NW-MCU creating a network security gateway, provides a solid setup for validation of the proposed security architecture. At the time of writing, the implementation described in Sect. 5 is a work in progress. The software for each of the three MCUs is in an working state, but not all features are completely done or well optimized yet. Therefore, comprehensive and sound validation results cannot be created at the moment. However, some basic performance measurements are presented to prove the viability of our architecture.

- Currently, the TLS handshake, including the secure element for authentication, takes around 1.2 s to complete. However, this process is not yet fully optimized.
- The delay caused by the processing chain of the NW-MCU and the Crypto-MCU is around 5 ms for network payload to finally reach the APP-MCU.
- DoS attacks are completely handled by the NW-MCU and the Crypto-MCU without affecting the actual functionality.

Based on these first promising results, the concept for the comprehensive validation of the system is already defined. Using the gateway functionality created within the current research project, the following tests, with additional comparison to other in this paper presented architectures, are planned for a future work.

- Measurement of the processing delay under different network traffic loads
- Behavior during and after different DoS attacks related to TCP and TLS
- Penetration tests regarding security aspects
- Tests related to functional safety and reliability of the system

7   Conclusion and Outlook

In this paper, a Multi-MCU security architecture has been presented. In addition to an APP-MCU running the actual application, two MCUs are added to provide security functionality in the form of TLS (Crypto-MCU) and a DoS protected network interface (NW-MCU). We showed that related work already has partial solutions against the identified attack vectors on SCADA and ICS systems relevant for this paper. However, all presented solution either lack proper security measures, do not provide the performance necessary in some of these critical systems or imply the need of a more powerful APP-MCU. Following this, we propose a new architecture featuring two additional MCUs for providing a secure network interface. One of them takes care of all network related functionality, while the second one is solely handling the security functionality. This physically isolates all cryptographically sensitive data from a remote access, highly increasing the security while providing protection against DoS attacks.

In conclusion, the current state of the prototype seems promising. The basic functionality is working as described in this paper, with no problems resulting from the use of a Multi-MCU architecture. In a future work, the architecture will be further verified against the dependability objectives like functional safety and IT-security. Also the performance characteristics will be analyzed.

References

1. IEC 61508: Functional safety of electrical/electronic/programmable electronic safety-related systems. Technical report International Electrotechnical Commission, April 2010
2. IEC 62351–3: Power systems management and associated information exchange - data and communications security; Part 3: Communication network and system security - Profiles including TCP/IP. Technical report International Electrotechnical Commission, October 2014
3. International Organization for Standardization: Identification cards - Integrated circuit cards - Part 3: Cards with contacts - Electrical interface and transmission protocols. Standard ISO/IEC, 7816–3 (2006)
4. International Organization for Standardization: Information technology - Security techniques - Evaluation criteria for IT security. Standard ISO/IEC 15408–1/2/3:2009, December 2009
5. Irmak, E., Erkek, I.: An overview of cyber-attack vectors on SCADA systems. In: 2018 6th International Symposium on Digital Forensic and Security, ISDFS, pp. 1–5, March 2018. https://doi.org/10.1109/ISDFS.2018.8355379
6. Liu, X., Qian, C., Hatcher, W.G., Xu, H., Liao, W., Yu, W.: Secure Internet of Things (IoT)-based smart-world critical infrastructures: survey, case study and research opportunities. IEEE Access 7, 79523–79544 (2019). https://doi.org/10.1109/ACCESS.2019.2920763
7. Mukhtar, M.A., Bhatti, M.K., Gogniat, G.: Architectures for security: a comparative analysis of hardware security features in Intel SGX and ARM TrustZone. In: 2019 2nd International Conference on Communication, Computing and Digital systems (C-CODE), pp. 299–304, March 2019. https://doi.org/10.1109/C-CODE.2019.8680982
8. Niedermaier, M., Merli, D., Sigl, G.: A secure Dual-MCU architecture for robust communication of IIoT devices. In: 2019 8th Mediterranean Conference on Embedded Computing, MECO, pp. 1–5, June 2019. https://doi.org/10.1109/MECO.2019.8760188
9. Schindler, W., Killmann, W.: A proposal for: Functionality classes for random number generators. Bundesamt für Sicherheit in der Informationstechnik, September 2011

10. Frauenschläger, T., Dentgen, M., Mottok, J.: Systemarchitektur eines Sicherheitsmoduls im Energiesektor. In: 2. Symposium Elektronik und Systemintegration: Intelligente Systeme und ihre Komponenten: Forschung und industrielle Anwendung, April 2020. https://www.haw-landshut.de/fileadmin/Hochschule_Landshut_NEU/Ungeschuetzt/ITZ_Cluster_Forschung/ClusterMST/Symposium-ESI/2020/Tagungsbandbeitraege/A1-3_OTH-Regensburg_Frauenschlaeger_ESI_2020.pdf

11. Urien, P.: Innovative TLS/DTLS security modules for iot applications: concepts and experiments. In: Mandler, B., Marquez-Barja, J., Mitre Campista, M.E., Cagáňová, D., Chaouchi, H., Zeadally, S., Badra, M., Giordano, S., Fazio, M., Somov, A., Vieriu, R.-L. (eds.) IoT360 2015. LNICST, vol. 169, pp. 3–15. Springer, Cham (2016). https://doi.org/10.1007/978-3-319-47063-4_1

Equally Distributed Bus-Communication Access Rights for Inter MCU Communication Using Multimaster SPI

Manuel Dentgen[✉], Sebastian Renner, and Jürgen Mottok

Laboratory for Safe and Secure Systems (LaS3), Technical University of Applied Sciences, Seybothstraße 2, 93053 Regensburg, Germany
{manuel.dentgen,sebastian1.renner,juergen.mottok}@oth-regensburg.de

Abstract. With the rising complexity and processing power of modern computer systems, the amount of MCU on a single PCB also rises. These microcontrollers often need to communicate with each other to exchange payload and control information in a bidirectional manner. Today's well-established communication protocols in MCUs either do not fit modern transmission speed requirements or do have an inappropriate master-slave attribute, which does not allow the communication partners to have equal bus access rights. Therefore, this paper introduces an extension of the Serial Peripheral Interface (SPI) to allow an equally distributed access right for the communication interface between two microcontrollers. It simultaneously does fit modern transmission speed requirements of a common network interface, so that the message transmission does not constitute a bottleneck in data processing. Besides the protocol design, we do also provide a first prototype implementation, which constitutes a proof of concept.

Keywords: Multimaster · SPI · Communication · Master · Slave · Bidirectional · Equally distributed transmission rights · Microcontroller · MCU · Embedded · Ethernet · Inter · Controller · Conversion · Flow control · Multimaster · Serial peripheral interface

1 Introduction

Within the context of the research project *Energy Safe and Secure System Module* (ES³M) [9] at the *Technical University of Applied Sciences* (Ostbayerische Technische Hochschule - OTH) in Regensburg, a module for the separation of the security protocol layer from the network stack is developed. To achieve this, the individual tasks of those layers are divided among several Microcontroller Units (MCUs) on a single Printed Circuit Board (PCB). The goal of this concept is to get a higher security level, since the sensitive security mechanisms are outsourced to a distinct centralized controller, which is not directly accessible from the external network. At the same time the controller, which can be accessed from the external network, has no security tasks. A third controller

© Springer Nature Switzerland AG 2020
A. Brinkmann et al. (Eds.): ARCS 2020, LNCS 12155, pp. 200–212, 2020.
https://doi.org/10.1007/978-3-030-52794-5_15

enables the module to communicate with an additional independent and isolated communication interface. This principle is shown in Fig. 1.

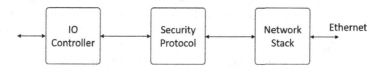

Fig. 1. Task separation of the security protocol layer and the network stack with the third Input/Output-controller on the left

1.1 Contribution

During the development of the research project it has become apparent, that the task separation principle used can easily be adopted to other application fields, e.g. for automotive or aviation. The third controller could communicate with an already existing sensor or actuator by connecting them via a standard communication interface. Our concept shall enable the conversion of low-level communication networks to Ethernet with an increased security level in those fields, without the need to exchange every single device, but by simply including this kind of module in a network.

However, the used MCUs only contain a single *Ethernet Media Access Control* (MAC) interface, which is used for the communication with the external network. This results in the necessity to implement another communication channel between the microcontrollers. The approach for this has to reach a similar transmission speed to what Ethernet already offers, to not create a bottleneck in data processing. It also has to allow bus access control on both sides with equal rights to allow an unconditional transmission in both directions. This paper will introduce such a communication interface.

1.2 Structure

The paper is structured as follows. In Sect. 2, some similar concepts to the one introduced in this paper are presented and compared to each other. It shall also be clarified why those are not fitting for our kind of task. Then in Sect. 3, the idea and theory behind the introduced architecture is presented, while considering the points previously mentioned. Section 4 focuses on the implementation of the concept within the context of the research project. Next, in Sect. 5 a proof of concept is presented, because the final implementation is not yet finished due to limitations of the current hardware. Section 6 summarizes the current state of the inter-controller communication and gives a brief outlook on future work.

2   Related Work

The idea of connecting several microcontroller units together and thereby generating a network of multiple controllers is not a new task in the embedded world. Various connection and design approaches have been made over the last years, all with the goal to achieve a fast, robust and secure communication between multiple controllers.

Niedermaier et al. [4] introduced a robust communication for the Industrial Internet of Things (IIoT) sector. They provide a concept to connect a communication interface with a following proof of concept. The presented architecture is similar to the one presented in this paper. However, they have used a standard serial peripheral interface for the inter-controller communication, with one of the controllers being the SPI master. This implies that the two communication partners are not equally permitted to access the communication bus. Besides other properties, this is not suitable for our project. We desire an inter-controller communication where both communication partners are fully authorized to access the bus.

Peng et al. [5] have presented a similar approach to our idea. They have realized an inter-controller communication using a dual-port Random Access Memory (RAM), and with that converting *RS232* or *RS485* to an Ethernet interface. However, they have developed a non-protected Ethernet endpoint, while we want to use a loop-through with an additional security mechanism.

Szekacs et al. [8] have implemented an inter-controller communication using the two interfaces SPI and Inter Integrated Circuit (I^2C) simultaneously. Their original goal was to connect a huge amount of sensors to one master using the I^2C-interface. As they have found out that they are not able to connect the estimated amount of sensors using only this communication type, they decided to extend their layout with several microcontrollers, all having their own connection to the sensors and communicating via SPI to the master. Maemunah et al. [3] have implemented a similar concept to them, by connecting multiple sensors to a MCU and sending all the measured data via a single interface to a processing master. The master is again the reason why we cannot use these approaches, since we want to use an equal bus access method.

The discussion shows that there are many inter-controller connection techniques, but none of them fitted perfectly for our task. Therefore, we have elaborated our requirements for the inter-controller communication more precisely and compared it to well established protocols with the goal to find a fitting interface.

3   Protocol Design

The previous chapter showed which elaborated communication systems are already available and why those are not suitable for the system presented here. Therefore, this chapter clarifies the requirements of the aspired communication interface. On the basis of this information, some well established communication protocols can be evaluated and eventually one is chosen.

3.1 Abstracting the Problem to Two Controllers

While speaking of three controllers for the research project prior to this section, the actual aspired communication interface represents a point-to-point (PTP) connection between two MCUs, which will be used twice originating from the centralized security controller. Therefore the problem can be abstracted to a data transmission between two controllers which is shown in Fig. 2. This represents another security benefit next to the task separation. The two connections are not implemented via a single bus system, but are separated from each other to prevent the data from being intentionally looped past the actual security controller. Thereby we achieve a higher security level, already during the hardware design phase.

Fig. 2. Communication principle broken down to two controllers

As mentioned before, an important setting for our communication protocol is the transmission speed between the controllers. The connection of the network controller can have a transmission speed of up to 100 Mbit/s. To not constitute a bottleneck in data processing, the inter-controller communication should also achieve a similar transmission speed to this extent. Another important property of the protocol is the fully equal transmission right in both directions. The reason for this is the possibility for both controllers to start a communication, as independent asynchronous data transmission is possible in our architecture. However, this results in the need for a full duplex transmission or the presence of a flow control between the two controllers, as no data shall be lost during transmission. These three aspects are the essential prerequisites for the transfer protocol.

3.2 Communication Protocols

With this information, some already well-established communication protocols can be elaborated and compared to each other. Communication protocols are sufficiently available, all having different advantages and disadvantages compared to each other. Examples for well-established communication interfaces, used by embedded devices in our daily life, are *UART*, *I²C*, *SPI*, *CAN* or *Ethernet*. Besides those, there are a lot of proprietary communication protocols, which are specially adapted to an application by the developer of a device. Besides the aspect that it is difficult to get access to these proprietary interfaces, we have decided to use and extend a widespread protocol to make it available for a wider range of microcontrollers.

As already mentioned, Ethernet is not included in the evaluation due to the insufficient amount of hardware-modules on a single MCU. If it was possible to connect the controllers via several Ethernet networks, this would be the preferred solution for our problem. To compare the well-established interfaces, some characteristics of them have to be clarified. This includes transmission direction and the usage of a clock signal.

Transmission Variants. Transmission protocols can be subdivided according to their possible transmission directions in relation to the time course. There are two different types of transmission types which can be considered for our application. They are called *Half-Duplex* and *Full-Duplex*. Half-Duplex describes the possible data flow in both directions, but not at the same time. This means that a message transmission between controller 1 and controller 2 can only take place in one direction at a time, which would be a clear limitation in our system. Full-Duplex on the other hand allows transmission in both directions at the same time. To make this possible, the transmission is usually realized on two different channels (lines). UART and SPI offer a Full-Duplex transmission, while I^{2}C and CAN are Half-Duplex due to restrictions caused by fewer lines.

Clock Line. Next to the transmission direction, the protocols can also be divided into the groups *asynchronous* and *synchronous*. The difference here is the presence or absence of a clock line. This means that with synchronous protocols there is an additional line over which a clock signal is transmitted. It is always generated by one of the communication partners and read by the others. A valid data bit can then be generated and detected at the falling or rising edge of the clock line. This allows independent operation of the two controllers and simultaneously synchronous data transmission, because edge sampling is one way of resynchronizing the transmission. When using an asynchronous interface, a valid data bit has to be detected by a specified bit length. The critical part with asynchronous protocols is, that the controllers have to work synchronously during a transmission. When the internal processing clock of the controllers and with that the calculation of the bit length gets out of sync, a reliable detection of the bit states can no longer be guaranteed. This effect gets worse when transmitting large messages. It also results in the fact that asynchronous protocols usually do allow a lower maximum transfer rate than synchronous protocols. While UART and CAN are asynchronous protocols, SPI and I^{2}C belong to the category of synchronous protocols. A further detailed comparison of several serial communication protocols can also be found at [2]. We have summarized the attributes described in this chapter in Table 1, including the four presented communication protocols:

Next to the comparison of the already mentioned aspects, it is also possible to compare the energy consumption. Solheim et al. [6] have done exactly that with I^{2}C and SPI. They found out that I2C has a higher energy consumption than SPI and assume that the necessary pull-up resistors for the I^{2}C bus are the reason for this.

Table 1. Comparison of the attributes of different communication protocols

	Transmission direction	Clock line
SPI	Full-Duplex	synchronous
I²C	Half-Duplex	synchronous
UART	Full-Duplex	asynchronous
CAN	Half-Duplex	asynchronous

3.3 Selected Communication Interface

The previous section shows clear advantages of SPI in comparison to the other interfaces presented. The higher transmission speed, the Full-Duplex attribute and the low energy consumption of SPI has led to the decision to use this interface in our system.

The well-established Serial Peripheral Interface was originally designed by Motorola Inc. to realize a fast, robust and synchronous data transmission between a single master and several slaves [7]. With this transmission protocol, the master always is the initiator of a message transfer, while a slave can only send an answer to a prior sent request. Furthermore, the master is generating the clock signal and with that the possibility of synchronizing the controllers. This concept fitted most implementations in the embedded world so far, because usually circuits had a single microcontroller which represented an intelligent unit, while all other integrated circuits have just been passive and non-intelligent (e.g. RaspberryPi[1], BeagleBoneBlack[2]). However, this method cannot fulfill our requirements of equally distributed communication rights between two microcontrollers. The one-sided initiation possibility always results in one of the controllers not being able to start a communication, which is not suitable for the in this paper described task. A consequence of this fact is the extension of the serial peripheral interface, while other attributes of the interface do already fit pretty good into our task.

Additionally Tongsan et al. [10] provide a software-defined inter-processor communication for embedded systems. They suggest to realize a software layer with a well-defined API to make the controlled hardware exchangeable. We have decided to use and integrate this technology into our system in order to remain flexible for possible extensions or changes as SPI still has its downsides.

4 Implementation of the Communication

After describing the theoretical background of the communication presented in this paper, we go on to the actual implementation. To do so, we briefly present aspects of the research project and clarify some necessary details of the specific controllers.

---

[1] https://www.raspberrypi.org/.

[2] https://beagleboard.org/black.

4.1   Context of the Research Project

The research project, for which this inter-controller communication was developed, essentially consists of the three microcontrollers, which do implement the task separation of security protocol and network stack. In the context of the project, the TLS protocol for the security mechanism with an underlying TCP connection is used. This is depicted in Fig. 3. The three controllers are of the type STM32H7[3], which provide many interfaces established in the embedded world, but, like already mentioned, just a single Ethernet interface. In theory, other MCUs would fit into our project, but we have chosen this one, as it has a high transmission speed Serial Peripheral Interface compared to other controllers. Nevertheless, future developments on other controllers should remain possible.

Like mentioned in the beginning of this paper, the main aspect of this multi-controller architecture is the separation of the security protocol from the network stack. The security protocol used in the project is *Transport Layer Security* (TLS) 1.2[4], implemented by the open source project *mbedTLS*[5], along with the network stack *LightweightIP*[6] licensed under the BSD license. For the MCUs the real-time kernel (version 10.3.1) *FreeRTOS*[7] for resource constrained systems with custom developed low level drivers are used, because they offer a smaller attack surface than e.g. a whole *Linux-distribution*, which has a higher amount of security vulnerabilities.

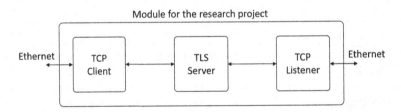

Fig. 3. Task separation of the currently developed research project

4.2   Transmission Speed

The MCU used in our system can run an internal clock speed of up to 480 MHz. This allows us to use the full SPI transmission speed of up to 133 MHz as master [1, p. 193], which results in the fact, that we should be able to realize the aspired 100 MBit/s transmission speed mentioned in Sect. 3. However, it is still necessary to extend the interface, as not all attributes specified are fulfilled by standard SPI.

---

[3] https://www.st.com/resource/en/datasheet/stm32h743bi.pdf.
[4] https://tools.ietf.org/html/rfc5246.
[5] https://tls.mbed.org/download.
[6] https://savannah.nongnu.org/projects/lwip/.
[7] https://www.freertos.org/index.html.

4.3   Necessary Connections of the Standard SPI

A standard serial peripheral interface has four lines to connect two communication partners. Those lines are the *Clock* (CLK), *Master Out Slave In* (MOSI), *Master In Slave Out* (MISO) and *Chip Select* (CS - sometimes called *Slave Select* (SS)). The last one is necessary when SPI is used as a bus system, where more than two controllers span the communication network. This is not intended for our project as we do only have two controllers. The resulting Point-To-Point (PTP) connection makes this line unnecessary for our concept.

4.4   Equal Transmission Rights

Another special characteristic, which is used within our system, is the so called unconventional *Multimaster SPI*. Using this setting, we do not have a distinct master of the SPI bus, like it is described in Sect. 3. Instead, the master of the communication is exchangeable to be always the transmitter of a message. At the same time, the receiver of data always has to be the SPI slave. This idea is visualized in Fig. 4. The advantage of this principle is an *equal transmission right* for both controllers, in contrast to the one-sided transmission right with normal SPI.

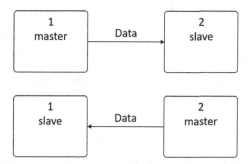

Fig. 4. Distribution of the SPI master attribute for the transmission of data

Simultaneously, when data is always transmitted by the master, there is no need for the Master In Slave Out line, as data will always be put on the *Master Out Slave In* line. This means, the only two connections necessary of the standard SPI communication are the CLK and MOSI lines, which are both controlled by the SPI master and read by the SPI slave. Using this method, the two controllers are always in SPI slave mode, as long as they do not want to transmit data themselves. If they again want to transmit a message, they switch to master mode and write to the lines. The downside of this concept is that there is no longer a Full-Duplex communication possible, as we do only have one line left for data transmission. Furthermore, it needs a kind of flow control to negotiate the transfer right for the prevention of a concurrent writing on the lines.

4.5 Flow Control

While two of the four original SPI lines were removed, additional lines for querying and confirming the transmission right have to be added. These lines get the names *Request To Send* (RTS) and *Clear To Send* (CTS), which are both implemented as *active low*. As the names suggest, the RTS signal of one controller is used to query the right for a transmission to the other controller. The second controller can then allow a transmission via its CTS line. To fully enable this functionality for both controllers, four pins are required, two inputs and two outputs each. The connection principle and line directions (input/output) is shown in Fig. 5. The result of these pins is a *flow control* of the data sent between the two controllers.

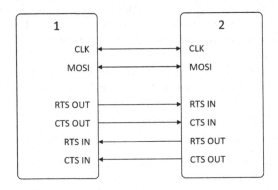

Fig. 5. Connection between the two controllers with additional RTS and CTS input and output lines

Starting a Communication. The procedure depicted in Fig. 6 is required to start a communication. Whenever there is no communication ongoing on the bus, a controller can request a transmission to its communication partner by pulling down its RTS output line. The request can be accepted by the communication partner by simply pulling its own CTS output, which is connected to the CTS input of the requesting controller, to low. This simple principle guarantees that both controllers are set correctly for the next transmission. After this sequence, the SPI master can initiate the transmission by generating a clock signal and putting the corresponding bit sequence onto the MOSI line. At the same time, the SPI slave will read a new bit for every rising edge on the clock pin. Both communication partners do have the information that there is a transmission ongoing due to the flow control mechanism and therefore no data can get lost because of an concurrent write on the lines.

If the requested controller does not acknowledge the transmission with a pull down of its CTS line, an error handling of the message transmission must occur. This can for example be realized by pulling up the RTS line of the requesting

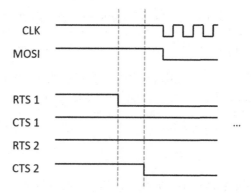

Fig. 6. Procedure for starting a communication

controller, with a following renewed pull down of the RTS line after a defined timeout.

The amount of transmitted bytes in a single transmission has to be set before the transfer itself. There are several ways to solve this task. We have simply added a header with a fixed length, which is sent prior to every payload data. With the constant amount of header bytes, both controllers can set their transmitting/receiving hardware for the right amount of bytes. The header then contains the amount of bytes which will be sent as data after the header block itself. This technique allows both controllers to always have information about the transmission size which is sent between them.

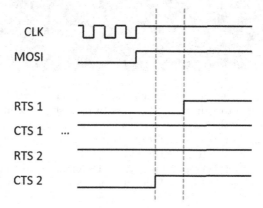

Fig. 7. Procedure for a finished communication

Finished Communication. A data transmission is finished or terminated with the sequence shown in Fig. 7. As both communication partners know the amount of sent bytes, the reading controller confirms the reception of the corresponding amount of bytes by pulling up its CTS line again. Following that, the sending controller pulls up its RTS line to signal the finished transmission. On the basis of this short sequence, both controllers are informed about the successful transmission.

After this sequence, the transmission of a single data block is finished and both controllers with all lines have reached their initial position. This means, both are ready for a new transmission to be set up.

5   Validation

The first implementation of the introduced protocol of this paper is already finished. We were able to connect two controllers using the multimaster SPI and the additional pins described in Sect. 4. Since we currently do not have a single PCB, to which the three controllers are attached, we are still working with patch wires that connect several NUCLEO boards from STM[8] with each other. This is the reason for using a lower transmission speed of 1 MHz, to avoid damage to the hardware by voltage overshoots on the lines.

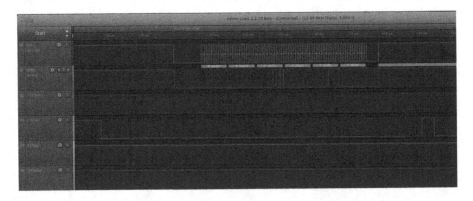

Fig. 8. Extract of an exemplary communication. Communication Partner 1 pulls its RTS line (orange) down to indicate a transmission request. Communication partner 2 replies to the request by pulling down its own CTS line (red) and with that accepting the following transmission. Subsequently the data transmission of the header (6 bytes) with the three 2-byte fields CRC, TYPE and LENGTH can be seen. The termination of the transmission includes the pull up of the CTS line from communication partner 2 with a following pull up of the RTS line of communication partner 1. (Color figure online)

Figure 8 shows the communication between our Point-To-Point connection using a logic analyzer. The described sequence of the corresponding RTS and CTS lines of the two controllers from Sect. 4 is well recognizable. In the figure

---

[8] https://www.st.com/resource/en/data_brief/nucleo-h743zi.pdf.

we do see a transmission of the mentioned header, which is 6 bytes long in our current implementation. The Header can easily be adapted to any other use case by just changing a few code lines in the software. Our message header is structured as follows. The first two bytes do include a to be implemented Cyclic Redundancy Check (CRC) for our communication. Bytes 3 and 4 include the message type. Those are adapted to the research project and in this case it means that payload data will be sent within the next block. The last two bytes include the data length of the following payload block. The sent data between the two controllers was the simple string *testing*. Every single character is sent as byte (ASCII) which results in the seven payload bytes depicted. The transmission of the data block would include another flow-control scheme described in Sect. 4, but this is not shown in the figure.

As we have not tested the higher transmission speed, this is just a *proof-of-concept*. We plan on making several tests when the PCB with all controllers is finished and ready to use. We will test especially, if we can actually reach the aspired data throughput of 100 MBit/s. However, this will take even more time for investigation and planning on testing and measuring methods and is therefore postponed to a future publication.

6   Conclusion

This paper presents an extended SPI communication interface using multimaster SPI, which was developed during a research project at the Technical University of Applied Sciences in Regensburg. It establishes a Point-To-Point connection of two MCUs, where both communication partners have a fully equal right to write on the bus. To prevent the loss of data because of a concurrent write on the lines, a flow control mechanism was implemented which allows the negotiation of the write permission. A prototype of the concept was successfully implemented, which constitutes the proof of concept. We believe that our prototype can be adopted to many other fields in the embedded world. Detailed load and performance tests are still missing, but will be presented and evaluated in a future publication.

References

1. STM32H742xI/G STM32H743xI/G, 32-bit Arm®Cortex®-M7 480MHz MCUs, up to 2MB Flash, up to 1MB RAM, 46 com. and analog interfaces, Rev. 7, April 2019. https://www.st.com/resource/en/datasheet/stm32h743bi.pdf. Accessed 12 Mar 2020
2. ElPROCUS: Overview on electronic communication protocols (2019). https://www.elprocus.com/communication-protocols/. Accessed 13 Jan 2020
3. Maemunah, M., Riasetiawan, M.: The Architecture of Device Communication in Internet of Things using inter-integrated circuit and serial peripheral interface method. In: 2018 4th International Conference on Science and Technology, ICST, pp. 1–4, August 2018. https://doi.org/10.1109/ICSTC.2018.8528663

4. Niedermaier, M., Merli, D., Sigl, G.: A secure dual-MCU architecture for robust communication of IIoT devices. In: 2019 8th Mediterranean Conference on Embedded Computing, MECO, pp. 1–5, June 2019. https://doi.org/10.1109/MECO.2019.8760188

5. Peng, D., Zhang, H., Li, H., Xia, F.: Development of the communication protocol conversion equipment based on embedded multi-MCU and Mu-C/OS-II. In: 2010 International Conference on Measuring Technology and Mechatronics Automation, vol. 2, pp. 15–18, March 2010. https://doi.org/10.1109/ICMTMA.2010.195

6. Solheim, T., Grannæs, M.: A comparison of serial interfaces on energy critical systems. In: 2015 Nordic Circuits and Systems Conference (NORCAS): NORCHIP International Symposium on System-on-Chip (SoC), pp. 1–4, October 2015. https://doi.org/10.1109/NORCHIP.2015.7364373

7. Hill, S.C., Jelemensky, J., Heene, M.R.: US Patent 4816996: Queued serial peripheral interface for use in a data processing system, March 1989. http://www.freepatentsonline.com/4816996.pdf. Accessed 13 Jan 2020

8. Szekacs, A., Szakaill, T., Hegykozi, Z.: Realising the SPI communication in a multiprocessor system. In: 2007 5th International Symposium on Intelligent Systems and Informatics, pp. 213–216, August 2007. https://doi.org/10.1109/SISY.2007.4342659

9. T. Frauenschläger, M. Dentgen, J. Mottok: Systemarchitektur eines Sicherheitsmoduls im Energiesektor, April 2020. https://www.haw-landshut.de/fileadmin/Hochschule_Landshut_NEU/Ungeschuetzt/ITZ_Cluster_Forschung/ClusterMST/Symposium-ESI/2020/Tagungsbandbeitraege/A1-3_OTH-Regensburg_Frauenschlaeger_ESI_2020.pdf. Accessed 12 Apr 2020

10. Tongsan, P., Piromsopa, K.: A software-defined inter-processor communication for embedded system. In: 2016 13th International Joint Conference on Computer Science and Software Engineering, JCSSE, pp. 1–6, July 2016. https://doi.org/10.1109/JCSSE.2016.7748848

Workshop on Computer Architectures in Space (CompSpace)

On the Evaluation of SEU Effects on AXI Interconnect Within AP-SoCs

Corrado De Sio, Sarah Azimi, and Luca Sterpone[(✉)]

Politecnico di Torino, Turin, Italy
{corrado.desio, sarah.azimi, luca.sterpone}@polito.it

Abstract. G-Programmable System-on-Chips offering the union of a processor system with a programmable hardware gave rise to applications that choose hardware acceleration to offload and parallelize computationally demanding tasks. Due to flexibility and performance they provide at low cost, these devices are also appealing for several applications in avionics, aerospace and automotive sectors, where reliability is the main concern. In particular, the interconnection architecture, and especially the AXI Interconnection for FPGA-accelerated applications, plays a critical role in these systems. This paper presents a reliability analysis of the AXI Interconnect IP Core implemented on Zynq-7000 AP-SoC against SEUs in the configuration memory of the programmable logic. The analysis has been conducted performing a fault injection campaign on the specific section of the configuration memory implementing the IP Core under test, which has been implemented within a benchmark design. The results are analyzed and classified, highlighting the criticality of the AXI Interconnect IP Core as a point of failure, especially for SEU-hardened hardware accelerator relying on mitigation techniques based on fine-grained and coarse-grained replication.

Keywords: AXI · Interconnecting · AP-SoC · FPGAs · SEUs · Fault injection

1 Introduction

In the last years, the advantages provided by the integration of a processor system and other components such as memories and programmable hardware on a single chip have become appealing for a wide range of applications within several domains. Especially, the reduction of cost and developing time along with the increasing of integration and flexibility is very interesting even in fields such as avionics, aerospace and automotive, where reliability is the main concern [1–3]. In particular, All-Programmable-System-on-Chips (AP-SoCs) combine on the same chip both a processor system and a Field Programmable Gate Array (FPGA), commonly referred as programmable logic. This architecture allows the designer to offload the processor system moving and parallelizing on the programmable logic the computationally demanding tasks as well as implementing customized hardware applications interacting with the processor and the other modules of the chips. Moreover, the time to design is shortened by the reuse of optimized IP blocks provided by vendors and third parties or developed through High-Level Synthesis (HLS) tools (even almost transparently to the user) [4, 5].

© Springer Nature Switzerland AG 2020
A. Brinkmann et al. (Eds.): ARCS 2020, LNCS 12155, pp. 215–227, 2020.
https://doi.org/10.1007/978-3-030-52794-5_16

Typically, the IP blocks are connected to each other and/or with the processor through an Advanced Microcontroller Bus Architecture (AMBA), mainly using an Advanced eXtensible Interface (AXI). However, the benefits provided by the on-chip SRAM-based FPGA come along with the reliability issues characterizing these devices. In particular, Single Event Upsets (SEUs) are a dominant source of error for these devices. SEUs can occur in the memory cells of FPGAs when they are exposed to ionizing radiation typical of the space environment, inducing undesired bitflips in the content of the memory cell struck by the ionized particle. However, the effect of SEUs are usually not permanent even if they may produce error states and outputs in the application. Though, when the corrupted memory cell belongs to the configuration memory of the FPGA it can undermine the correctness of the implemented design causing semi-permanent misbehaviors. Indeed, the behavior of the configurable hardware is defined by a bitstream downloaded in the configuration memory of the device where it programs the basic programmable elements of the FPGA (i.e. LUTs, Flip-Flops, DSP, PIP, etc.). Hence if the corrupted memory cell of the configuration layer was configuring a critical resource of the implemented design, the fault will affect the application until the configuration memory is rewritten with the correct content. To mitigate the SEUs induced errors, several techniques have been proposed, such as periodic refresh of the configuration memory to scrub accumulated faults (scrubbing) and replication of the resources to detect and correct misbehavior (e.g. Dual Module Redundancy, Triple Module redundancy).

In this work, we perform a reliability analysis of the AXI Interconnect IP Core by Xilinx for connecting one or more AXI memory-mapped master devices or cores to one or more memory-mapped slave devices or cores, usually used in the AP-SoC as standard mean to interconnect the processor system and the IP cores implemented on the programmable logic. At first, we proposed a benchmark design, subsequently implemented on an AP-SoC Zynq7000, based on the hardware acceleration paradigm. The reliability analysis is carried out through a fault injection campaign addressing the specific section of the configuration memory related to the AXI Interconnect block under test. The experimental results have been aggregated and analyzed to classify produced errors. Finally, the criticality of the AXI Interconnect IP Core as a point of failure even with the hardening of the hardware-accelerated core has been exposed in the conclusion.

The paper is organized into six sections. Section 2 is dedicated to related works, Sect. 3 reports the background of AP-SoC, reliability of programmable devices against SEUs and the AXI Interconnection IP Core by Xilinx. Section 4 describes the evaluation workflow, the design under test and fault injection platform. In Sect. 5, the performed fault injection campaign is described, and the obtained results are reported, classified and analyzed. To conclude, in Sect. 6, we discuss the results and future work.

2 Related Works

Related works focus mainly on the reliability of HLS generated IP Cores and their interfaces. In [6, 7], the reliability evaluation of AXI Interfaces implemented using Vivado HLS is reported. The authors evaluate the reliability of different versions of a custom IP core characterized by different interfaces and hardened solutions against multiple bit upsets. However, the adopted mitigation techniques are restricted to the HLS core, leaving aside the AXI Interconnection IP Core and only one of the proposed configurations implements a hardened AXI Interface (i.e. triplicated AXI-Stream Interface). Even though the interface is triplicated, the AXI Interconnect IP Core is still unhardened and not replicated. Most importantly, it is in common between the instances of the replicated interface. Indeed, AXI Interconnect IP Core is usually used also for mapping in memory of registers of initialization, status, and management of the AXI-DMA IP Core, that manage direct memory access between the memory and devices and cores implementing AXI4-Stream interfaces. The authors perform injections considering the AXI-DMA IP Cores and AXI Interconnect IP Core as a single module, reporting that it is a weak link even after interface replication. In [8], the authors perform analysis on the previously described configuration, reporting the same trend for replicated interfaces connected to a single unhardened AXI Interconnect IP Core.

3 Background

3.1 AP-SoC

The AP-SoC is an electronic device integrating a hard processor system and an FPGA into the same chip. Figure 1 shows the general scheme of the Zynq-7000 AP-SoC architecture. However, the block architecture of different AP-SoCs is very similar and they differ mainly for the I/Os, the characteristics of the processor systems as well as for the size and technology of the programmable logic. In this paper, we carry out our experiments and analyses on the Zynq-7000 AP-SoC which consists of a dual-core ARM Cortex-A9 processors and a 28 nm Series 7 programmable logic [9].

The presence of both processor system and programmable hardware enables the possibility to easily combine software programmability with custom hardware acceleration. An FPGA, and so the integrated programmable logic of the AP-SoC, consists of two layers named Application Layer and Configuration Layer. The Application Layer is composed of the resources available to the user to implement the desired hardware application. The resources are programmable logic elements, such as DSPs, LUTs, flip-flops, and programmable routing elements, such as Programmable-Interconnection-Points (PIPs). The logic functions of these resources and their interconnection are univocally defined by the content of the configuration memory. Indeed, the programmable logic is programmed by downloading and storing a bitstream into the configuration memory. The configuration memory is the main component of the Configuration Layer. Different sections of the configuration memory configure different sections and resources of the Application Layer. The bitstream can be generated by the user using vendor tools starting from the netlist of a target circuit. Additionally, the rise of HLS tools has made the development of core for hardware acceleration easier, providing optimization and interface management through high-level directives [10].

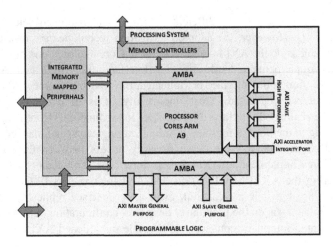

Fig. 1. General overview of Zynq-7000 AP-SoC.

3.2   SEUs in FPGAs Configuration Memory

Single Event Effects (SEEs) are a phenomenon that can occur when the silicon of an integrated circuit is hit by ionizing radiation and particles. The interaction between the silicon of the integrated circuits and the particles can cause several effects in the device, leading to displacement in the lattice of the material, transitory glitches of current, and change the status of bistable elements. In particular, SEUs are one of the most dominant SEEs [11, 12]. They are soft-errors caused by the change of the content of a memory cell when it is struck by a charged particle and so affecting the device functionality for a short period without undermining the device integrity. However, since FPGAs configuration memory data are not usually rewritten during device execution, an SEU corrupting a configuration memory cell will affect the application behavior permanently until the next power cycle or reconfiguration. Figure 2 shows an example of how an interconnection can be disabled by a bitflip in the configuration memory. In the figure, a charged particle striking the memory cell generates an open fault in the interconnection line that can be fixed only by rewriting the correct content in the configuration memory.

In order to mitigate the effects on the application layer induced by the SEUs in the configuration memory, several techniques have been proposed. In particular, SEU-hardening design techniques for FPGAs involve either replication at the gate level (fine-grained) or at the module level (coarse-grained) to detect and eventually correct the errors [13].

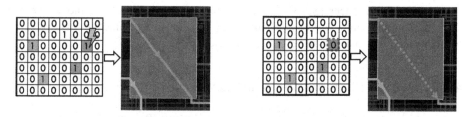

Fig. 2. SEUs affecting the configuration memory section programming a switch matrix.

3.3 AMBA and AXI Interconnect IP Core

AMBA is a standard developed by ARM for the interconnection of blocks in a system-on-chip. AMBA supports high-performance and high-frequency communication and includes the specification for AXI4 interfaces. In particular, AXI4, AXI4-Stream, and AXI4-Lite have been adopted by Xilinx for IP blocks interfacing and on-chip communication [14]. Additionally, as previously illustrated in Fig. 1, AXI ports for general purpose and high-performance communication, as well as the AMBA AXI interconnect, are present on Xilinx AP-SoCs.

The AXI Interconnect IP Core is a logic core provided in the Xilinx IP catalog to be implemented in the programmable logic [15]. It allows connecting AXI masters and AXI slaves modules transparently to the user accordingly with the interface characteristics of any IP block. The AXI Interconnect IP Core can be configured to support various communication models (i.e. 1-to-N, N-to-1, N-to-M).

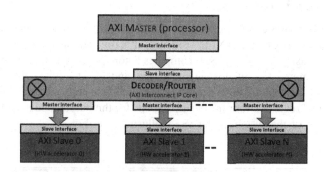

Fig. 3. Single master-multiple slaves AXI architecture.

In this paper, we will focus on the 1-to-N interconnect model, typical of hardware-accelerated systems architecture. In the 1-to-N model, a single master is present and it can access several memory-mapped slaves to use the AXI interconnection module. Figure 3 shows a schema of the 1-to-N communication model. Generally, in the hardware accelerator paradigm, the processor system acts as master, demanding computationally expensive tasks to the hardware modules (slaves). The slave modules can perform different operations if different tasks need to be accelerated on the hardware or perform the same operation on different data vector if a highly parallel computation is desired.

Additionally, the architecture can be used to perform the same function on the same data as mitigation techniques based on the replication, and compare obtained results from the hardware modules to detect and eventually correct errors.

4 Evaluation Platform and Workflow

For analyzing the reliability of the AXI Interconnect IP Core, we developed a benchmark design based on the hardware-accelerator paradigm. The hardware-accelerator module has been replicated emulating a dual with comparison approach for the detection of the misbehaviors in the programmable logic, with the detection check implemented on the processor side. The fault injection campaign has been carried out using a previously developed fault injection platform. The platform can perform automatized fault injection campaigns on the sections of the configuration memory related to the specific modules under test. Moreover, it provides insight into the structure of the configuration memory under test. The platform runs on a host computer connected to the AP-SoC managing of the generation of faulty configuration bitstream as well as of the download in the configuration memory. The test routine executing on the processor system stimulates the hardware accelerators with a randomly generated test vector. The outputs are compared by the processor system with the expected results and sent the execution report to the host computer. Then, the errors are classified accordingly with their characteristics and patterns. In the following subsections, the evaluation platform and the adopted workflow are reported in detail.

4.1 Benchmark Design

The benchmark design consists of a duplicated hardware accelerator connected to the processor system through the AXI Interconnect IP Core. The hardware accelerator has been developed using Vivado HLS. It computes a non-linear signature from four 32 bit fixed-point parameters (22 bits for the integer part and 10 bit for the decimal part). The custom IP core implements also an AXI4-Lite interface that provides access to six memory-mapped registers, four for the inputs, one for the output, and a control register. The architecture of the system under test is illustrated in Fig. 4.

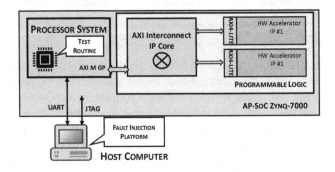

Fig. 4. The overall scheme of the evaluation platform architecture.

The processor system is connected to two instances of the hardware accelerator by the AXI Interconnect IP Core configured as single master-multiple slaves. Both the two hardware accelerators as well as the AXI Interconnect IP Core are implemented in the AP-SoC programmable hardware. Additionally, the AP-SoC is connected with a host computer. The host computer can configure the FPGA using the JTAG interface and can start the test routine running on the processor system through a serial connection with the processor. On the same channel, it can receive the report generated by the test routine.

4.2   Test Routine

The test routine running on the processor system consists of three parts: a preamble, a body, and an epilogue. In the preamble, the routine initializes the software data structures for using the hardware accelerator IPs and verify that they are in a correct state. In the body, the routine stimulates alternately each hardware with 1000 different inputs. For each input, it collects the result and verify its correctness or detects if the IP under test hangs. In the epilogue, the routine reports the status of the IP cores to the fault injection platform and signals the end of the test routine. During all the phases, the processor system reports the status of the test routine and IP cores executions results to the host computer which stores them for future analysis.

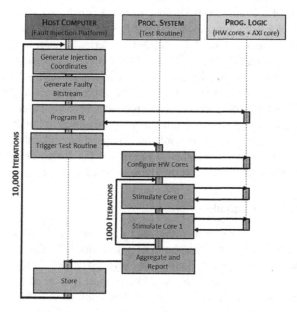

Fig. 5. Fault injection workflow.

4.3   Fault Injection Workflow

An enhanced version of the fault injection platform presented in [16] has been used for the fault injection campaign. PyXEL can interface with Vivado to retrieve the list of the resources used for implementing a specific hierarchical cell (e.g. the AXI Interconnect IP Core) and provide to the user the coordinates in terms of frames and bits where they are programmed. Moreover, it allows generating a visual representation of the content of the configuration memory facilitating the definition of the constraints for the location of the injections. Using these features, it has been possible to limit the fault injection coordinates to the configuration memory section implementing the specific module under test. The platform runs on the host computer and manages the experimental workflow. In detail, it controls the generation of the injection locations and injected bitstreams, the download of the faulty bitstreams in the configuration memory, the trigger of the test routine, and the collection of results. All the injections steps are automated and executed by the platform without user interaction. A representation of the described workflow is reported in Fig. 5

5   Experimental Analysis and Results

The reliability analysis of AXI Interconnect IP Core has been performed through a fault injection campaign. The AXI Interconnect IP Core has been implemented in the programmable logic of a Zynq-7000 AP-SoC within a benchmark design based on the hardware accelerator paradigm. Zynq-7000 AP-SoC integrates on the same chip a Dual-core ARM Cortex-A9 and a 28 nm Xilinx Series 7 programmable logic. The performed fault injection campaign emulates SEUs effect in the configuration memory through bitflips in the bitstream. The amount of injection has been selected accordingly with the target confidence and error margin. The coordinates of injection have been chosen in order to affect only the AXI Interconnect IP core under test. Results are reported in terms of overall error rate computed as the number of faulty bitstreams that generated an error in one or more on-hardware computation out of the amount of faulty bitstream tested. Additionally, incorrect behaviors of the design under test have been classified in different categories accordingly to their effect on the system.

5.1   Fault Injection Campaign

To perform an analysis of the errors produced by emulating radiation-induced SEUs in the configuration memory affecting the AXI Interconnect IP Core, a fault injection campaign has been carried out. We singularly injected 10,000 bitflips in the configuration memory section configuring the AXI Interconnect IP Core under evaluation. The configuration memory section selected for injection consists of 338,446 bits and spans over 196 frames belonging to a single clock region. Figure 6 shows the floorplanning of the implemented benchmark design as shown by the Vivado device view. The resources implementing the AXI Interconnect IP Core are represented in blue and highlighted by a yellow square. In this paper, we will focus on the 1-to-N interconnect model, typical of hardware-accelerated systems architecture. In the 1-to-N model, a single master is present and it can access several memory-mapped slaves to use the AXI interconnection module. Figure 3 shows a schema of the 1-to-N communication model. Generally, in the hardware accelerator paradigm, the processor system acts as master, demanding computationally expensive tasks to the hardware modules (slaves). The slave modules can perform different operations if different tasks need to be accelerated on the hardware or perform the same operation on different data vector if a highly parallel computation is desired. Additionally, the architecture can be used to perform the same function on the same data as mitigation techniques based on the replication, and compare obtained results from the hardware modules to detect and eventually correct errors. In the top-left corner is represented the processor system with the hard interconnections. Similarly, Fig. 7 reports a subsection (from the frame 1800 to the frame 7400) of the configuration memory as shown by the fault injection platform. The part to inject is highlighted by the yellow square.

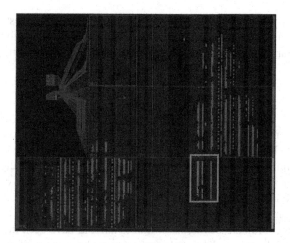

Fig. 6. The Vivado view of the design, and the part selected for the injection (yellow square). (Color figure online)

Please notice that a single frame spans only over a single clock region and frames belonging to the same clock region are sequential in the configuration bitstream and accordingly in the configuration memory view produced by PyXEL. Though, the sequence of clock region in the bitstream is out of order compared to the device view exposed by Vivado. Therefore, blocks in Fig. 7 result displaced compared to their position in Fig. 6.

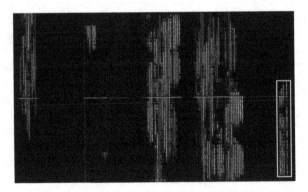

Fig. 7. A Section of the Configuration Memory view of the benchmark generated by PyXEL and the subsection selected for the injection campaign (yellow square). (Color figure online)

Accordingly with (1), 10,000 injections allow to conservatively estimate with 0.01 of margin error (e) and 95% confidence level the probability that a bitflip in the injected section of configuration memory can be a source of error for the system under test [17].

$$n = \frac{N}{1 + e^2 \times \frac{N-1}{t^2 \times p \times (1-p)}} \tag{1}$$

In particular, n is the minimum number of injections needed to meet the target margin of error e. N is the population size (i.e. the 338,446 injectable bits) and p is the estimated probability of a fault to result in an error. We conservatively chose p = 0.5 which maximizes the value of n. The parameter t is the cut-off point corresponding to the desired confidence level computed with respect to the Normal distribution. We choose a 95% confidence level for which the value of t is 1.96.

The injection coordinates, in terms of frames and bit, have been independently and randomly generated subsampling with replacement the section of the configuration memory under test. The fault injection campaign required about 25 h to complete.

5.2 Analysis of Results

As a result 306 out of the 10,000 faulty bitstream have generated errors in the circuit. The fault injection campaign showed an overall error rate of 3.06% with a 1% margin error and a 95% confidence interval. Please notice that only a subset of the resources related to the configuration memory section under test is used and consequently the number of bits with value 1 is significantly lower than the number of bits with value 0. Nonetheless, they are more likely to generate errors in the application when corrupted [18]. In detail, only 10% of the injected faults were 1 to 0 bitflips but 18% generated errors. Therefore about 50% of errors were generated by injections from 1 to 0 despite the asymmetry in the subsampling. Table 1 reports a summary of the injections and results they generated.

Table 1. Summary of SEUs injections and results

Injected fault	Amount	Generating errors
0-to-1	9155 (91.55%)	154 (1.6%)
1-to-0	845 (8.45%)	152 (17.9%)
Total	10 000 (100%)	306 (3.06%)

5.3 Classification of Faulty Results

The results have been classified accordingly with the issue they produced in the system. As reported in Table 2, more than 88% of errors provoked a failure of both the hardware accelerators. Please notice that even if for clarity faults are classified accordingly with the effect they generate on the communication with the hardware accelerator cores, given the injection process previously reported, all the faults are caused by a malfunction of the AXI Interconnect IP Core. In detail, in 49.35% of the detected misbehaviors, both the hardware accelerator cores cannot be initialized correctly or stopped to work after few successful communications. In 32.68% of the cases, both the hardware cores can be reached by the processor system but their computations are faulty. In 4.90% of cases, only one core out of two can be reached by the test routine but the results it returns are wrong. Only in the 11.76% of the faulty cases, we have one of the two core behaving correctly, while the other does not respond to the stimuli. The results are summarized in Table 2.

Table 2. Classification of system faults

Class	Amount
Both HW cores hang	151 (49.35%)
Both HW cores fail	100 (32.68%)
Single HW core fails	36 (11.76%)
HW core fails + HW core hang	15 (4.90%)
Others	4 (1.31%)
Total	306 (100%)

Additionally, it has been observed that when both the cores produce erroneous computation, the returned values are the same. Therefore, it is impossible to detect the fault without comparing them with the golden result even with the replication of the hardware accelerator.

6 Conclusions and Future Works

In this paper, we evaluated the reliability of AXI Interconnect IP Core against SEUs. The study has been carried out through a fault injection campaign in the configuration memory of Zynq-7000 programmable logic. Errors have been classified accordingly with their effect on the system and type. The analysis has shown as AXI Interconnection IP Core can be a source of errors for architecture exploiting hardware acceleration. Additionally, it has been shown as errors generated in the interconnection core can thwart mitigation techniques based on the replication of hardware modules. As future work, the design of a hardened the AXI Interconnect IP core needs to be performed to perform a comparative analysis

References

1. Flesch, G., Keymeulen, D., Dolman, D., Holyoake, C., McKee, D.: A system-on-chip platform for earth and planetary laser spectrometers. In: 2017 IEEE Aerospace Conference, Big Sky, MT, pp. 1–12 (2017)
2. Sabogal, S., George, A., Crum, G.: ReCoN: a reconfigurable CNN acceleration framework for hybrid semantic segmentation on hybrid SoCs for space applications. In: 2019 IEEE Space Computing Conference, SCC, Pasadena, CA, USA, pp. 41–52 (2019)
3. Shea, E., George, A.: OPIR video preprocessing and compression for on-board aerospace computing. In: 2017 IEEE National Aerospace and Electronics Conference, NAECON, Dayton, OH, pp. 142–148 (2017)
4. Vaidya, B., Surti, M., Vaghasiya, P., Bordiya, J., Jain, J.: Hardware acceleration of image processing algorithms using Vivado high level synthesis tool. In: 2017 International Conference on Intelligent Computing and Control Systems, ICICCS, Madurai, pp. 29–34 (2017)
5. Toft. J.K., Nannarelli, A.: Implementation of hardware accelerators on Zynq, Kgs. Lyngby: Technical University of Denmark. DTU Compute-Technical Report-2016, No. 7 (2016)
6. Benevenuti, F., Kastensmidt, F.L.: Reliability evaluation on interfacing with AXI and AXI-S on Xilinx Zynq-7000 AP-SoC. In: 2018 IEEE 19th Latin-American Test Symposium, LATS, Sao Paulo, pp. 1–6 (2018)
7. dos Santos, A.F., Tambara, L.A., Benevenuti, F., Tonfat, J., Kastensmidt, F.L.: Applying TMR in Hardware Accelerators Generated by High-Level Synthesis Design Flow for Mitigating Multiple Bit Upsets in SRAM-Based FPGAs. In: Wong, S., Beck, A.C., Bertels, K., Carro, L. (eds.) ARC 2017. LNCS, vol. 10216, pp. 202–213. Springer, Cham (2017). https://doi.org/10.1007/978-3-319-56258-2_18
8. Benevenuti, F., Kastensmidt, F.L.: Analyzing AXI Streaming Interface for Hardware Acceleration in AP-SoC Under Soft Errors. In: Voros, N., Huebner, M., Keramidas, G., Goehringer, D., Antonopoulos, C., Diniz, Pedro C. (eds.) ARC 2018. LNCS, vol. 10824, pp. 243–254. Springer, Cham (2018). https://doi.org/10.1007/978-3-319-78890-6_20
9. Xilinx, Inc.: Zynq-7000 All Programmable SoC: Technical reference manual, San Jose, CA, USA, User Guide, UG585, July 2018
10. Xilinx, Inc.: Vivado design suite user guide: high level synthesis, San Jose, CA, USA, User Guide, UG902, December 2018
11. Quinn, H.: Radiation effects in reconfigurable FPGAs. Semicond. Sci. Technol. **32**(4), 044001 (2017)
12. Du, B., et al.: Ultrahigh energy heavy ion test beam on Xilinx Kintex-7 SRAM-based FPGA. IEEE Trans. Nucl. Sci. **66**(7), 1813–1819 (2019)

13. Siegle, F., Vladimirova, T., Ilstad, J., Emam, O.: Mitigation of radiation effects in SRAM-Based FPGAs for space applications. ACM Comput. Surv. **47**(2), 34 (2015). Article 37

14. Xilinx, Inc.: Vivado Design Suite: AXI Reference Guide, San Jose, CA, USA, User Guide, UG1037, July 2017

15. Xilinx, Inc.: AXI Interconnect v2.1: LogiCORE IP Product Guide, San Jose, CA, USA, Product Guide, PG059, December 2017

16. Bozzoli, L., De Sio, C., Sterpone, L., Bernardeschi, C.: PyXEL: an integrated environment for the analysis of fault effects in SRAM-based FPGA routing. In: 2018 International Symposium on Rapid System Prototyping, RSP, Torino, Italy (2018)

17. Leveugle, R., Calvez, A., Maistri, P., Vanhauwaert, P.: Statistical fault injection: quantified error and confidence. In: 2009 Design, Automation & Test in Europe Conference & Exhibition, Nice, pp. 502–506 (2009)

18. De Sio, C., Azimi, S., Bozzoli, L., Du, B., Sterpone, L.: Radiation-induced single event transient effects during the reconfiguration process of sram-based FPGAs. Microelectro. Reliab. **100**, 113342 (2019). ISSN 0026-2714

Satellite Onboard Data Reduction Using a Risc-V Core Inside an RTG4-Based Data Processing Pipeline

Gasper Skvarc Bozic[⊠], Thomas Unterlinner, Tanja Eraerds,
Sabine Ott, and Markus Plattner

Max Planck Institute for Extraterrestrial Physics,
Giessenbachstr. 1, 85748 Garching, Germany
gaskvarc@mpe.mpg.de

Abstract. The Wide Field Imager (WFI) is one of two scientific instruments onboard the next generation European x-ray observatory ATHENA. It will orbit Lagrange point L2 and send the acquired science data to a single ground station with a downlink that is available for several hours once per day. The data rate of the downlink is a bottleneck, which limits the amount of science data that can be transferred.

Measurement data of the eRosita satellite which is in operation since mid of 2019 shows that a high radiation background generates parasitic sensor data that adds to the science data. In order to remove the parasitic data from the science data stream onboard, a Risc-V softcore processor implementation in the RTG4 FGPA has been studied. Depending on the observation scenario, the data rate is reduced by a factor of more than 50.

Within this article, we describe the WFI onboard processing architecture, the sensor effects on space radiation and the hard- and software architecture of the Risc-V softcore that can be implemented to reduce the data rate on board. Three test cases are defined and executed to verify the performance of the data reduction scheme.

Keywords: ATHENA · WFI · Risc-V · RTG4 · Real-time · Onboard processing

1 Real-Time Data Processing Onboard ATHENA WFI

The Wide-Field-Imager (WFI) is one of two science instruments onboard the next generation x-ray space telescope ATHENA (Advanced Telescope for High ENergy Astrophysics) [1]. Its camera system consists of four large and one fast sensor, sensitive in the energy range from 0.2 eV up to 10 keV. The sensors are based on DEPFET (DEpleted P-channel Field-Effect Transistor) technology, 2-dimensional arrays of 512×512 (large), and 64×64 (fast) pixels, respectively. The sensors are operated in parallel, independent from each other, in rolling shutter mode. This means that 511 (63) rows are active and record incoming x-ray photons while one row is readout. Since the detection principle shall also resolve the energy of each incoming x-ray photon, the sensors have to be read out at rates of more than 50 Mega-Pixel per second to avoid a pile-up.

© Springer Nature Switzerland AG 2020
A. Brinkmann et al. (Eds.): ARCS 2020, LNCS 12155, pp. 228–238, 2020.
https://doi.org/10.1007/978-3-030-52794-5_17

In order to achieve the pixel read-out rate, each sensor is read out with eight channels operated in parallel. The eight data streams of one sensor are processed in real-time parallel processing pipelines that are implemented inside a Microchip RTG4 FPGA. The processing steps of each pipeline are:

- Offset correction: Every pixel has its individual offset value that is subtracted from the current measurement value.
- Common Mode Correction: Variations in the read-out ASICs cause an offset value common to all values of one read-out line. This offset is subtracted from all 64 pixels of one channel.
- Event and Pattern Filter: The pixel (energy) values are compared to thresholds that span the valid energy range. Pixels within the valid range are flagged as "valid". In case several neighboring pixels show valid values, the pattern is analyzed [2].
- Event List Generator: Dependent on the operational mode, the valid events are selected and spatial coordinates, as well as timestamps, are added to them.

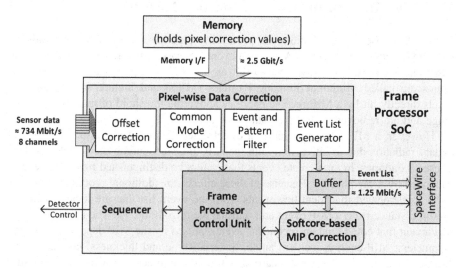

Fig. 1. Block diagram of FPGA (red: real-time processing pipeline, blue: softcore). (Color figure online)

All of these pipeline stages are based on pixel-wise data processing, i.e. each stage executes operations on the data stream of its detector channel without dependency on neighboring channels, see [3] for details. The output of the data processing pipeline is an Event List that includes all event data of the frame, i.e. coordinates of an event (pixel that was hit by x-ray photon), the energy (ADC value) and the time stamp (arrival time of the x-ray photon sampled with the frame rate). The event list of a frame is stored in an FPGA internal buffer (block RAM).

In addition to the real-time data processing pipeline, the FPGA accommodates

- a Sequencer block that generates all dynamic signals required for detector control in rolling shutter mode
- a Frame Processor Control Unit based on a finite state machine
- a Risc-V softcore that processes the event list (see Sect. 3)

The downlink data rate for a given satellite is limited. On the other hand, we want to transfers as much relevant science data to a ground station as possible. It is beneficial if the system allows it to do some data processing on the satellite itself and thus reduce the required downlink data rate. The described RTG4 FPGA processing pipeline already significantly reduces the science data rate. However, since RTG4 FGPA provides a flexible implementation environment, we investigated if the science data rate can be further reduced by implementing a Risc-V softcore for executing a Minimum Ionizing Particles (MIPs) exclusion algorithm.

2   Science Data Disturbance by Ionizing Particles

In the ideal case of observation, the processing pipeline can be adjusted to all the required observation scenarios. Additional events, however, are created in reality due to radiation that is existing in the halo orbit around L2. The particles that cause such events are called Minimum Ionizing Particles (MIPs) and include mainly protons. Pixels directly hit by a MIP receive energies above the threshold of maximum energy range and are removed within the data processing pipeline.

However, a MIP not only creates a direct detector hit but can also generate secondary radiation due to interaction with the structure surrounding the detector system. These secondaries, in turn, create events that cannot be distinguished from valid events generated by x-ray photons. Because of these effects, an additional processing step has to be implemented that identifies events from the event list that are located within a certain distance from a MIP event and remove them from the list. The area around the MIP event that could contain secondary events caused by the MIP depends on several parameters: MIP energy, incident angle, material (type and thickness) crossed by the MIP, etc. Geant4 simulations are carried out, taking into account these characteristics of incoming particles and the detector surroundings.

This simulation approach has been verified using data from the eRosita mission [4]. Although eRosita has a different type of sensor, the sensitivity regarding MIPs is comparable. Measurement results obtained by the eRosita cameras in orbit around Lagrange point L2 have been used for model correlation and yield an agreement within 10% between simulation and measurement results. Applying the same approach to ATHENA WFI with an adapted simulation model yields an average rate of 2 MIP/cm^2/s and an average count of 10 pixels that are hit by one MIP directly. This results in an average value of 0.41 MIP per frame of a large sensor and 10^{-4} MIP per frame of the fast sensor.

3 RISC-V Softcore Architecture and MIP Removal Algorithm

As described in Sect. 1, the real-time data processing is implemented in FPGA-based pipelines. Data from all pixels flow through the pipeline stages and additional information based on the processing stages is added in the form of flags. At the end of the pipeline, that Event List Generator selects the valid events and forwards them into an FPGA internal buffer memory. This is the place, where the raw data has been reduced by two to three orders of magnitude. Based on the nature of the task responsible for identifying the events within the defined region of a MIP as described in Sect. 2, it would be difficult to implement the required logic in the FPGA fabric. Therefore, a softcore microprocessor is used to perform the required task.

3.1 Softcore Microprocessor Architecture

Figure 2 depicts the softcore microprocessor architecture where blue and green blocks represent components implemented in the FPGA fabric. Whereas, red blocks represent components external to the FPGA. Green blocks indicate fabric interfaces with the physical world. The architecture is based on a 32-bit Risc-V CPU with a 32-bit AHB internal interconnect. For the design presented in this paper a Risc-V soft IP core (MiV_RV32IMA_L1_AHB) from Microsemi was used. This Risc-V soft IP core has a separate bus for memory and memory-mapped peripherals. The memory bus is connected to a DDR3 memory controller which interfaces the external DDR3 memory where program data is stored.

Several different peripherals were implemented. The most important is the dual-port SRAM with APB wrapper. This is the interface between the fabric parallel data pipeline and softcore microprocessor as depicted in Fig. 1. Other peripherals such as GPIO and UART are used for debugging purposes and provide an interface between the microprocessor and a PC. All peripherals are connected via the APB bus and through the AHB to APB bridge to the main interconnect. A second APB bus is used as an interface between the CoreABC processor and the memory controller. The CoreABC is a small co-processor used for external memory configuration and initialization. After power-up, certain configuration registers in the DDR3 external memory have to be configured.

The softcore microprocessor implementation was designed for the RTG4 target device with a system clock running at 50 MHz. The JTAG component included in the architecture enables the programming of the microprocessor and advanced debugging capabilities.

As an interface between fabric and microprocessor two options are possible. One is the dual-port SRAM and the other is FIFO buffers. At this point, dual-port memory was chosen as it simplifies testing. Currently, we do not have a dummy data generator that could fill the FIFO buffer and mimic the parallel data pipeline, because the interface between parallel data pipeline and softcore microprocessor is not yet completely defined. With SRAM we can write the generated event list at the beginning of program execution to the SRAM. The dual-port memory is connected to the APB peripheral bus for simplicity. In case the memory penalty is significant then the SRAM can be moved directly to the AHB bus and improve the performance as long as the burst transfer mode of the AHB bus is utilized.

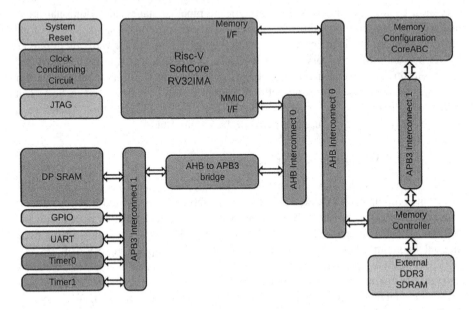

Fig. 2. Softcore microprocessor architecture with AHB internal interconnect. (Color fgure online)

3.2   Event List Structure

The input to the algorithm running on the Risc-V microprocessor is an Event List, which is the output of the frame processing pipeline. Its structure is shown in Fig. 3. For each frame, the Event List header is generated that contains the time stamp in the form of the frame counter and additional housekeeping data e.g. threshold values used in the pipeline stages. Each event is represented as one line that contains amongst others the following data:

- Energy value (bits number 36 down to 23): The 14-bit output of the ADC represents the energy of the pixel
- Line address (bits number 22 down to 14): The 9-bit value corresponds to line number 0–511
- Pixel address (bits number 13 down to 5): The 9-bit value corresponds to the column number 0–511
- Flags (bits number 4 down to 0): Information gained by the pipeline stages and added to each event indicating, for example, the results of threshold comparison.

Figure 3 illustrates the event list and shows a frame. The blue dots represent pixels illuminated with x-ray photons.

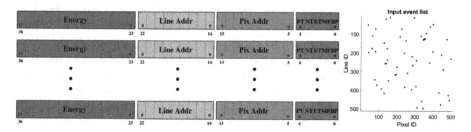

Fig. 3. Event list format and example frame. (Color figure online)

3.3 MIP Pixel Exclusion

Since the input to the algorithm is already a reduced dataset in from of an Event List it is not beneficial to reconstruct the frame in the microprocessor as this introduces substantial memory penalty and usage. Therefore, the generated Event List is considered as data point dataset. Each MIP event is represented by multiple pixels where each pixel corresponds to one data point in the generated Event List. When the Event List is passed to the processor, the processor does not know which event pixels belong to one MIP event even though this would be obvious if one would plot the data points. Therefore, it is necessary to perform a clustering algorithm in order to identify different MIP events and the number of them. However, because prior to clustering the number of clusters is unknown a hierarchical clustering algorithm or some other form of non-parametric clustering algorithm is needed.

The algorithm presented in this paper uses the DBSCAN clustering algorithm [5] since it is a non-parametric density-based clustering algorithm and suits this application well. Once all the clusters or rather MIP event groups (tracks) are identified it can be determined if other events occurred within the MIP event region. In order to do this, the region around each MIP event has to be defined. In our case, an elliptical exclusion area around the MIP tracks was chosen. First, a centroid is calculated for each cluster and other ellipse parameters based on mathematical equations presented in [6]. Based on these parameters an ellipse border is computed and with it the region around the MIP. Afterward, the non-flagged events can be checked if they fall into any of the computed regions if they do, they are flagged which indicates that they belong to a MIP event as explained in Sect. 2.

The algorithm depicted in Fig. 4 was first tested as a MATLAB script where one can also visualize all the results and prove the algorithm correctness. After successful test with MATLAB scripts the algorithm was rewritten in C to test it on the Risc-V microprocessor.

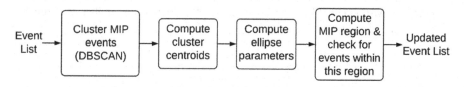

Fig. 4. Secondaries detection algorithm flow diagram.

Prior to described algorithm above, we used a simpler algorithm for detecting MIP events. It is based on an insertion sort algorithm with time complexity of $O(n^2)$, which is comparable to the worst-case time complexity $O(n^2)$ of the DBSCAN algorithm. Based on the results from Tables 1 and 2 it was determined that an algorithm with time complexity $O(n^2)$ is a feasible solution for our target application. However, the algorithm based on insertion sort had a significant drawback as it could not distinguish between two MIP events with either the same Line addresses (y coordinate) or the same Pixel addresses (x coordinate). Therefore, a new algorithm for identifying MIP events was needed.

Table 1. Performance for processing one event list with one MIP event (insertion sort)

Number of events	Flagged events	Cycles	Execution time [ms]
750	189	382500	7,65
500	113	256700	5,10
350	22	171100	3,42

Table 2. Performance for processing one event list with multiple MIP events (insertion sort)

Number of events	Flagged events	Cycles	Execution time [ms]
780	206	515900	10,30
505	101	328100	6,97
350	22	202400	4,04

As can later be seen from results in Sect. 4, the current C implementation of the new algorithm is nowhere near required timing constraints. However, we are confident that with optimized range query function we can achieve similar results as we did with the insertion sort based algorithm, if not better.

4   Experimental Results

Three different scenarios have been tested for the new algorithm:

- Test 1 has been performed with a constant number of ~ 50 events with an increasing number of MIP events (with an average of 10 pixels per MIP).
- Test 2 always included 3 MIP events per frame and the number of events has gradually been increased.
- Test 3 has been performed with a constant number of ~ 50 events, a constant number of MIP events (3 MIPs per frame), and an increasing number of pixels per MIP event.

Test 2 and test 3 demonstrate the timing complexity of the DBSCAN clustering algorithm which is expected to be $O(n^2)$ in the worst case, result of using a linear search. Algorithm is affected by the Event List growth and it does not matter which number of events increases be it either MIP or regular events. However, test 2 has worse performance as significant number of regular events introduces additional timing penalty because of another linear search in the last block of the algorithm depicted in Fig. 4.

It should be pointed out that these results can be affected by the size of a MIP region since more events can fall into a region. However, this is only significant when a large number of events are present in a frame, and more events need to be processed. Moreover, for each test case, a random Event List was generated.

Figure 5 depicts the result from the measurement of the execution time of the function executing algorithm as described in Fig. 4. The execution time linearly increases with the increasing number of MIP events. The dotted trendline (linear approximation) also confirms this behavior.

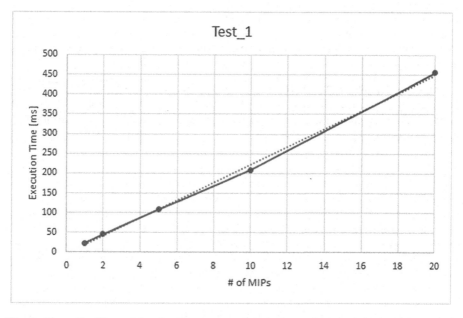

Fig. 5. Execution Time of the algorithm compared to the increasing number of MIP events per frame

Figure 6 depicts the relation between the execution time and the increasing number of events per frame. As seen by the dotted trendline the execution time follows an $O(n^2)$ the worst-case timing complexity characteristic in the case of the DBSCAN algorithm.

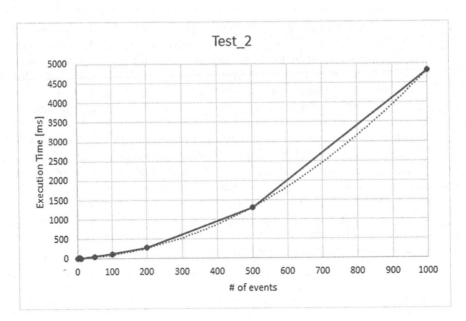

Fig. 6. Execution Time of the algorithm compared to the increasing number of events per frame

Figure 7 depicts the measurement result when the number of pixels per MIP event is increased. As seen by the dotted trendline the execution time follows an $O(n^2)$ the worst-case timing complexity characteristic in the case of the DBSCAN algorithm.

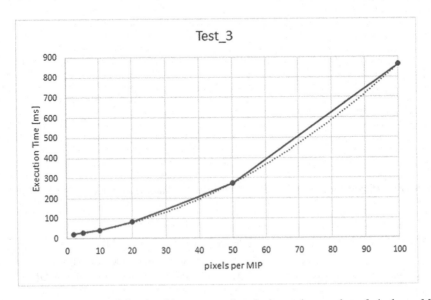

Fig. 7. Execution Time of the algorithm compared to the increasing number of pixels per MIP

Figure 8 depicts visual results from the algorithm described in Sect. 3.3. Generated Event List is shown in the left figure where events are represented by blue dots. Generated Event List is plotted in a 512 × 512 pixel frame in order to have a visual representation of the sensor array. The figure on the right depicts detected MIP events with their elliptic regions. The color of MIP events is not important and it is there just to visually distinguish between different MIP events. Two sizes of ellipse regions are shown, where smaller regions marked with the red color include fewer events from the Event List as opposed to larger regions marked with blue color.

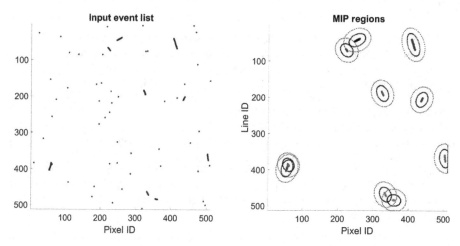

Fig. 8. Visualization of the algorithm results described in Sect. 3.3. (Color figure online)

5 Conclusion

In this paper, a use case of a softcore microprocessor in space application was presented. In particular, a MIP pixel exclusion algorithm running on a Risc-V softcore microprocessor as part of the WFI onboard processing architecture. The softcore microprocessor architecture was based on a 32-bit Risc-V RV32IMA CPU with a 32-bit AHB internal interconnect.

Two different approaches were tested for the MIP pixel exclusion algorithm. One based on an insertion sort algorithm, which proved that algorithms with time complexity $O(n^2)$ are a feasible solution for our application. However, it turned out it is not suitable for all scenarios. Therefore, a second more robust algorithm concept based on data clustering DBSCAN algorithm was presented. Its executions times were far off from required timing constraints. The most significant drawback of the current DBSCAN based algorithm is the range query function. Currently it is implemented as naïve linear search of the Event List which results in saver timing penalty and thus making the DBSCAN algorithm of timing complexity $O(n^2)$. Mover, another search for elements is performed in the final stage of the new algorithm which introduces additional timing penalty.

Nevertheless, with DBSCAN having a worst-case time complexity of $O(n^2)$ we are confident that with an optimized range query function based on r*-tree or kd-tree data indexing structure we can achieve similar results, if not better, as with the insertion sort based algorithm. With the use of data indexing structure the expected timing complexity of DBSCAN is $O(n * log(n))$.

Our next steps are to write an optimized C code for the range query, run the test on the Risc-V softcore microprocessor, and see if our speculations are correct.

References

1. Nandra K., et al.: The hot and energetic universe – a white paper presenting the science theme motivating the ATHENA + Mission. http://www.the-athena-x-ray-observatory.eu
2. Schanz, T., et al.: A fast one-chip event-preprocessor and sequencer for the Simbol-X LowEnergy detector. Nucl. Instrum. Methods Phys. Res. A **624**, 392–395 (2010)
3. Plattner M., et al.: WFI electronics and on-board data processing. In: Proceedings SPIE 9905, Space Telescopes and Instrumentation 2016: Ultraviolet to Gamma Ray, 99052D, 11 July 2016. https://doi.org/10.1117/12.2235375
4. Meidinger, N., et al.: Development of the focal plane PNCCD camera system for the X-ray space telescope eROSITA. Nucl. Instrum. Methods Phys. Res. A **624**, 321–329 (2010)
5. Ester, M., Kriegel, H.P., Sander, J., Xu, X.: A density-based algorithm for discovering clusters. In: KDD-96 Proceedings, pp. 226–231. AAAI (1996)
6. Haralick, R.M., Shapiro, L.G.: Computer and Robot Vision, vol. 1. Addison-Wesley Publishing Company, Boston (1992)

Workshop on Parallel Systems and Algorithms (PASA)

Accelerating Real-Time Applications with Predictable Work-Stealing

Florian Fritz[(✉)], Michael Schmid, and Jürgen Mottok

Laboratory for Safe and Secure Systems - LaS³,
Regensburg University of Applied Sciences, Regensburg, Germany
{florian2.fritz,michael3.schmid,juergen.mottok}@oth-regensburg.de

Abstract. Modern compute architectures often consist of multiple CPU cores to achieve their performance, as physical properties put a limit on the execution speed of a single processor. This trend is also visible in the embedded and real-time domain, where programmers are forced to parallelize their software to keep deadlines. Additionally, embedded systems rely increasingly on modular applications, that can easily be adapted to different system loads and hardware configurations.

To parallelize applications under these dynamic conditions, often dispatching frameworks like Threading Building Blocks (TBB) are used in the desktop and server segment. More recently, Embedded Multicore Building Blocks (EMB²) was developed as a task-based programming solution designed with the constraints of embedded systems in mind.

In this paper, we discuss how task-based programming fits such systems by analyzing scheduler implementation variants, with a focus on classic work-stealing and the libraries TBB and EMB². Based on the state of the art we introduce a novel resource-trading concept that allows static memory allocation in a work-stealing runtime holding strict space and time bounds. We conduct benchmarks between an early prototype of the concept, TBB and EMB², showing that resource-trading does not introduce additional runtime overheads, while unfortunately also not improving on execution time variances.

Keywords: Real-time · Parallel programming · Work-stealing

1 Introduction

Modern processors rely on multiple cores and accelerating hardware to achieve their performance, as the execution speed of a single processor is physically limited by heat output and power draw. Consequently, developers have to explicitly parallelize their applications to achieve faster execution. Doing this manually can be tedious and error prone, therefore most industries have adopted dispatching frameworks to help with this process. The key idea behind these libraries is that programmers only declare how their work can be split up into individual tasks, while the framework's runtime schedules the work dynamically

© Springer Nature Switzerland AG 2020
A. Brinkmann et al. (Eds.): ARCS 2020, LNCS 12155, pp. 241–255, 2020.
https://doi.org/10.1007/978-3-030-52794-5_18

onto available system resources. Common examples are Intel's Threading Building Blocks (TBB), Microsoft's Parallel Patterns Library (PPL) and the Open Multi-Processing (OpenMP) standard. While task-based programming is a de facto standard in desktop applications and scientific computations, these frameworks are still uncommon for embedded systems due to their highly dynamic nature. A first contender entering this domain is Embedded Multicore Building Blocks (EMB^2), by specifically focusing on requirements like task priorities and static-memory allocation.

In sight of these various implementation variants, we investigate how different scheduling approaches and their concrete implementations affect their suitability for high performance embedded systems. Specifically, we take interest in using task-based programming to gradually parallelize individual real-time applications (Sect. 2). For this, we first recapitulate the commonly used work-stealing algorithm [3], draw implications for the predictability on embedded devices and discuss what challenges practical implementations face. As two examples, we study the internals of TBB, a representative of modern desktop implementations, and EMB^2, a contender specifically for the embedded space (Sect. 3). We find that work-stealing fits our use-case from a theoretical standpoint, but no implementation guarantees static memory usage and strict theoretical bounds. Following this, we introduce a novel resource-trading algorithm that enables us to implement a C++ work-stealing library with static memory allocation and strict theoretical bounds (Sect. 4). Finally, we analyze how the three libraries perform on an octa-core ARM system. We conduct tests on both an isolated and multiprogrammed system using small problem sizes to evaluate how viable the frameworks are for embedded real-time applications (Sect. 5).

2   System Model and Requirements Context

We consider the acceleration of applications executing on an operating system (OS) scheduling threads onto a symmetric multicore processor using a real-time schedule, e.g. preemptive fixed priority scheduling. Each application[1] τ_i periodically performs work by releasing a sequence of threads to be executed by the OS. To be applicable for real-time and embedded use-cases, the applications must guarantee predictable time and memory bounds, as unexpected deadline misses are not acceptable.

Looking at a single application τ_i, we consider the process of gradually parallelizing it. For this a programmer can use the aforementioned dispatching frameworks to introduce sections of task-based parallelism to speed up compute intensive algorithms. This process breaks down the algorithms into a series of individual tasks, resulting in a Directed Acyclic Graph (DAG) where vertices denote computations and edges represent ordering constraints between them. Figure 1 shows a small example DAG, further discussed in the following section.

---

[1] Usually in real-time literature applications are referred to as tasks and threads are called jobs, however, this conflicts with the notation in task-based programming.

The dispatching framework creates a pool of P_i worker threads within the application τ_i to execute the tasks. A variety of techniques exist to schedule the DAG cooperatively among this thread pool. A simple method is to distribute the work statically. However, this can result in poor load balancing for irregular workloads, or in multiprogrammed systems if single workers are preempted. On the other hand, there exist a variety of dynamic dispatching algorithms which aim to improve load balancing. Variations include, among others, list scheduling (GNU OpenMP), work-sharing (EMB^2) and work-stealing (TBB).

From the point of view of the OS, applications are therefore following a fork-join structure. Each application starts with a single, main thread, until a parallel algorithm is executed on a pool of P_i worker threads (fork). When the workers have completed all tasks, the application joins back into a single serial thread. The fork-join procedure can be repeated multiple times. This leads to a two level scheduler: the OS preemptively schedules jobs onto physical processor cores, the application internally executes tasks cooperatively on the worker threads.

3   State of Task-Based Programming

In theory, list schedulers provide optimal bounds for distributing task-based programs. However, they suffer from memory contention in real implementations which can lead to bad average case runtimes. Because of this, work-stealing variants have prevailed instead. The idea is to associate each processor with its own deque (double ended queue) in which tasks are pushed and popped locally as long as the worker thread does not run out of tasks. The processor only interacts with other deques when it has no more work, in which case it tries to steal work from another processors deque.

Work-stealing therefore acts mostly decentralized, avoiding contention on shared data structures like a central task queue. This makes it perform well on modern microarchitectures, both in theory [3] and practice [2,10]. However, implementation details can significantly affect memory usage and runtime properties of work-stealing frameworks. To assess the use of such libraries in real-time systems, we first recapitulate the proven bounds of classic work-stealing and discuss how it maps to practical libraries implementing it. Next, we analyze the schedulers used in TBB and EMB^2, to show where practical task-parallel libraries are heading in general and in the embedded space.

3.1   Classic Work-Stealing

Blumofe proves the first good space and time bounds for fully strict computations [3]. Figure 1 shows part of a strict DAG with three potentially parallel computation strands shaded in gray. Dotted edges are called spawn edges and allow the control flow to diverge, curved edges are data dependencies between strands of execution, enforcing ordering of tasks. Parallel strands form a parent-child relationship, where a parent spawns a child. For a computation to be fully strict, data dependency edges must only go from child to parent.

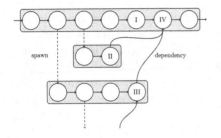

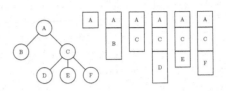

Fig. 1. DAG of computation in classic work-stealing

Fig. 2. Invocation tree (left) and resulting call-stacks (right)

While at first seeming restrictive, strict computations are those that are intuitively well-formed, i.e. spawning a child strand corresponds to an asynchronous subroutine call. Listing 1 shows an example program that could result in a DAG similar to Fig. 1, spawning two potentially parallel sub procedure calls in lines 5 and 6, then synchronizing to wait for their completion in line 8. The API shown in the example is known as nested fork-join parallelism [7] and implemented in libraries like Cilk [5] and TBB [8]. Interpreting parallelism as asynchronous subroutine calls allows us to view the execution as walking over an invocation tree (Fig. 2), where a serial execution is a preorder walk of the tree and parallel execution schedules walk the tree asynchronously[2].

In the randomized work-stealing algorithm there are four main events when worker threads interact with the scheduler and diverge from this serial execution [3]: (1) spawning, i.e. pushing a task to the bottom of their local deque; (2) enabling a blocked task, i.e. being the last predecessor in the DAG to finish; (3) executing the last vertex in a string of execution; (4) stealing, i.e. running out of local work and stealing uniformly at random from the top of other deques.

To analyze the time and space requirements of invocation trees under work-stealing variants, three properties are of interest: (1) S_1 is the space required for a serial execution, which is the peak memory usage when run on a single thread. In the invocation tree on the left side of Fig. 2, this corresponds to the deepest stack on the right side (A, C, D); (2) T_1 is the total work in the DAG and equals execution time on a single thread; (3) T_∞ is the critical, or longest path in the DAG. It is equal to the execution time on unlimited workers, as the ordering constraints of the critical path force it to execute serially.

---

[2] Fork-Join parallel APIs and invocation trees hide details compared to fully-strict DAGs and have not the same expressive power. However, we use them to simplify our arguments and all proofs hold on the DAG, too.

```
1   int fib(int n) {
2     if (n <= 1) return n;
3
4     int a, b;
5     spawn([&]() { a = fib(n - 1); });
6     spawn([&]() { b = fib(n - 2); });
7
8     sync();
9     return a + b;
10  }
```

Listing 1: Example of a nested fork-join parallelism API.

Following the above rules and definitions, one can show that the active part of the parallel invocation tree, i.e. all tasks that are executing, waiting for predecessors or enqueued in a deque, have the busy-leaves property [3]: each leaf of the active invocation tree has a processor working on it. When run on P_i worker threads, at most P_i branches of the tree can be active, as each branch has a leaf and therefore one of the processors working on it. Each branch uses a maximum of S_1 memory, leading to the space bound in Eq. (1).

$$S_P \leq S_1 P_i \tag{1}$$

The proof leading to the time bound of randomized work-stealing uses a more complicated delay sequence argument [3]. Intuitively, the proof shows that it is very unlikely that there are many steal attempts without stealing a task that makes progress on the critical path. The expected number of time steps used to perform steals is $T_\infty P_i$. To finish a computation the steals $T_\infty P_i$ and the work T_1 are added up and divided by the number of workers, leading to the expected time bound in Eq. (2). Additionally, the execution time can be bounded to a fixed value with a high probability. Similar bounds hold for multiprogrammed environments [1].

$$T_P = O(T_1/P_i + T_\infty) \tag{2}$$

A framework holding the busy-leaves property and the time bounds can therefore be practical for a soft real-time application requiring a bounded memory footprint and a certain quality of service.

3.2   Work-Stealing Implementation Challenges

The main challenge for work-stealing implementations is to adapt the programming language's serial semantics to a parallel execution, as compiled languages like C/C++ are designed with a stack based, linear execution in mind. For example while work-stealing both D and F in Fig. 2 can execute concurrently, having one thread observe the stack (A, C, D) and a second one observe (A, C, F) at the same time. Building such a diverging stack is known as a cactus-stack in language design. In order to keep time and space bounds, as well as stick close to serial semantics, a work-stealing scheduler has to maintain a cactus-stack and make sure that tasks are never blocked by the implementation. If for example a thread executing Listing 1 encounters the sync (vertex I in Fig. 1) and has to wait for children to complete (vertex II and III), it must make the rest of the function (vertex IV) executable by another worker. Additionally, implementations must amortize their scheduling overheads against the work T_1/P and span T_∞ of the computation, e.g. if the stealing process incurs overheads they must be considered as a factor in the T_∞ term.

To understand how implementations can approach this challenge, we present some common variants found in frameworks below.

Heap Allocated Stack Frames – One solution to build a cactus-stack is to allocate each function frame on the heap instead of the stack. This allows for non-blocking execution and strict space bounds, as only the active stack frames of the invocation tree are kept allocated and stacks are independent of worker threads. Cilk [5] implements this principle and therefore holds both theoretical time and space bounds. The drawback to this approach is that it requires compiler support or exhaustive manual code transformations to adopt a heap-stack-frame calling convention, making it less interoperable with existing software and incurring overheads on every function call.

Execute on Worker Stacks – Another approach is to execute tasks directly on the linear stacks of each worker thread. This method requires no special language constructs, but problems occur when a synchronization point is reached. If a thread reaches e.g. the sync() in line 8 of Listing 1 and has to wait for children to finish, the function frame lies on top of the stack. To stay greedy, the worker has to start stealing, but executing the stolen task directly on top of the worker's stack leads to two problems: (1) the stack can grow unbounded, as the worker can pile up multiple stolen stacks, (2) the task waiting at the sync() is blocked until all stolen tasks above have finished, as it is buried in the call stack.

This technique therefore violates both strict time and space bounds. To prevent unbounded space usage sometimes **restricted stealing** approaches are used, limiting work-stealing attempts to a subset of tasks. Examples for this are leapfrogging [4,15] and depth-restricted stealing [8]. However, restricting steals can potentially lead to near serial execution times [13].

One Stack per Steal – To keep the portability of execution on regular stacks but not block in tasks, an option is to always execute a stolen task on a new stack. This technique holds strict time bounds, but uses $S_1 N_{steals}$ memory proportional to the number of active stolen tasks. As with restricted stealing, some implementations like Cilk Plus limit the parallelism in favor of bounded memory usage, setting a fixed amount of stacks and stopping stealing if they are exhausted.

Memory Mapped Cactus-Stack – This solution uses an OS modification for thread local memory mapping, allowing the runtime system to give each worker thread the illusion of having a linear stack [9], holding strict bounds.

The main drawbacks are frequent memory mappings and either OS support or tricks around processes and virtual memory.

3.3   Case Study: TBB and EMB²

Looking at actual implementations of task-based programming, we first examine TBB, the industry leading task-parallel library in C++. The framework offers a low level fork-join task-parallel API, high level parallel patterns, concurrent data-structures and includes an optional scalable memory allocator. Overall, TBB's goals are to achieve high throughput by offering a composable, portable task-based API that does not require compiler support and can be gradually incorporated to existing applications.

Internally, TBB [8,14] resembles mostly classic work-stealing for scheduling tasks, with decentralized LiFo deques and randomized stealing. It uses a combination of the 'execute on worker stacks' and 'heap allocated stack frames' strategy for task execution. When using the high level fork-join APIs that are easily added to existing code (like in Listing 1), it executes the tasks on the worker threads, loosing strict bounds. Alternatively, one can re-write code with explicit task and continuation objects, manually building up a heap-allocated cactus-stack. This looses normal call-stack semantics, but in return mostly keeps classic bounds. The parallel patterns internally use this style for efficiency. In case a worker stack becomes too deep, TBB stops stealing, restricting parallelism in favor of application stability.

In contrast to this general purpose library, the EMB² [12] task scheduler specifically targets the embedded market. It is based on the Multicore Task Management API (MTAPI) [6] specification, an industry standard for lightweight task scheduling on resource constrained embedded systems with heterogeneous hardware. Specifically, EMB² implements a MTAPI standard compliant task scheduling environment in C, which can be used directly, but is also utilized by parallel patterns offered by EMB²'s high level C++ API. The framework offers support for acceleration hardware, supports core affinity as well as task priorities and allocates all runtime resources exclusively during startup. Overall, EMB² offers a portable solution to dispatch tasks onto different components of a resource constrained system, acting more like a 'whole system scheduler' similar to an OS and is not restricted to strict fork-join parallelism on the CPU.

Looking at EMB²'s scheduling and task management, we only discuss execution on the CPU. Each thread is associated with multiple FiFo queues for different task priorities, with workers pulling tasks in either local-first or priority-first order. Task execution uses the 'run on workers stacks' technique and tasks are blocked in the stack while stolen tasks are executed above. Newly spawned tasks are distributed to threads in a round robin fashion. The combination of work-sharing and FiFo queues leads to a fair task execution, i.e. old tasks are executed first, ensuring that no single task is buried in queues. This fits the 'whole system scheduler' style of MTAPI, i.e. a system that continuously spawns mostly independent tasks needing to finish in a timely manner. However, no formal bounds can be provided and especially tree-like computations use much memory as the schedule results in a breadth first execution of the invocation tree. To make use of the static resource allocation, the programmer has to manually find the maximum number of spawned tasks.

In summary, TBB sticks as close to classic work-stealing as possible, while focusing on portability and average system throughput. When necessary, it diverges from theoretical bounds in favor of a portable and simple implementation. This trend can be seen in most general purpose implementations. EMB^2 in contrast offers a task-based API, similar to TBB, but tunes its scheduler for fair task execution and offers specialized features like static resource allocation at startup.

4   Work-Stealing with Static Memory Allocation

EMB^2 shows that static, predictable resource usage and clean task-based parallel APIs are in demand on embedded platforms. However, their fair scheduling model is better suited for controlling the whole system rather than gradually introducing parallel sections in individual applications. Classic work-stealing on the other hand is a good fit for this purpose and can also ease the reasoning on upper memory bounds. A combination of work-stealing and static memory allocation at startup can therefore lead to predictable application behavior. Unfortunately, modern frameworks like TBB intentionally hurt the tight bounds of randomized work-stealing and make liberal use of a general purpose memory allocator. On a desktop machine occasional usage of more memory or longer execution times are well worth the trade-off. For an embedded system, in contrast, unpredictability can cause major issues.

To bring work-stealing closer to the embedded domain, we explore how a `C++` library implementation can provide tight and predictable memory bounds while also keeping the runtime properties of classic work-stealing and a natural fork-join API. The core of the prototype – called Predictable Parallel Patterns Library for Smart and Scalable Systems (P^{3}LS^3) – is a novel resource-trading scheme that integrates memory management into the stealing procedure. This allows the implementation to allocate all memory statically at startup, guaranteeing a maximum application footprint after a single, serial measurement run.

4.1   Resource-Trading Algorithm

Existing implementations like Cilk and TBB allocate all resources used during scheduling on the heap. This adds a multithreaded memory allocator as an abstraction layer to be considered in a pessimistic analysis. The different orders of allocation that can happen must be taken into account for exact memory requirements, as well as the sporadic work involved in balancing memory between threads or requesting new pages from the OS.

To avoid this issue, the resource-trading algorithm incorporates the balancing of memory into the stealing process. This amortizes the management overhead into the T_∞ term of the time bound and allows for a strict space bound. The starting point is the maximum amount of resources R_S a serial invocation tree can allocate. Figure 3 shows R_S exemplary as the dark shaded areas, indicating the active part of the deepest invocation tree (we use R_S instead of S_1 to more accurately describe our implementation later on).

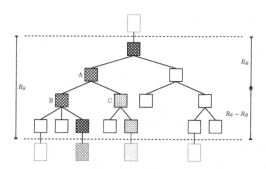

Fig. 3. Invocation tree with resource-trading

Resource-trading has the same linear growing bound $R_S P_i$ as work-stealing. Each worker thread is associated with R_S resources at startup, with no additional allocations during runtime. By proofing that a worker thread never runs out of resources with this initial configuration, the bound $R_S P_i$ follows trivially. Specifically, we show that a thread always starts stealing with R_S resources and these are enough to run until returning to the stealing state.

A serial execution of the invocation tree has by definition enough resources, therefore the interactions during the work-stealing algorithm are of interest. The critical point where a thread loses resources of its initial R_S pool are synchronization points where another thread stole part of the work and is not yet finished. Figure 3 shows this situation. The first, dark shaded thread eventually returns from task B, requiring task C to be finished before continuing working on task A. However, task C is currently being executed by the second, light shaded thread. To not idle the first worker has to start stealing. Unfortunately, all resources including A and upwards must be kept allocated, making the first thread lose R_B blocked resources.

To solve this, each thread trades in resources to compensate for potentially blocked resources of another worker on a steal. In the example in Fig. 3 the second thread trades R_B of its initial R_S resources to task A when stealing C. This leaves the worker with $R_S - R_B$ resources for the remaining invocation tree, which are sufficient for executing it, as R_S equals the longest branch. Following this trade-in rule and the busy-leaves property, each task t with n active child tasks has $n - 1$ traded resources associated with it. The first $n - 1$ children finishing can not execute t, but can combine their free resources with one of the traded in resources to enter the stealing state with the initial R_S resources. The last child finishing does not require spare resources, as it can continue working on the parent task, freeing its resources when finishing it.

Following this simple trade-in rule, resources can be balanced between the workers only on steal and synchronization events, leading to strict space bounds. The trading affects the time bounds by adding the work to trade resources to the steal procedure. When the work required for stealing is proportional to c_∞, the expected time bound in Eq. (3) follows.

$$T_P = O(T_1/P_i + c_\infty T_\infty) \tag{3}$$

4.2 Prototype Implementation

In order to keep the busy-leaves property and strict time bounds, the prototype must implement a cactus-stack and not block in threads. The system model suggests that parallel sections are clearly defined and should be predictable in resource usage, having the execution switch from a serial to a parallel section explicitly. Figure 3 shows this with a switch from the serial stack (shaded) to the parallel invocation tree at the top, dotted line. We decide to build a cactus stack by executing each spawned task on a small stackful coroutine[3], as spawns tend to be dense in a parallel section, requiring only a small stack per task. Calls into purely serial code that potentially uses more stack space are run on a separate, bigger stack, as indicated with the bottom, dotted line in Fig. 3. By doing this, P^3LS^3 holds strict theoretical bounds and implements the API in Listing 1.

The previous section on the resource-trading algorithm introduced abstract resources R_S that can be split and united at any point. However, memory can not be split and united at will, as computers rely on continuous blocks of memory in the virtual address space. Our first prototype therefore trades fixed size memory blocks managed in a linked list, i.e. it trades the stackful coroutines to execute tasks. Each thread starts with D blocks equal to the deepest spawn depth and trades are performed by slicing and concatenating parts of the lists. The time c_∞ to perform a steal is therefore $c_\infty = O(D)$.

The stealing procedure integrating resource-trading is implemented in a non-blocking manner, thus holding bounds on a multiprogrammed environment [1]. During stealing, a flag is atomically updated from a thief to acquire a task, similar to Wool [4]. The new value indicates both the stolen state of the task and contains the traded in resources, making the action of stealing and trading in resources atomic. Each task additionally holds a stack of currently traded in resources, which is also used to implicitly synchronize as the last finishing child encounters an empty resource stack.

During development the program must be executed once to measure the maximum size of the coroutines and the computation depth D by triggering the biggest possible invocation tree. These measured values are then used to configure the scheduler, which during startup acquires the $S_P = O(P_i(S_1 + D))$ memory required for the execution. This way of finding the static memory

---

[3] The resource-trading algorithm can work with any other choice of cactus-stack and non-blocking scheduler. We choose coroutines as we are interested in exploring a pure library solution with a clean API.

footprint is very accessible for the developer, as it only depends on few metrics and the model of an invocation tree is simple to reason about.

5 Performance Analysis

We evaluate the performance of P^3LS^3 by comparing it to TBB (2019, interface version 11000) and EMB^2 (v1.0.0). All benchmarks are executed on a Banana Pi M3 as an example of a high performance embedded system. The board is equipped with an A83T ARM SoC housing a Cortex-A7 octa-core processor clocked at 1.6 GHz and runs the vendor supplied linux operating system, which is based on the 3.4.39 smp preemp kernel. The benchmark applications are compiled with GCC v5.4 using optimization level -03.

We first analyze the scheduling overhead of the frameworks using the synthetic load of unbalanced tree search [11], followed by an embarrassingly parallel row wise matrix multiplication. Further benchmarks where conducted, but are not shown for brevity. However, they all show the same trend as seen in the following evaluation. Each benchmark is discussed in one of the following subsections, with diagrams showing the resulting speedups and full execution time distributions. The box plots indicate the 95th and 5th percentile execution times with whiskers and all fliers are included.

All measurements are performed in both isolated and multiprogrammed system conditions. Isolated tests are executed with minimal influences from other processes running on the system, by isolating the benchmark processor cores and using the round robin real-time scheduler. These isolated measurements are most common in other benchmarks, and thus can be used for comparison. To simulate a multiprogrammed system, we intentionally run one higher priority process per CPU core, potentially preempting the currently running benchmark. The processes are periodically performing work and memory access, resulting in a measured per core utilization of an average 25%.

5.1 Unbalanced Tree Search

Unbalanced tree search [11] constructs and traverses a highly unbalanced tree by calculating a hash value at each node. The benchmark spawns a task for each node, resulting in very unpredictable load with many synchronization points, revealing the frameworks scheduling overhead. For our test, we choose to spawn an initial 140 nodes at the tree root and eight children with a probability of $q = 0.124875$. This leads to a tree with about 71,000 nodes and therefore the same amount of spawned tasks. We repeat each benchmark 50 times.

Figure 4a shows that TBB and P^3LS^3 both achieve a near identical speedup in this test, while EMB^2 can not accelerate the computation, even introducing a significant slowdown at low core counts. This confirms the assumption that decentralized work-stealing and its depth-first tree traversal is superior to the work-sharing scheduler used in EMB^2 for this kind of fine-grained, recursive tasks. Turning to the time distributions in a multiprogrammed environment,

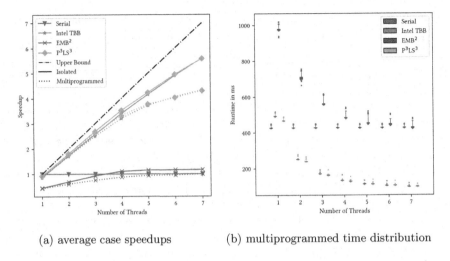

(a) average case speedups   (b) multiprogrammed time distribution

Fig. 4. Results of the unbalanced tree search benchmarks.

shown in Fig. 4b, we can see generally low dispersion for TBB and P^3LS^3, close to the serial measurements. EMB^2 in contrast shows by far the biggest irregularity in execution times. This trend is also visible in non synthetic divide and conquer algorithms like a fast Fourier transform, although it is less pronounced.

5.2 Matrix Multiplication

We implement a row wise matrix multiplication as an example of an embarrassingly parallel algorithm. Using the frameworks `parallel_for` constructs, rows are executed concurrently, making the libraries handle splitting up data and load balancing internally. We choose a matrix size of 128×128 and repeat each benchmark 5000 times.

The measured average speedups compared to the serial implementation are shown in Fig. 5a. All three frameworks nearly reach the theoretical upper bound of a perfect, linear speedup when being executed on an isolated system, with TBB being the fastest by a slight margin. When looking at the multiprogrammed environment, all frameworks show worse speedups. Interestingly, EMB^2 slows down more drastically than the other two frameworks on lower core counts, suggesting problems with either load balancing or synchronization. Looking closer at the time distributions in Fig. 5b, we notice a trend of more consistent execution times with increasing thread count and observe that the libraries do not introduce more variance than a serial execution, suggesting that the overall system jitter by the higher priority workers dominates.

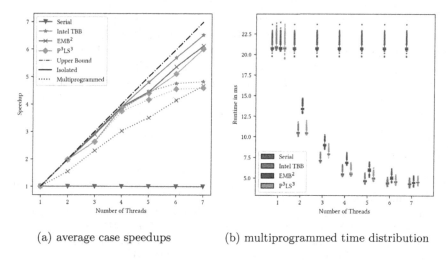

(a) average case speedups   (b) multiprogrammed time distribution

Fig. 5. Results of the matrix multiplication benchmarks.

6   Conclusion

We analyzed how task-parallel programming and dispatching frameworks fit into the embedded and real-time domain. We argue that classic work-stealing offers good theoretical bounds and our tests verify that it leads to consistently fast execution times even on small problem sizes. Specifically, the benchmarks show that EMB^2 suffers from load balancing issues, while TBB and P^3LS^3 perform almost equally well on all tests. This behavior results from P^3LS^3 and TBB using a lock-free work-stealing scheduler, while EMB^2 uses a mostly work-sharing implementation and therefore, find the former to be superior for parallelizing individual applications. Furthermore, all benchmarks show that the use of work-stealing frameworks does not increase the dispersion of the execution times compared to a sequential execution. The uncertainty from randomized stealing is dominated by other system effects.

Our remaining concern with existing dispatching frameworks is their liberate use of dynamic memory management and occasional deviation from classic work-stealing bounds in favor of mainstream usability. As embedded systems can require static resource allocation, we implemented a prototype work-stealing library in C++, offering both static memory allocation and strict theoretical bounds. Our time measurements show that our early prototype P^3LS^3, implementing the proposed resource-trading approach, can keep up with the industry leading TBB. Unfortunately, P^3LS^3 can not improve execution time variances compared to TBB, even though TBB implements blocking style work-stealing and uses dynamic memory management. Under our current measurement conditions, we can therefore not detect any sporadic, negative effect on execution times resulting from dynamic memory allocations.

Currently, we focus on the performance of individual applications, in future work we would like to investigate the behavior of multiple task-parallel applications running concurrently on a real-time OS. We would also like to refine our measurements, by including memory usage and by looking at smaller problem sizes. Lastly, we want to explore if resource-trading can be integrated into parallel patterns that require structured memory allocations, like e.g. divide and conquer algorithms with temporary buffers.

References

1. Arora, N.S., Blumofe, R.D., Plaxton, C.G.: Thread scheduling for multiprogrammed multiprocessors. In: Proceedings of the Tenth Annual ACM Symposium on Parallel Algorithms and Architectures, SPAA 1998, Puerto Vallarta, Mexico, pp. 119–129. ACM (1998). https://doi.org/10.1145/277651.277678
2. Atkinson, P., McIntosh-Smith, S.: On the performance of parallel tasking runtimes for an irregular fast multipole method application. In: 13th International Workshop on OpenMP, IWOMP 2017. LNCS, vol. 10468, pp. 92–106. Springer, Cham (2017). https://doi.org/10.1007/978-3-319-65578-9_7
3. Blumofe, R.D., Leiserson, C.E.: Scheduling multithreaded computations by work stealing. In: Proceedings 35th Annual Symposium on Foundations of Computer Science, pp. 356–368, November 1994. https://doi.org/10.1109/SFCS.1994.365680
4. Faxen, K.: Efficient work stealing for fine grained parallelism. In: 39th International Conference on Parallel Processing, pp. 313–322, September 2010. https://doi.org/10.1109/ICPP.2010.39
5. Frigo, M., Leiserson, C.E., Randall, K.H.: The Implementation of the Cilk-5 multithreaded language. In: Proceedings of the ACM SIGPLAN 1998 Conference on Programming Language Design and Implementation, PLDI 1998, Montreal, Quebec, Canada, pp. 212–223. ACM (1998). https://doi.org/10.1145/277650.277725
6. Gleim, U., Levy, M.: MTAPI: parallel programming for embedded multicore systems. Technical report (2013)
7. Halpern, P.: Strict fork-join parallelism. Technical report N3409, September 2012
8. Kukanov, A., Voss, M.J.: The foundations for scalable multi-core software in Intel® threading building blocks. Intel Tech. J. **11**, 309–322 (2007). https://doi.org/10.1535/itj.1104.05
9. Lee, I.T.A., Boyd-Wickizer, S., Huang, Z., Leiserson, C.E.: Using memory mapping to support cactus stacks in work-stealing runtime systems. In: Proceedings of the 19th International Conference on Parallel Architectures and Compilation Techniques - PACT 2010. Vienna, Austria, p. 411. ACM Press (2010). https://doi.org/10.1145/1854273.1854324
10. Li, J., Dinh, S., Kieselbach, K., Agrawal, K., Gill, C., Lu, C.: Randomized work stealing for large scale soft real-time systems. In: IEEE Real-Time Systems Symposium, RTSS, pp. 203–214, November 2016. https://doi.org/10.1109/RTSS.2016.028
11. Olivier, S., et al.: UTS: an unbalanced tree search benchmark. In: International Workshop on Languages and Compilers for Parallel Computing, LCPC 2006. LNCS, vol. 4382, pp. 235–250. Springer, Heidelberg (2007). https://doi.org/10.1007/978-3-540-72521-3_18
12. Schuele, T.: Embedded multicore building blocks - parallel programming made easy. In: Embedded World 2015 (2015)

13. Sukha, J.: Brief announcement: a lower bound for depth-restricted work stealing. In: Proceedings of the Twenty-First Annual Symposium on Parallelism in Algorithms and Architectures, SPAA 2009, Calgary, AB, Canada, pp. 124–126. ACM (2009). https://doi.org/10.1145/1583991.1584025
14. Voss, M., Asenjo, R., Reinders, J.: Pro TBB. Apress, Berkeley (2019)
15. Wagner, D.B., Calder, B.G.: Leapfrogging: a portable technique for implementing efficient futures. In: Proceedings of the Fourth ACM SIGPLAN Symposium on Principles and Practice of Parallel Programming, PPOPP 1993, San Diego, California, USA, pp. 208–217. ACM (1993). https://doi.org/10.1145/155332.155354

Author Index

Printed in the United States
By Bookmasters